The Texas Art Review

Les Krantz

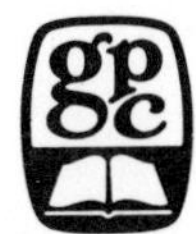

Gulf Publishing Company
Book Division
Houston, Texas
in conjunction with
The Krantz Company Publishers, Inc.

Les Krantz
Editor and Publisher

Janice Feldstein *Associate Editor,* Bill Marvel *Contributing Editor,*
Igor Alexander *Contributing Editor,* Marjorie G. Krantz *Research Director,*
Bill Lowry *Cover Design* (Photography by Les Krantz), Typography by
Siemens Communications Graphics.

Library of Congress Catalogue Number 82-83197

ISBN 0-87201-018-X

Manufactured in The United States of America

To Manny, who traveled every
highway and byway of Texas,
relating magical stories to two small
boys waiting at home.
Thanks Dad.

CONTENTS

Book III: **HOUSTON AND SOUTHEAST TEXAS**

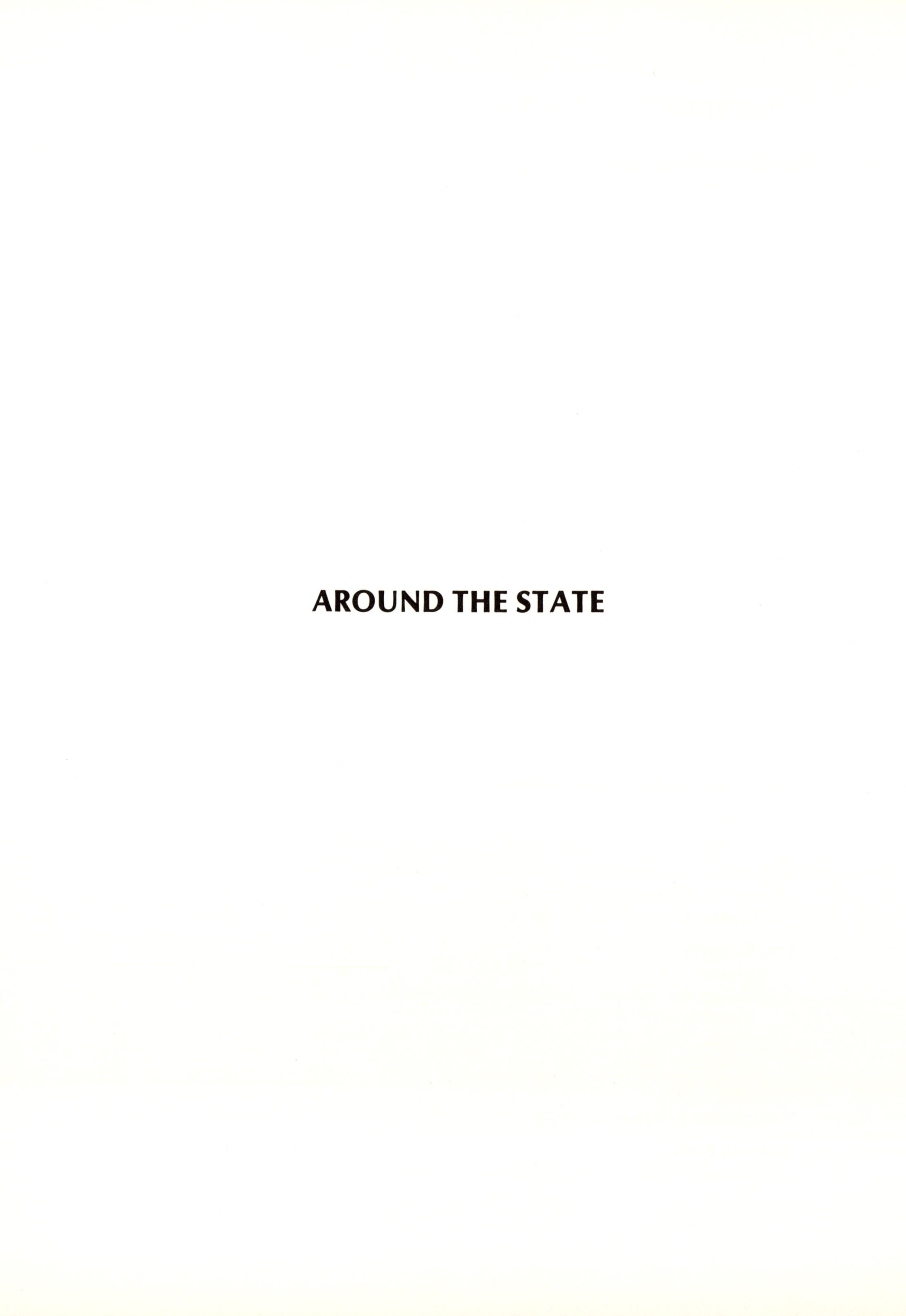

AROUND THE STATE

Geographical Cross References

Additional exhibiting facilities may be found in Parts II and III
of this volume.

Abilene
Museums: Abilene Fine Arts Museum

Amarillo
Museums: Amarillo Art Center
Galleries: James M. Haney Gallery

Austin
Museums: Dougherty Art Center, Archer M. Huntington
Art Gallery, Lyndon B. Johnson Library and Museum,
Laguna Gloria Art Museum, Leeds Gallery, Texas
Memorial Museum
Galleries: Country Store, Galerie Ravel, Rue de Lamar
Gallery

Brownsville
Museums: Brownsville Art League Museum

Corpus Christi
Museums: The Art Museum of South Texas, The Japanese
Art Museum, South Texas Artmobile (Center for the Arts),
Weil Gallery

El Paso
Museums: El Paso Museum of Art, El Paso Museum of History,
Wildnerness Park

Kingsville
Museums: John E. Connor Museum

Lubbock
Galleries: Double-T-Ranch, Lubbock-Light Artists' Co-op

Midland
Museums: Museum of the Southwest
Galleries: Hanging Tree Gallery

San Antonio
Museums: Institute of Texas Cultures, Marion Koogler
McNay Art Institute, San Antonio Museum of Art,
Witte Memorial Museum
Galleries: Charlton Art Gallery, Mission Gallery, Shown-
Davenport, Texas Trails

Victoria:
Museums: The Nave Museum

Wichita Falls
Museums: Wichita Falls Museum and Art Center

Museums and Public Exhibition Spaces

Abilene Fine Arts Museum   801 S. Mockingbird   Abilene 79605
(915) 673-4587   Tuesday-Friday: 9-5; weekends: 1-5

Abilene Fine Arts Museum

The Abilene Fine Arts Museum was organized in 1937. The permanent collection includes contemporary graphics, antique fans, historical artifacts, and regional painting.

The exhibition program is active and varied, and ranges from classical and contemporary painting to wild and Western.

The contemporary graphics collection includes works by Robert Motherwell, Joseph Albers's *Homage to the Square: Hard Edge, Soft Edge,* and artists' books by Dieter Roth, Oskar Kokoschka, and others.

A red figure and a black figure Attic Lekythos from the fourth century B.C. are included in the study collection.

Amarillo Art Center   2200 S. Van Buren   Amarillo 79178
(806) 372-8356   Tuesday-Friday: 10-4; Saturday-Sunday: 1-5;
Wednesday: 7-9:30; closed in August

Amarillo Art Center

The Amarillo Art Center is housed in a beautiful, functional building that was designed by Edward Durell Stone and completed in 1972. It is part of a fine-arts complex on the campus of Amarillo College, and though closely related to the college operates as a separate entity.

The center has a small but growing permanent collection which focuses on twentieth-century American art. There are more than 400 photographs, including work by Russell Lee, Dorothea Lange, Paul Hester, Edward Steichen, Walker Evans, Paul Strand, and Michael Smith.

The works of Jack Boynton, a contemporary Texas artist who has made important contributions to the arts of the Southwest for over three decades, are exceedingly well represented. Recent acquisitions also include works by Bob Camblin, Lucas Johnson, Eric

Anderson, Philip Renteria, Dan Traverso, Gerald Patrick, and Ben
Woitena.

Ten to twenty exhibitions are mounted each year, half of which
are organized by the Amarillo staff. The exhibits cover many
periods and styles, but again the emphasis is on twentieth-
century art. Most exhibits are accompanied by publications and
interpretive programs.

Art Museum of South Texas

The Art Museum of South Texas   1902 N. Shoreline   Corpus
Christi 78403   (512) 884-3844   Tuesday-Saturday: 10-5; Sunday:
1-5

The Art Museum of South Texas is housed in a building designed
by architect Philip Johnson of New York City. Mr. Johnson has
called the building "the most exciting he has ever done." It is of
reinforced concrete formed and cast in place. The usable space is
over 30,000 square feet. There are three levels to the museum. The
lower level houses construction areas, shipping and receiving,
storage areas, and offices. The first floor is a sweep of pure white,
unimpeded space which houses large collections from private
sources and other loan exhibitions. The second-floor level has a
spectacular 60-foot walkway which provides a view of the Great
Hall below as well as access to the outdoor sculpture court and the
skylighted Upper Gallery. The building opened in 1972.

exhibitions

Over 60 exhibitions covering a broad range of periods and
media have been presented in the past decade. Over 50 new works
have been added to the museum's collection, including a drawing
collection which was made possible through matching-grant
funds. A series of French Impressionist paintings have been made
available through a long-term loan from the National Gallery of
Art. An exhibition of classical Greek sculpture was presented on
long-term loan from the Boston Museum of Fine Arts. A long-term
loan of eighteenth- and nineteenth-century paintings was also made
available from the Boston Museum of Fine Arts collection.

The educational program includes guest lecturers, art
documentary films, slide lectures, art classes, and a docent tour
program which reaches all the fifth and sixth grade students in the
local school district. The research library contains over 3,000
volumes.

To reach the museum take the I-37 to Water St; turn left to
Hirsch St., then turn right.

Brownsville Art League Museum

Brownsville Art League Museum   230 Neale Drive   Brownsville
78520   (512) 542-0941   Monday, Wednesday, Thursday, and
Friday: 9:30-3:30; Tuesday: 1-4; open weekends for loan exhibits

In 1950 Mr. and Mrs. Hector del Valle offered the Brownsville Art
League a permanent home as a permanent studio—the old Neale
home. The Neale home was built in 1836 by the grandfather of

Mrs. del Valle, William Neale, who had immigrated from England
to Mexico in 1827. He later moved to Brownsville where he built
his last home. In 1975 funds were raised to build a concrete, air-
conditioned museum 75 feet northwest of Neale House. It now
houses the League's valuable collection of paintings, etchings,
and drawings and is said to be the only small art museum in Texas
possessing its own permanent collection of art works.

The permanent collection consists of paintings in oils, acrylics, *collections*
watercolor, collages, woodcuts, drawings, and etchings by James
McNeil Whistler, Augustus E. Johns, N.C. Wyeth, Dale Nichols,
Hayward Veale, Frederic Taubes, Harry Anthony De Young,
Alexander Calder, Milford Zornes, and others.

Recent exhibitions have included an exhibit of modern art and
an exhibit of etchings and aquatints by Goya on loan from the
Sarah Campbell Blaffer Foundation; an exhibition of the work of
Bartolome Mongrell Mestra, artist and instructor from Matamoras,
Mexico; and Mexico and the Revolution/Portrait of an Era—
photographs and prints.

Museum activities include lectures, gallery talks, arts festivals,
workshops, formal education programs for adults, and permanent,
temporary, and traveling exhibitions.

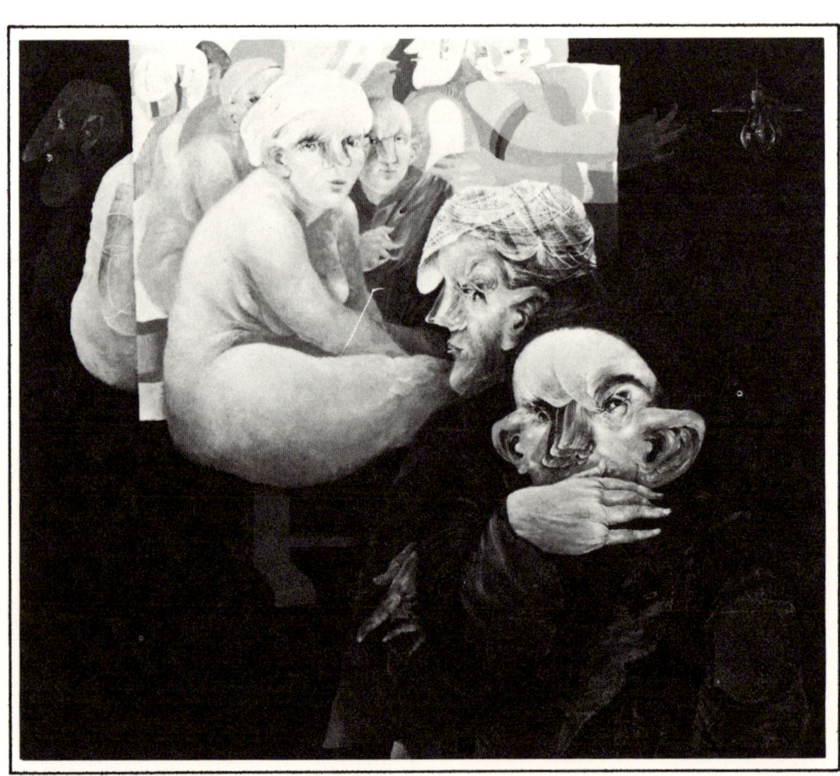

Gonzalo Cienfuego, *Dia De fiesta en la plaza,* 35" x 43", oil on canvas.
Archer M. Huntington Art Gallery.

John E. Conner Museum   Texas A & I University   Kingsville
78363   (512) 595-2819   Monday-Friday: 10-5; Sunday: 2:30-5

The Conner Museum is a general museum of South Texas with
collections in natural history, archaeology, anthropology, history,
and art. The museum's temporary exhibit gallery displays shows
dealing with a wide variety of topics, including local and nonlocal
art.
  As a general museum of South Texas, the Conner Museum's
gallery specializes in the art of the region. Two of the significant
artists of the area who have been shown here are Jerry Smith,
wildlife photographer, and Guy Morrow, egg-tempera realist
painter. Folk arts such as retablos and pinatas have also been
displayed.
  Traveling exhibits which fall outside the general areas of
specialization have included the Goya etchings, *The Disasters of
War,* and the Western sculpture of Jim Deutch. Upcoming exhibits
include Morning Sun: American Graphics of the 1920s and 1930s,
and Works by Women, with paintings by Mary Cassatt, Georgia
O'Keeffe, and others.

Dougherty Art Center   1110 Barton Springs Rd.   Austin 78767
Address mail to Box 1088   Tuesday-Friday: 11-5; Saturday-
Sunday: 1-4

Dougherty Arts Center is part of the Cultural Arts Programs, Parks
and Recreation Department, City of Austin. There is a large
exhibition space, along with classrooms, an auditorium, dance
rehearsal space, and offices.
  The center hosts exhibits for many city arts organizations, such
as Women and Their Work, the League of United Chicano Artists,
and Waterloo Watercolors. All types of two- and three-dimensional
works are exhibited.
  Classes are given in the visual and the performing arts.
  The Dougherty Art Center is funded by proceeds from the hotel
occupancy tax.

El Paso Museum of Art   1211 Montana Ave.   El Paso 79902
(915) 541-4040   Wednesday-Saturday: 10-5; Sunday: 1-5

The museum is housed in an imposing classic structure built in
1910—the home of State Senator and Mrs. W. W. Turney. It was
opened as a museum in 1947, but was incorporated as the El Paso
Museum of Art in 1959.
  The core of the holdings is the Samuel H. Kress Collection of
Fourteenth to Seventeenth Century European Art, a beautiful
group of almost sixty paintings which includes works by Bellini,
Botticelli, Crespi, Tiepolo, Ribera, and Van Dyck.
  Decorative arts of the eighteenth, nineteenth, and early

Connor Museum

Dougherty Art Center

El Paso Museum of Art

twentieth centuries are displayed in the Heritage Gallery.

Remington's *Sign of Friendship* and Inness's *Landscape* are special attractions.

The museum also exhibits pre-Columbian pottery and artifacts and Mexican colonial paintings and sculpture.

To reach the museum, take I-10 to North Mesa; North Mesa to Montana Avenue.

transportation

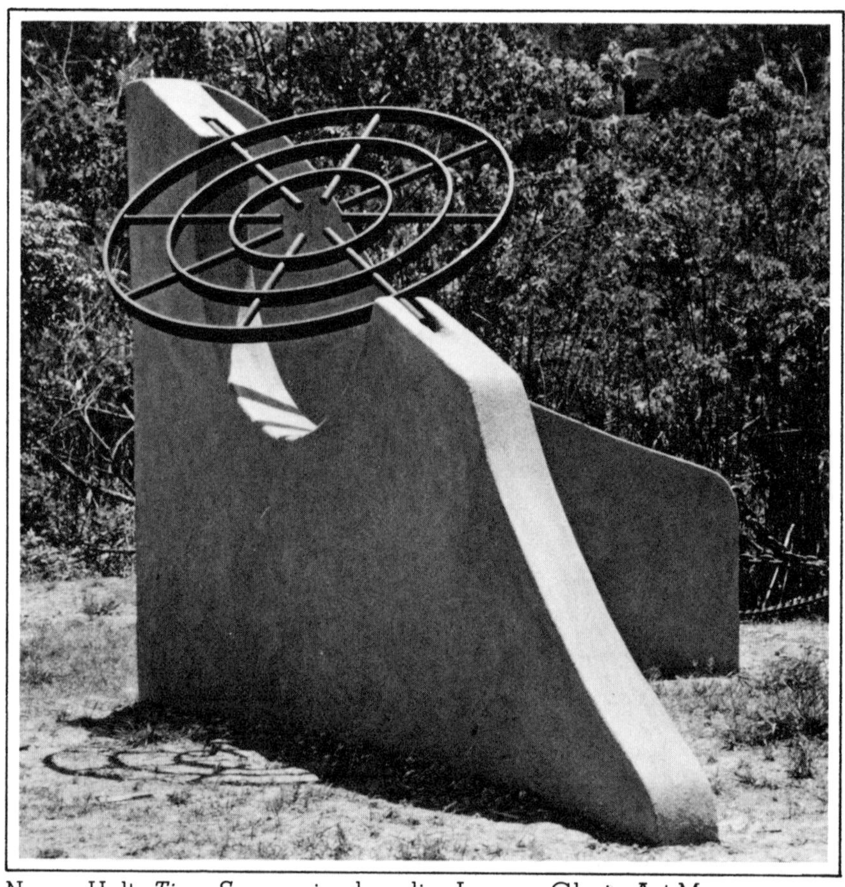
Nancy Holt, *Time Span*, mixed media. Laguna Gloria Art Museum.

El Paso Museum of History (formerly the Cavalry Museum)
12901 Gateway West   El Paso 79927   (915) 858-1928
Wednesday-Saturday: 9-5; Sunday: 1-5

El Paso Museum of History

This history and military museum is a city facility connected with the El Paso Museum of Art.

The collections feature guns, horse gear, photographs, cavalry gear, and costumes. Six walk-up dioramas depict various aspects of the Paso del Norte: The Coming of the Spanish, The Coming of the Trains, The Mexican Revolution and Pancho Villa, A Shoot-out on Old El Paso Street, and the Mexican Punitive Expedition with "Black-Jack" Pershing (1916-1917).

Huntington Art Gallery

Archer M. Huntington Art Gallery   University of Texas at Austin   23rd & San Jacinto (Art Building) and Harry Ransom Center (21st & Guadalupe)   (512) 471-7324   Monday-Saturday: 9-5; Sunday: 1-5

In 1927 Archer M. Huntington, a well-known scholar and philanthropist, and his wife, the sculptress Anna Hyatt Huntington, deeded property to The University of Texas for the "use and benefits" of a future art museum on the campus. The gallery was established in 1963 in part with funds from the Huntington endowment.

collections

The Huntington Art Gallery sponsors exhibitions at two locations on The University of Texas campus: in the gallery in the Art Building and in the gallery in the Harry Ransom Center.

The Art Gallery's growing permanent collection includes Greek and Roman art, a very extensive collection of nineteenth- and twentieth-century American art, contemporary Latin American art, and approximately 4,000 prints and drawings of every historical period.

The permanent collection is supplemented by temporary loan exhibitions which bring to the university art of diverse cultures and periods. The Art Gallery organizes short-term exhibitions of objects from its permanent collection and works of art borrowed from other major museums and private collections. In addition to serving regular academic courses, the Art Gallery provides regular Wednesday-noon gallery talks, special mini-courses, symposia, lecture series, films, and performances relating to the exhibitions. The Art Gallery's education staff currently implements, with the aid of federal funds and the cooperation of the Austin Independent School District, an Art Enrichment Program for gifted children in the fourth, fifth, and sixth grades.

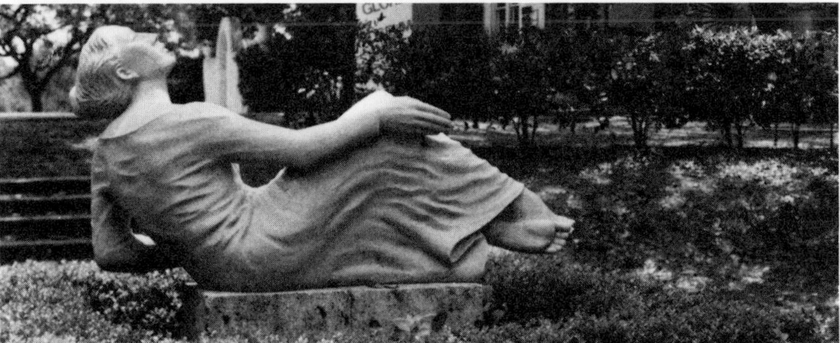

Charles Umlauf, *Poetess,* cast stone. Laguna Gloria Art Museum.

tours

Special tours of the permanent collections and temporary exhibitions are available. The tours, which are conducted by volunteer docents, well-trained in the history of art, should be scheduled in advance. Those interested in individual or group tours are invited to contact the Art Gallery office (471-7324) to make arrangements.

Institute of Texan Cultures, The University of Texas   801 S. Bowie
St. at Durango Blvd.   San Antonio 78205   (512) 226-7651
Tuesday-Sunday: 9-5

Institute of Texan Cultures

A unique educational center that annually attracts half a million
visitors from all over the world. Built in 1968 as the Texas Pavilion
for San Antonio's world's fair, it remains in the heart of downtown
on HemisFair Plaza.

Although the Institute's exhibit floor is the size of a football field,
it is not a museum in the usual sense of the word. It owns no
collections. Every item in its varied exhibits is borrowed from more
than 1,000 individuals and museums. As a result, the institute's
exhibits change constantly.

The modern, colorful displays are designed to tell the stories of
the 30 major ethnic, cultural, national, and racial groups that
settled and developed Texas. The exhibits are brought to life by a
variety of audiovisual devices and by interpreters who make
history as vital as tomorrow's headline. Demonstrations in Indian
lore, cowboy life, and pioneer living are presented regularly,
along with crafts such as quilting, spinning, and weaving. In the
Music Room, visitors not only see and touch instruments from
many lands but play the only juke box in San Antonio stocked with
authentic recordings from around the world.

In the Dome Theater, *The Faces and Places of Texas* is shown
twice daily on 36 screens. Other films and multimedia shows are
also presented.

In the institute's Lower Gallery there are ever-changing exhibits
related to the heritage of Texas, and varying from folk art and
crafts to historical presentations to fine art.

The educational programs travel throughout the state and
beyond, and special outreach programs are familiar sights in
schools, libraries, museums, and shopping centers.

The Japanese Art Museum   426 S. Staples   Corpus Christi
78401   (512) 883-1303   Monday-Friday: 10-4; Sunday: 2-5

Japanese Art Museum

The Japanese Art Museum was incorporated in January 1974 with a
grant from the Billie Trimble Chandler Arts Foundation, Inc.,
which provided a permanent collection of Asian art and artifacts,
which has steadily grown.

A diorama of the Japanese emperor and empress in the Imperial
Palace greets the visitor as he comes into the entry area. Also on
display are the legendary Seven Gods of Good Fortune and
hundreds of figures of children.

The wall cases in the next exhibit all present a history of the
performing arts of Japan—with figures depicting traditional
festival dances, masks for ceremonial performances, Bunraku
puppet heads, masks and figures of the Noh and Kabuki theaters,

and fans used for many purposes. Around the perimeter of the
other walls are dioramas of a bamboo forest home, a Shinto shrine,
and other historical characters in their native environments. There
is also a display featuring the kimono and the obi, the traditional
Japanese dress. Cloisonne, lacquerware, porcelain, woodcarving,
and metalworks from many Asian cultures are displayed.

Two large cases of earthenware figures and containers represent
the evolution of pottery production in Japan over thousands of
years. Bronze vases and incense burners, and porcelains from
Japan and China are also displayed.

The Imperial Room contains commissioned portraits of every
emperor of Japan throughout history, as well as oil paintings of the
Imperial Palace, an Imperial ceremony, and two scenes from the
Japanese Creation mythology.

Imperial Room

Displays of Buddhist sculpture and ritual items and paintings of
Buddhist and Hindu deities are mounted when temporary
exhibitions do not pre-empt the large exhibit hall. Some of the
special exhibitions planned for the remainder of 1982 are: Folk
Arts—Japan and Mexico; Boys Day; Ukiyo-E—Woodblock Prints;
Raku Pottery; and Jean Despujols: Scenes from Southeast Asia.

The museum is honored to display the works of Fona Celis
Cabrera, who has resided in Corpus Christi for the past few years.
The works are watercolors that reflect the seventeenth-
and eighteenth-century two-dimensional art tradition of Japan.

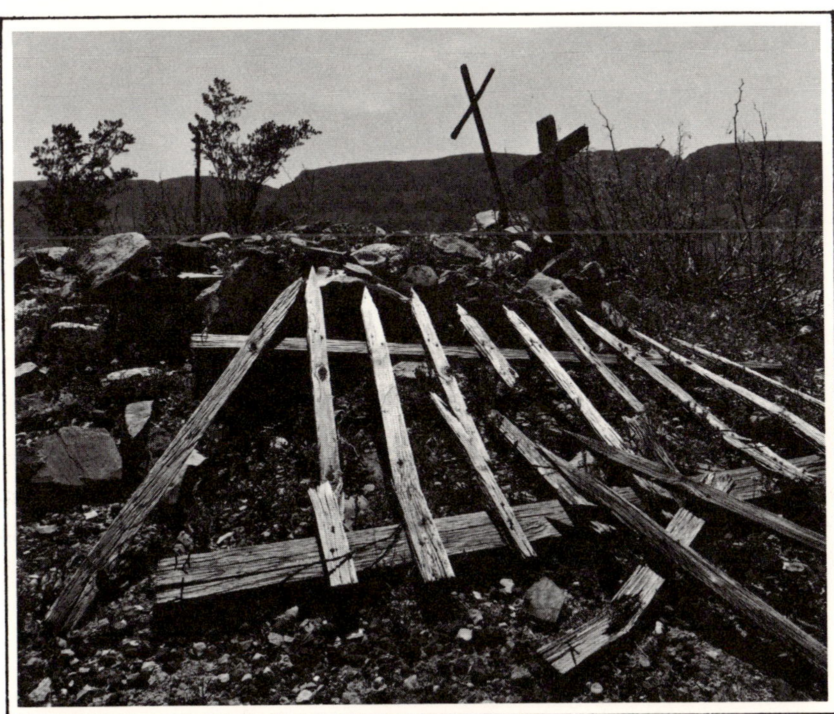

Frank Armstrong, *Teringua Abaja,* Big Bend National Park 1981, copy-
righted photo. Laguna Gloria Art Museum.

Lyndon B. Johnson Library and Museum   2312 Red River
Austin 78705   (512) 397-5137   Daily: 9-5

The Johnson Library and Museum is administered by the National
Archives and Record Service, General Service Administration.
The archives house 31 million papers—the largest collection of
documents in any of the six presidential libraries in the United
States. The bulk of the holdings consists of 17 million presidential
papers, 6 million pre-presidential pages, 6 million papers donated
by associates of LBJ, and 2 million federal records. This is
primarily a library for scholarly research.

The museum houses a collection of more than 35,000 historic
objects. Its holdings include the personal possessions of President
Johnson and a bounty of materials that are acquired only by those
who serve in the nation's highest office: 15,000 gifts to the
president from the American people; 1,000 gifts from heads of
state; and 3,000 original political cartoons. Holdings range from a
T'ang Dynasty tomb sculpture to a rock brought back from the
first manned landing on the moon.

The most popular exhibit is the replica of the Oval Office. It is a
7/8 reproduction accurate to the smallest detail. Many temporary
and touring exhibitions fill the exhibit calendar each year.
Exhibits organized by the Johnson Library and Museum widen the
range of its influence by traveling throughout the country.

There is an active program of symposia at the library that make
it a national forum for the free exchange of ideas. All programs,
usually jointly sponsored by the University of Texas, are open to
the public without charge.

Laguna Gloria Art Museum   3809 W. 35 St.   Austin 78763
(512) 458-8191   Tuesday-Saturday: 10-5; Sunday: 1-5;
Thursday: 10-9

Laguna Gloria Art Museum is the only museum in Texas and the
Southwest devoted exclusively to American art of the twentieth
century. It is an exciting combination of historical place and
contemporary purpose. The museum is housed in a Mediterranean
style villa which was built in 1916 by Clara Driscoll Sevier and
deeded in 1943 to the Texas Fine Arts Association for use as a
museum.

Continually changing exhibitions represent the diversity and
richness of American art. There is no permanent collection, other
than the sculpture on the grounds, which includes an installation
by Nancy Holt.

Recent exhibitions have included the work of Dan Flavin,
Miriam Schapiro, Howardena Pindell, Christo, and Robert
Smithson. Regional and Texas artists are an important area of
concentration: Amado Pena, Frank Armstrong (photography),
Janet Kastner, John Huke, and Randy Smith-Huke.

**Johnson
Library
and
Museum**

Oval Office

**Laguna
Gloria
Art
Museum**

exhibitions

An ongoing exhibition series entitled New Works presents the work of leading artists of the region. Highlights of the coming months will include the Texas Fine Arts Association National Exhibition, juried by Howard N. Fox, Assistant Curator for Exhibitions, Hirshhorn Museum and Sculpture Garden, Smithsonian Institution; Recollections: Ten Women of Photography; and New Works by Austin Artists: Another Look.

programs

The Program Department presents a variety of lecture, performance, film, and video programs to large audiences throughout the year. Some programs are designed to augment and expand the scope of the museum's exhibitions. Films, ranging from works by independent filmmakers to films by or about artists, reveal the vitality of the film movement and its place within American art as a whole. Lectures by scholars, artists, and critics serve to interpret and enhance current exhibitions, while the museum's performance programs of dance and literature focus on the emerging artist and underscore the interrelatedness of all the arts.

The museum is at the end of west 35th St. The MoPac Freeway is adjacent to it, and the West 35th St. cutoff leads to the museum's front gate.

Leeds Gallery

Leeds Gallery   Humanities Research Center   University of Texas at Austin   Austin 78712   Academic Center 414   (512) 471-4664   Monday-Friday: 8-4:45

Humanities Research Center at the University of Texas at Austin was created in 1957 by the chancellor, Harry Huntt Ransom, as a repository for the special collections purchased or donated to the university since 1883. Holdings include rare books and manuscripts, photography collections, theater arts, and art works.

The Art Collection consists of approximately 40,000 items, primarily nineteenth- and twentieth-century literary research materials, 1,000 etchings, engravings, woodcuts from the fifteenth through the nineteenth century; 10,000 portraits in all media; and major collections of book illustration, typography, and wood-engraved blocks.

Individual works by well-known artists include: Rossetti, Lucas Cranach, Sir Joshua Reynolds, Jacob Epstein, Max Beerbohm, Eric Gill, Joseph Pennell, Edmund Burne-Jones, Arthur Rackham, Jean Cocteau, e.e. cummings, Joe Brown, Sir Peter Lely, Mary Beale, Romeyn de Hooghe, Hans Sebald Beham, Wyndham Lewis, William Rothestein, John Singer Sargent, von Ostade, and Rembrandt.

The Eric Gill collection is substantial. Gill (1882-1940) was a sculptor, engraver, draughtsman, and typographer, and examples of his work in every media are in the collection—about 3,000 pieces.

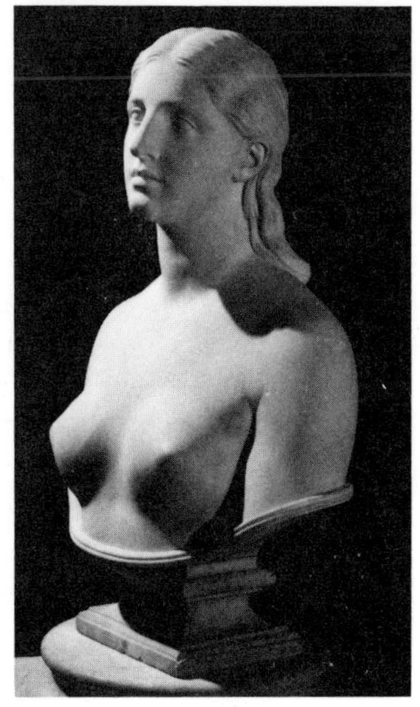

Hiram Powers, *Eve Disconsolate,* 1859, 24″ high, marble. Archer M. Huntington Art Gallery.

Significant features of the French art collection are the works by
Jean Cocteau, his drawings and designs, as well as works by
Valentine Hugo, Odilon Redon, and 600 portraits of French
literary figures.

Sculptured works in marble and bronze feature nineteenth-
century artists Elisabet Ney and Bailly and Houdon.

The thrust of the collections centers on the literary worlds of the
last two centuries and encompasses primarily the works of Great
Britain, France, and the United States. Art works from the
sixteenth through the eighteenth centuries, however, include
examples from all of Europe.

The fourth floor of the Academic Center features, as well as the
H.R.C. Art Collection and the Leeds Gallery, Special Collections
Rooms which house the following art works and libraries: Alfred
and Blanche Knopf library; J. Frank Dobie Collection; Jack Josey
Room; Edward Larocque Tinker Collection; and the Erle Stanley
Gardner Study. The lobby area contains tapestries by the Gobelin
Factories and a portrait of Falstaff by Gainsborough Dupont.

McNay Art Institute

Marion Koogler McNay Art Institute   6000 N. New Braunfels Ave.
San Antonio 78209   (512 824-5368   Tuesday-Saturday: 9-5;
Sunday: 2-5

Marion Koogler McNay was a discriminating collector, a generous
patron, an earnest student of the fine arts, and a philanthropist of
the first magnitude. She created and endowed a museum to be
devoted to the modern and early arts, to collecting and preserving
them, and to presenting them to a public with which she was eager
to share.

the building

The mansion which was to become the museum was begun in
1927 under the skillful direction of Atlee B. Ayres. It was one of the
most elaborate in San Antonio at the time—the culmination of Mr.
Ayres's extensive studies of Mexican and Mediterranean architecture. Like Isabella Stewart Gardner of Boston, Mrs. Atkinson
participated actively in the design, construction, and embellish-
ment of the residence.

The museum opened in November 1954. The collection offers a
broad survey of modern French painting, with masterpieces by
Cezanne, Gauguin, Redon, and Picasso. Mrs. McNay had virile
tastes, and rather than Impressionism, she was inclined toward the
Expressionist traditions. She also assembled a rich group of
American watercolors, headed by Winslow Homer, Childe
Hassam, and Maurice Prendergast, as well as an exemplary
collection of New Mexican folk art.

Other bequests have enhanced the collection greatly. The
Oppenheimer collection of medieval and gothic arts was particularly rich in German and Netherlandish wooden sculpture, in
both Northern European and Italian panel paintings, and in

notable French stone sculpture. The Lang collection of 62
important works of art included major paintings by Shahn,
O'Keeffe, Dubuffet, Klee, and Braque, and sculpture by Calder,
Degas, Matisse, Picasso, and Giacometti.

Robert L.B. Tobin, an ardent collector and generous patron, has
aided the collection's growth in every area, notably through a
large group of stage designs by Robert Indiana and blocks of prints
by Jacques Villon and paintings and prints by George Grosz. His
contributions of rare illustrated books of the twentieth century and
of master modern prints are also extensive.

Ten color prints by Mary Cassatt, given by Mrs. Edgar Tobin,
are the *pieces de resistance* of the print cabinet.

A selection of 100 prints from the permanent collection will be
on exhibit from June to August, 1982. Art of New Mexico will be
featured in June and July, 1982. Other 1982 exhibits will be: The
Goya *Disasters of War,* which will be traveling to several museums
in Texas; the Graphic Work of Toulouse-Lautrec; Collectors'
Gallery XVI, a selection of works borrowed from New York
galleries and on sale to the public; and in early 1983, American
prints from the McNay's permanent collection.

To drive to the McNay Art Institute go out U.S. 81 (Austin
Highway) to N. New Braunfels Ave. It is also possible to go by bus:
the Broadway-Terrel Heights bus from Houston & North St. Mary's
Sts. or Broadway & Houston St.

Museum of the Southwest   1705 W. Missouri Ave.   Midland
79701   (915) 683-2882   Monday-Saturday: 10-5; Sunday: 2-5

The Museum of the Southwest was incorporated on September 25,
1965, under the auspices of the Junior League of Midland. In 1968
it moved to its present home, a house designed for Juliette and
Fred Turner, Jr., by Anton F. Korn, a Dallas architect.

There are over 4,000 square feet of exhibition space on the first
and second floors. The original porch has been enclosed to form
the Thomas Gallery.

The permanent collections focus on the art and anthropology of
the Southwest. Parts of the collection include the Fred T. and
Novadean Hotan Collection of the Taos Society of Artists, an
international print collection, works of Merritt Mauzey,
contemporary and traditional Southwestern works in all media,
costumes, Native American Indian art and artifacts, the works of
Colonel "Bud" Bissell, a West Texas archaeology collection, an
eighteenth- to twentieth-century fan collection, and decorative
arts.

Major exhibitions during the past year have included both
traveling and in-house exhibits: Afghanistan; Confluence of
Tradition and Change: 24 Contemporary Indian Artists; Painters
in Taos: The Eiteljorg Collection: History of American Quilts;

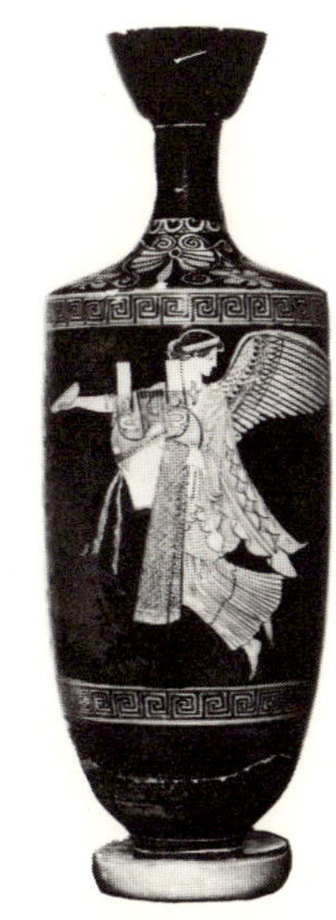

Oionokles Painter (Southern
Italian), *Red Figure Lekythos*
(c. 470 B.C.), 15" high. Archer
M. Huntington Art Gallery.

transportation

Museum of the Southwest

Merritt Mauzey Graphics and Paintings; and Western Art: A
Collection of Legendary Graphic Observations by Bob Bell.

   The annual Southwestern Area Art Show, held every summer,
presents works of local artists from the greater Southwestern
region. All media are eligible for the juried competition.

Nave Museum

The Nave Museum   306 W. Commercial   Victoria 77901
(512) 575-8227   Tuesday-Sunday: 1-5

The Nave Museum is an art museum operated by the Victoria
Regional Museum Association. The building was designed by San
Antonio architect Atlee B. Ayres and was erected as a memorial to
Texas artist Royston Nave following his death in 1930. The museum
owns a collection of Nave's paintings and a small number of
contemporary works, primarily by Texans. The museum maintains
an active exhibition program, opening new exhibitions every six
weeks. Exhibits are organized by the museum or are borrowed
from other museums, exhibition services, and private collectors.

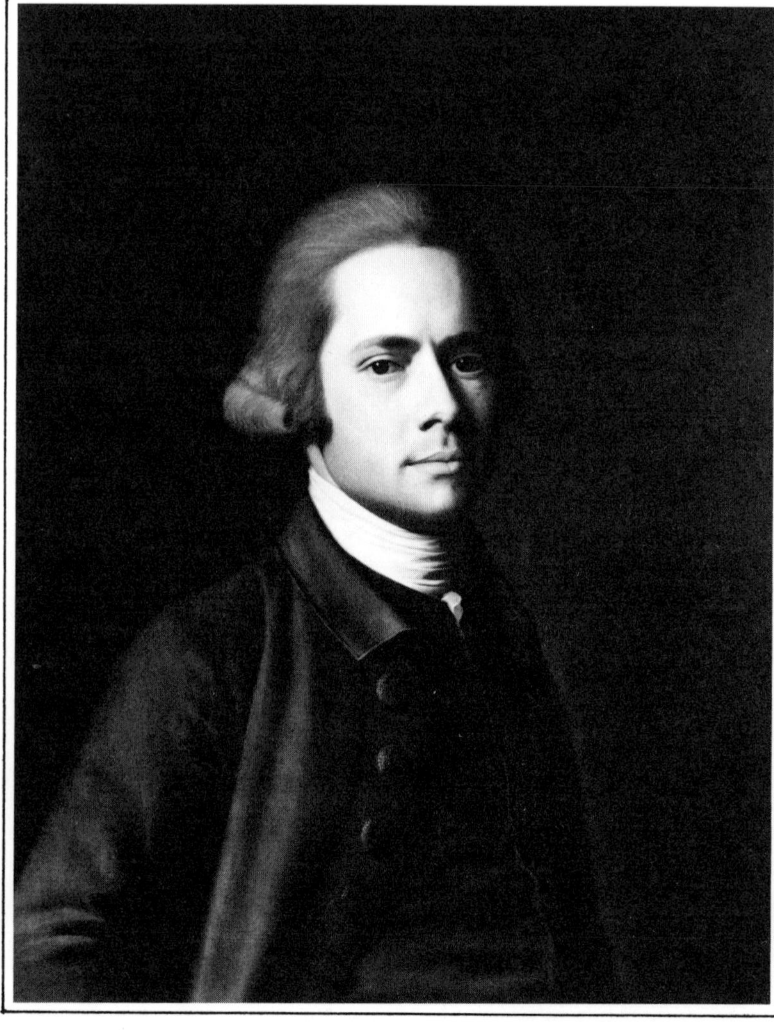

John S. Copley, *Portrait of a
Man in Blue,* 30" x 25", oil on
canvas. San Antonio Museum
Association.

San Antonio Museum of Art   200 W. Jones Ave.   San Antonio
78209   (512) 826-0647   Daily: 10-5; June 1-August 31: 10-6
Admission: $2 adults; $1 children under 12. Saturday and
Sunday: free until noon

The San Antonio Museum of Art is one of three facilities operated
by the San Antonio Museum Association, which was founded in
1923. The association also operates the Witte Museum and the San
Antonio Museum of Transportation.

the building

The museum is housed in a group of buildings originally
constructed for the Lone Star Brewing Company, which was
chartered in 1883. A major San Antonio enterprise for more than
30 years, during the early 1900s the Lone Star became the state's
largest brewery, producing a variety of labels and serving a
market that stretched from Texas westward to California and south
to Mexico. Adolphus Busch of the Anheuser-Busch Brewing
Association of St. Louis served as principal owner of the brewery,
and it was he who launched a major expansion program adding
the castlelike towers that house the art collections of the San
Antonio Museum Association.

In the early 1970s, at a time when the brewery complex had
fallen into disrepair, the San Antonio Museum Association saw the
buildings as an ideal location for a municipal art museum; it was
close to the San Antonio River and the downtown area and could
be easily adapted into an art facility. It was decided that the main
building would become the art museum, and the seven ancillary
buildings could be restored for offices, shops, storage, and a
restaurant. Only a few minutes from the inner city, the brewery-
turned-museum has towers and turrets of modified Romanesque
design with details reminiscent of medieval fortifications. Its
ceilings are 20 feet high in some areas, and numerous ornate
columns adorn the 16 spacious galleries. The two principal towers
are connected by a glass-enclosed skywalk, a contemporary
addition, which offers a view of the city and the picturesque banks
of the river. Glass-enclosed elevators inside each tower carry
visitors through four levels of galleries.

collections

The permanent collection of paintings, sculpture, and
decorative arts emphasizes regional materials and the arts of the
Americas. Some highlights of the collections are as follows:

Photography: American photography since 1920, including the
works of Ansel Adams, Diane Arbus, Imogene Cunningham,
Edward Weston, Dorothea Lange, Walker Evans, and Edward
Steichen.

Contemporary and modern art: paintings and sculpture by
Frank Stella, Wayne Thiebaud, Philip Pearlstein, Ron Davis,
Richard Diebenkorn, Mark Di Suvero, George Segal, Robert
Tiemann, Hans Hofmann, and Larry Bell.

Texas furniture, paintings, and decorative arts: one of the best collections of Texas art in the country. Multi-colored quilts, Texas campaign dinnerware, furniture. Paintings by William Samuel, Carl G. von Iwonski, Theodore Gentilz, Hermann Lungkwitz, and Rudolph Mueller.

Eighteenth- and nineteenth-century art: paintings by Gilbert Stuart, Edward Hicks, John Singleton Copley, Benjamin West, Asher Durand, Jasper Cropsey, William Merritt Chase, and John Linton Chapman.

Nineteenth- and twentieth-century art: paintings by Ernest Lawson, Marsden Hartley, Robert Henri, Lyonel Feininger, Arthur B. Davies, and Julian Onderdonk.

In addition the collection includes American Indian and pre-Columbian art, Mexican folk art, and Spanish colonial art.

Some recent exhibitions have included: Russell Lee, one of the greatest documentary photographers of American social history; Between Continents/Between Seas: Pre-Columbian Art of Costa Rica; and American Landscape, a photography exhibit organized by the Museum of Modern Art in New York.

The museum is just north of downtown—west of Broadway and east of St. Mary's St.

transportation

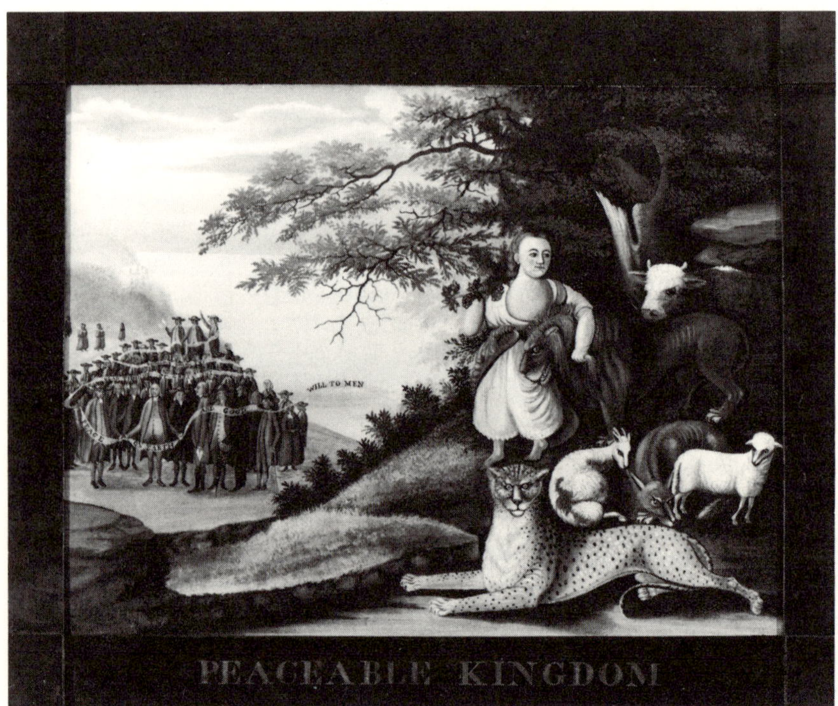

Edward Hicks, *Peaceable Kingdom with Quakers Carrying Banners* (1830-35), 17½″ x 23½″, oil on canvas. San Antonio Museum Association.

South Texas Artmobile   Center for the Arts   Corpus Christi
State University   6300 Ocean Drive   Corpus Christi 78412
(512) 991-6810, Ext. 369   Monday-Friday: 8-4 (September-May)

The South Texas artmobile is a nonprofit organization sponsored
by Corpus Christi State University and the James R. Dougherty,
Jr., Foundation. Founded in 1969 the mobile gallery travels from
September to May displaying original works of art to 36
communities throughout South Texas. The self-contained art
gallery provides an opportunity for schoolchildren and adults to
view two touring exhibits each year which include a wide variety
of styles, media, and processes. Background material and
explanation are given by a curator from the staff.
   The exhibits are organized by the university art-gallery staff.
Works are acquired through loans from individual artists,
galleries, museums, and collectors.
   Since its opening in 1969, over twenty centuries of art have been
presented to the communities of South Texas. The exhibits were
selected to introduce to the viewers different periods and styles,
ranging from the prehistoric Indian period of Mexico to the
modern and contemporary period in American art.

South Texas Artmobile

Texas Memorial Museum   2400 Trinity   University of Texas at
Austin   Austin 78705   (512) 471-1604   Monday-Friday: 9-5;
Saturday-Sunday: 12-5

The museum was built for the Texas Centennial in 1936 on the
grounds of the University of Texas at Austin. Exhibits and
collections focus on anthropology, history, geology and
paleontology, and natural history.
   The geological exhibits include explanations of how rocks are
made and how certain minerals are mined and processed, with
collections of meteorites, tektites, and other rocks and minerals.
The internationally renowned Barron Collection of gems and
minerals is displayed in a sizable alcove. Exhibits in paleontology
include fossils, and casts and pictures of amphibians and reptiles,
dinosaurs, and fossil insects.
   Natural-history exhibits feature the animals and plants of Texas.
Exhibits in the Hall of Man relate the story of man, with emphasis
on Native American cultures: North, Central, and South.
Demonstrations of how man has created cloth and pottery
complement such exhibits as the Huaxtec ceramic figurines,
pre-Columbian Peruvian pottery, and weaving from the
southwestern United States.
   Other outstanding exhibits in the Hall of Man are the Great
Stone Head of La Venta (a cast of an artifact of the Olmecs—
the oldest civilization of the Americas); a collection of beautifully
carved wooden ceremonial relics from New Guinea; a series of

Texas Memorial Museum

paintings done by contemporary Native American artists; and the
Paul Perez collection of masks of southern Mexico.

Special exhibits include the current show, Ties, Rails, &
Spikes, developed by the museum staff, and Implements of
Women's Work, an exhibit of nineteenth-century patent models.
Costume exhibits from Czechoslavakia and Mexico are currently
featured.

Weil Gallery   Center for the Arts   Corpus Christi State
University   6300 Ocean Drive   Corpus Christi 78412   (512)
991-6810   Monday-Friday: 9-5

Weil Gallery

The Weil Gallery was opened in 1979 in the Center for the Arts, a
multidisciplinary building dedicated to integrating visual and
performing art. Works shown are from an international selection of
all media, which range from traditional to contemporary works.

Traveling exhibitions arranged by other institutions as well as
shows organized by the university art gallery staff comprise the
program here.

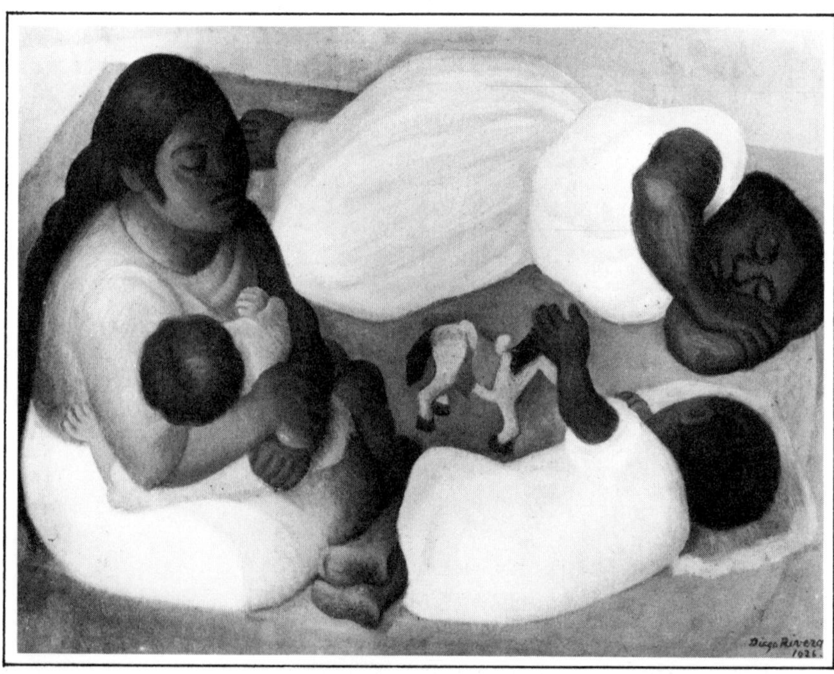

Diego Rivera, *La Siesta,* 1926, oil on canvas.
San Antonio Museum Association.

Wichita Falls Museum

Wichita Falls Museum and Art Center   2 Eureka Circle
Wichita Falls 76308   (817) 692-0923   Monday-Saturday: 9-4:30;
Sunday: 1-5

The Wichita Falls Museum and Art Center has a relatively small
but top-quality collection of American prints ranging from the
early colonial period to the present. The collection begins with A
Map of New England (Wine Hills Map), 1677, produced by John
Foster, America's first printmaker, and extends through the
contemporary printmakers of today. Several important artists who
are represented include: Paul Revere, George Catlin, Winslow
Homer, James Abbott McNeil Whistler, Asher B. Durand, Mary
Cassatt, Edward Hopper, John Marin, Jackson Pollock, Roy
Lichtenstein, Jasper Johns, Robert Indiana, Claes Oldenberg, and
Louise Nevelson.

Wilderness Park Museum

Wilderness Park Museum   2000 Trans-mountain Rd.   El Paso
79924   (915) 755-4332   Wednesday-Saturday: 9-5; Sunday: 1-5

A branch of the El Paso Museum of Art, the Wilderness Park
Museum is devoted to archaeology and science.

The collection includes Pueblo and early area Indian pottery;
artifacts of the Paleo-Indian and more recent American Indian
cultures.

Large dioramas depict A Cave Valley Pueblo in Old Mexico, A
Hueco Tanks Indian Scene, the Paleo-Indian Kills a Mastodon in a
Bog, The Hunting and Gathering Era, and A Pit-House Habitat.

A wilderness foot trail, a pit-house picnic area, and
archaeological excavation replicas are on the site.

Witte Memorial Museum

Witte Memorial Museum   Brackenridge Park   San Antonio
78209   (512) 826-0647   Monday-Friday: 9-5; Saturday, Sunday,
Holidays; 10-6   Admission: voluntary donation; Adults $.50;
children, $.25

The oldest of the three museums under the aegis of the San
Antonio Museum Association, the Witte Memorial Museum was
founded in 1926 by Ellen Schulz Quillan. Originally a history and
science museum, the Witte now includes exhibits related to the art
of the Americas: American contemporary painting and sculpture,
photography, decorative arts, Texas furniture and decorative arts,
and an American Indian collection.

There are four historic early Texas houses and a furnished log
cabin on the grounds. Slide presentations depict the highlights of
San Antonio history.

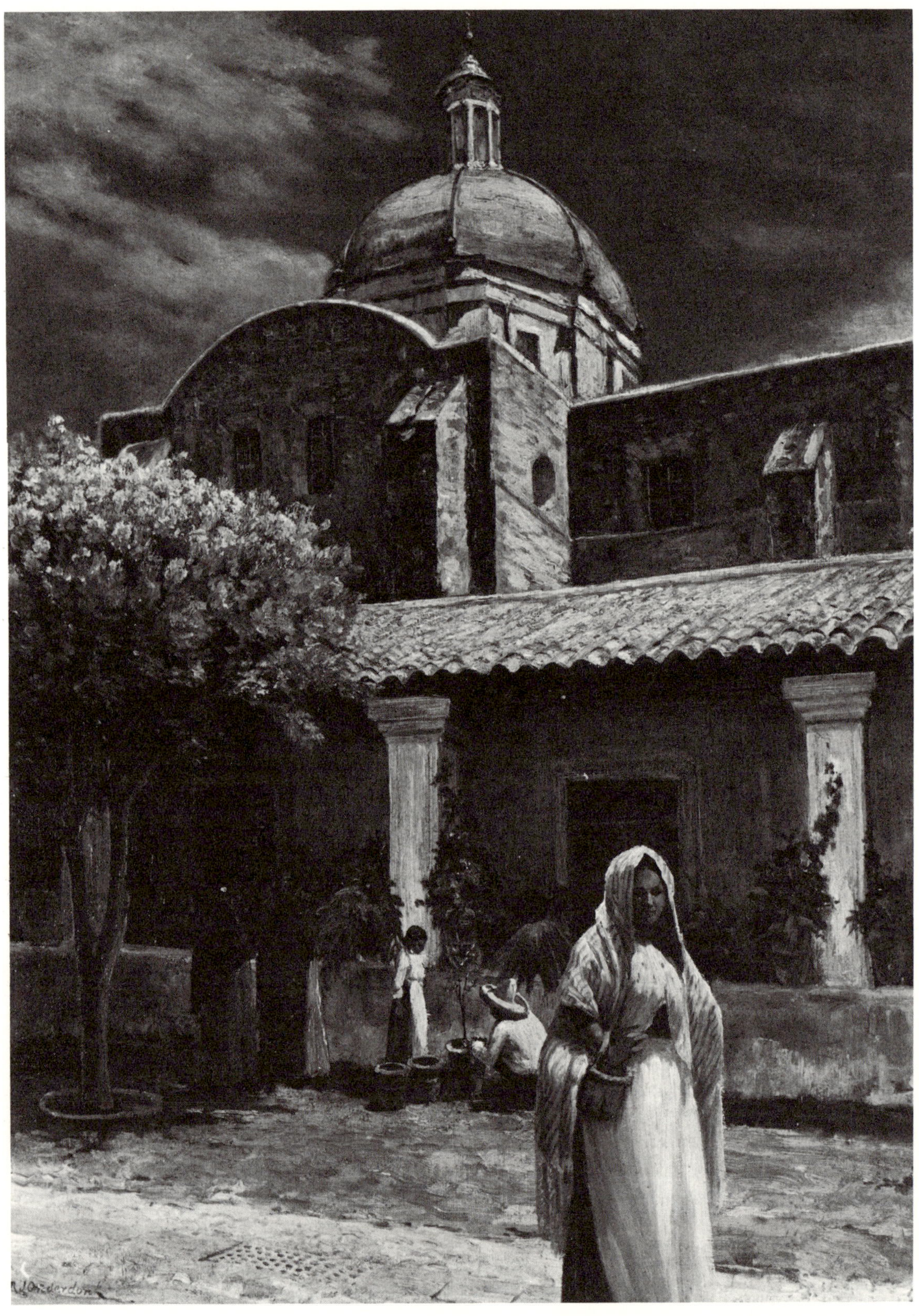

Robert J. Onderdonk, *Catholic Sister's Home in Mexico,* 1911, 24″ x 18″, oil on canvas.
San Antonio Museum Association.

The Galleries

Charlton Art Gallery   308 N. Presa   San Antonio 78205
(512) 223-2181   Monday-Saturday: 10-5:30

Contemporary regional artists are featured here—paintings, drawings, prints, sculpture, ceramics, and photographs.

The media are varied: the abstract sand paintings of David McCullough; Brad Braune's representational watercolors; Gilberto Tarin's figurative fantasies in acrylic; E.O. Goldbeck's panoramic photographs; and the vibrantly colored aquatints of Dan Allison.

A comfortable setting for viewing local talent.

Charlton Art Gallery

Country Store Gallery, Inc.   1304 Lavaca   Austin 78701   (512) 474-6222   Monday-Friday: 8:30-6; Saturday: 9-1

The Country Store Gallery rests on foundations of tradition and heritage. The building which houses the Country Store is a landmark in Austin. Originally, it was a mid-nineteenth-century plantation home. Square nails which were used in the construction are still in evidence in portions of the building. Other features of the original house include an indoor, spring-fed well, and basement-level slaves' quarters.

As early Austin spread out from the banks of the Colorado, the farmland became part of town. The plantation home became a boardinghouse operated by a Mrs. Key. During the construction of the Capitol, the architect and the project superintendent boarded with Mrs. Key.

In more recent times, the old building has been a landmark for the commemoration of heritage through the presentation of fine art. It is appropriate that this building which is, itself, a part of history, should play a role in the continuing salute to our heritage through the display of Texas and Western art.

Country Store

This gallery has made all types of fine paintings available to buyers throughout the Southwest and the United States for many decades. These fine, original paintings also include those of great artists from all periods, including Old Masters and the French Impressionist school, as well as American artists of quality.

The Country Store Gallery continues to be a significant part of the tradition and heritage which are unique to Austin.

Double-T-Ranch Gallery   5302 D. Slide Road   Lubbock 79414   (806) 792-2306   Monday-Saturday: 10-6

Double-T-Ranch

The Taylors, who had previously owned a Western store for 10 years, opened the gallery in March 1979 as an outgrowth of their long interest in Western and Indian art.

Principal artists shown here include Alfredo Rodriguez, a young portraitist; Jodie Boren, who works in watercolors and oils on Western themes; and James Ralph Johnson, an expert on cavalry.

Bronzes by Cowboy Artists of America—some deceased—include: John Hampton, Byron Wolfe, Shorty Shope, Ned Jacob, James Boren, John Kittelson, and Fred Harmon.

Also included in the Double-T-Ranch inventory are beautiful Navajo woven rugs, Indian pottery, and paintings by Indian artists such as Abeita, Benciti, and Hunting Horse.

The back room is devoted to limited-edition prints from nationally known artists. There is a good selection of out-of-print prints as well as recent issues. The gallery tries to deal in a wide range of prices.

The James M. Haney Gallery   4500 I-40 West   Amarillo 79106   (806) 358-3653   Monday-Saturday: 10-5

Haney Gallery

James M. Haney, the southwestern artist, opened his gallery in February of 1980. Although much of the original and limited-edition work shown in the gallery is southwestern in influence, the gallery also offers antique European painters, contemporary work, ceramic sculpture, hand-carved decoys, and bronze sculpture.

Most of the painters have worked in oils or acrylics and are representational in style. James M. Haney, southwestern still-life; Marlin Adams, traditional still-life, landscape, and portrait painting; Neal White, energy-related landscapes depicting life in the oil fields; and Truman Kluck, beautiful hand-carved decoys of ducks, geese, and swans are the main attractions here.

Some of the most unique sculpture offered in the gallery is that of Santa Fe artist Mary Ann Gerber. Her ceramic sculpture depicts the native American Indian in fully detailed one-of-a-kind pieces. Her "Indian Madonnas," Indian women with children, are the most popular with collectors.

Graphic works shown in the gallery include signed and

numbered limited-edition offset lithographs by James M. Haney,
Marlin Adams, and Neal White, plus works by a host of other
well-known artists. A highlight are the original silkscreens by artist
and master printer Jeffrey Sims. His subtle treatment of flowers is
quiet and beautiful.

Hanging Tree

Hanging Tree Gallery   #102 San Miguel Sq.   Midland 79703
(915) 694-9772

Hanging Tree Gallery opened in March 1976 under the direction
of Carol Swain. The gallery features works by noted professional
artists and specializes in subjects of the Southwest ranging from
small-scale sculpture and prints to mammoth bronzes. A staff of
consultants give personalized service and advice to corporate
accounts.

The storytelling art of Gerald Farm portrays the nostalgia and
the tender side of the Old Wild West. Robert Summers, one of the
country's leading bronze artists, also paints the contemporary
cowboy in a combination of soft impressionistic landscape and
realistic detail. Amada Pena's serigraphs depict his own Hispanic
culture in bold graphic design. Jerry Ruthven paints landscapes of
his native Texas hill country. The smooth brush technique of D.R.
Parker and his dramatic use of light give his works wide appeal.

The canvases of Bettie Felder reflect the artist's own self. A
Felder painting is love—peace—joy—a drama featuring children
in a storybook world.

Life-size song birds and game birds and wood carvings by J.J.
Fox complete the inventory.

Lubbock Lights

Lubbock Lights Artists' Co-op Gallery   1701 Ave. Q   Lubbock
79401   (806) 744-2218   Tuesday-Sunday: 12-6

The gallery began in 1978 as the only contemporary gallery within
a 100-mile radius. It was started and operated by Lora Hunt and
Debbie Milosevich until the business became too distracting to
their own artistic production. In January 1980 it turned into a co-op
with approximately 23 members, many with young, national
reputations. As a co-op it has continued to handle the work of
contemporary artists from other parts of Texas and from New
Mexico.

The gallery has a wide range of media from painting, prints,
drawings, and photography to ceramics, jewelry, neon, and
textiles. Quickly gaining national repute are the Expressive
Symbolist prints and paintings of James W. Johnson, the bitingly
romantic serigraphs of Future Akins, the impeccably beautiful
functional ceramics of James Watkins, the delicate porcelain
pieces of Cecily Smith-Garnett, and the bizarre sculptural jewelry
of Ron Davis.

Other interesting work by the members includes the unique woven bead necklaces of Linde Stewart Carneiro, the engaging neon/mixed-media sculpture of Jennifer or Tony Greer, the sensual, humorous ceramics of Esmeralda Delaney, and the elegant jewelry of Joan Harvey. Some of the work of nonmembers includes the prints and drawings of Suzy Klotz-Reilly, prints and drawings by Ken Saville, the records of Terry Allen, and the earcuffs of Dell Fox.

Other members are Ashton Thornhill and Gilbert Boucher, photography; Lora Hunt, prints and music boxes; Susan Budge and John Chinn, ceramics; Amy Blackburn-Fiel, prints and drawings; Joanna Moss, paintings and drawings; Jim Carlin, paintings; Valerie Komkof-Hill and Starr Shelton, textiles.

Three rooms of the gallery are devoted to an assortment of members' and nonmembers' work, while one room is maintained for featuring one- to three-person exhibitions and an annual Christmas show.

Mission Gallery

Mission Gallery   112 Mission St.   San Antonio 78210   (512) 271-3643   Monday-Friday: 8-5; Saturday: 8-12

The gallery opened in 1981 in the King William Historic District. Emphasis thus far has been on exhibiting watercolors by contemporary Texas artists. Among those to exhibit have been Henry Rayburn, Joseph Polley Paine, and Joe L. Lopez.

Henry Rayburn's subject matter ranges from early Texas scenes, to florals, to abstractions. His style varies from near-photographic realism to free-flowing lyrical brushstrokes. His color schemes range from subdued sepia washes to brilliant opaque splashes of color. Works of Joseph Polley Paine encompass a wide range of objective and nonobjective concepts in paintings and graphics. Joe L. Lopez's subject matter is normally the Hispanic people of Texas and Mexico. He has a continuing series titled "Hermosa Vida."

The intricate pen-and-ink works of David Honhorst are also featured. His works use limited subject matter and precision tools to reveal possible variations on a theme.

Also available are prints from Argentina and Uruguay, functional stoneware pottery by David Chohlis, and original stained-glass designs by Carol Halbrook.

The gallery is available for one-to four-week shows. Opening receptions are held on either Saturday or Sunday. Exhibition space is approximately 1,000 square feet in four rooms. A layout and photographs of the gallery will be provided upon request. Fees and services are flexible to meet individual requirements.

Galerie Ravel   1210 W. 5th   Austin 78703   (512) 474-2628
Tuesday-Saturday: 11-5

Galerie Ravel

Galerie Ravel, which opened in 1976, carries an extensive
collection of contemporary original prints by European,
American, and Latin American artists. The major focus at this time
is on Latin American works.

Examples range from surrealism to figurative works, in both
prints and paintings. There are works by such major artists as
Armando Morales, paints and oils; Tamayo, prints and mixografia
prints; and prints by Zuniga and Carlos Merida. Also included are
European prints by Appel, Clave, Miro, Wunderlich, Antes,
Vasarely, and Coignard; and American prints by Rauschenberg,
Dine, Calder, Lindner, and Oldenberg.

One gallery has five to six showings a year of the work of
established as well as promising young artists such as Kenneth
Hale, printmaker and painter; Yvonne Burk, printmaker and
painter; Pauline van Bavel-Kearney, ceramist; Teodulo Romulo,
painter and printmaker.

There are two exhibition areas, a small, intimate area in front
with a large room in the rear. An excellent reference library is
available.

Rue de Lamar Gallery   8738 N. Lamar   Austin 78753   (512)
837-7040   Monday-Saturday: 10-5

Rue de Lamar

Mary McCluskey opened the gallery in September 1971 and
moved it to its present location in November 1980. The gallery is
traditional in style, with fine antiques throughout.

Original traditional oil paintings and watercolors are featured:
impressionist works by F. Gall, A. Gisson, Esra and Americo
Makk, A. Collins, H. Dubois, and others. Fine landscapes by
R.D. Enright and A.D. Greer have an enthusiastic audience.
Floral oils by O. Leevis and paintings by P. Salinas and Robert
Wood are also featured.

The gallery motto is "Something for everyone, sensibly priced."

Shown-Davenport Gallery   Austin and Tenth Sts.   San Antonio
78209   (512) 828-7515   Wednesday-Sunday: 11-4

**Shown-
Davenport**

Co-directors John Shown and Don Davenport opened the Shown-
Davenport gallery in March 1980. They change exhibits every
week and have up to this time shown 200 artists, mainly from the
local area. However, as the gallery's reputation has increased,
artists from California and New York have contacted the gallery
and have shown here. The gallery is completely open-minded, but
generally the work is contemporary, including performance
pieces and installation and conceptual art.

Artists who are regularly shown here include New York

printmakers Robert Adsit and Larry Young and local artists Shown
and Davenport, artists in their own right. Others include Rayburn,
Ray Chavez, and Brad Braune.

Stitcheries, including John Shown's well-known "house portrait"
series, are on exhibit throughout the year. A room separate from
the rest of the gallery space houses the Shown-Davenport ceramics
where gift items designed by Don Davenport can be purchased.

The fast-paced changing exhibits have in the past featured rock
bands and video. The gallery does not necessarily concentrate on
avant-garde work, however; realistic painters such as Eva
Templeton also exhibit here.

The gallery is a meeting place for young area artists, and the
weekly openings are a perfect place to get together and discuss
what is going on in the art world. The gallery has several annual
theme shows. The Salon des Refuses (rejects from the San Antonio
Art League's annual show) is typical.

Texas Trails Gallery   245 Losoya   San Antonio 78205   (512)
227-1541   Monday-Saturday: 10-6; Sunday: 10:30-5:30

Texas Trails

Texas Trails Gallery has been in operation for twelve years, five of
which have been at the present location on the famed San Antonio
Riverwalk in the heart of the major hotel district.

Among the examples of Western and Indian art which are the
specialty here are works in oil and watercolor by Don Trioni, a
historical painter who knows his uniforms; acrylics by Jean Bales,
an Iowa Indian who paints scenes of the everyday life of her tribe;
watercolors of the contemporary West by Scott Kennedy;
watercolors of ranch life by Clif Cavini; and acrylics of Texas
wildlife by Andrea Peyton.

One gallery space is devoted to original paintings and working
studies by Henry J. Soulen who died in 1965. All of these works
appeared in the Curtis Publications.

Sculptures by Frank Polk, David Lemon, Bill Nebecker, Don
Smith, and Wah Ming Chan; ceramics by Pat Pauli; and Navaho
rugs can also be seen.

A rear gallery space is devoted to limited-edition prints by John
Clymer, James Boren, James Reynolds, Tom Lovell, Range Hood,
Jerome Tiger, and Kelly Haney.

Dallas-Fort Worth
and Northcentral Texas

Museums and Public
Exhibition Spaces

Amon Carter Museum   3501 Camp Bowie Blvd.   Fort Worth
76101   (317)738-1933   Tuesday-Saturday: 10-5; Sundays &
holidays: 1-5:30

Amon Carter
Museum

Amon G. Carter, founder and publisher of the Fort Worth *Star-Telegram*, began his collection of Western American art with the purchase of a group of watercolors by Charles N. Russell, the "cowboy artist" of Montana. The collection continued to grow, and he left instructions in his will that a museum be built to house it after his death so that the works of art could be made available to the people of Texas, and the study and documentation of Western North America should be furthered.

    The building, designed by the well-known architect Philip Johnson, was opened to the public in 1961. It is a graceful and dramatic structure built of native Texas shell-stone. Five arches on tapered columns form an expansive, shaded porch that looks on to shady garden terraces. The building focuses on the magnificent main gallery from which open ten smaller, more intimate galleries. The museum also houses a large reference library specializing in American art and history, and a small theater and bookstore.

the building

    Although in the beginning the Amon Carter Museum emphasized Western art, under its founding director, the late Mitchell A. Wilder, the institution broadened its perspectives to take in the art and history of the American frontier, that is, the entire Western movement from sea to shining sea. Today the museum is one of the finest museums of American art in the land, with a wide-ranging collection of painting, sculpture, and photography that has grown far beyond the boundaries of any specific region or period. Nevertheless the permanent collection does primarily reflect the nineteenth and early twentieth centuries. The collection of Remingtons and Russells remains one of the finest in the world and surveys show that a large percentage

collections

of the museum's visitors come here just to see paintings and bronzes by these two artists.

There are scores of Remington paintings in the museum, but perhaps the most popular is *A Dash for the Timber,* a large, dramatic oil depicting a horseback skirmish between troopers and Indians. Almost as popular is the Remington bronze sculpture showing a foursome of cowboys off on a toot, *Coming Through the Rye.* The collection of Russells numbers well into the hundreds and incudes sketches, bronzes, paintings and examples of that artist's humorous illustrated letters.

Among the other artists and illustrators of the Old West represented in the museum's vast collection are the landscape painters that accompanied early survey parties, such as Alfred Jacob Miller, Albert Bierstadt, Thomas Moran, Thomas Worthington Whittredge, and John Mix Stanley; Buffalo Meat, a Cheyenne warrior who created charming drawings of tribal life while a prisoner of the U.S.; cowboy artists Edward Borein and William James; E. Irving Couse, one of the original members of the Taos Society of Artists; Henry Farny; Harry Jackson; Frank Tenney Johnson; and Olaf Seltzer.

While the casual visitor may come to see these, the reputation of the museum's collection of major nineteenth-century paintings is also growing. Winslow Homer's *Crossing the Pasture,* the only Homer oil in the permanent collection of any Southwestern museum, portrays an idyllic, rural scene typical of an earlier, simpler America. Martin Johnson Heade's dark, dramatic *Thunderstorm Over Narragansett Bay* is one of the finest American seascapes while *Two Hummingbirds above a White Orchid*, by the same artist, is an almost voluptuous picture of nature.

Remington collection

nineteenth century painting

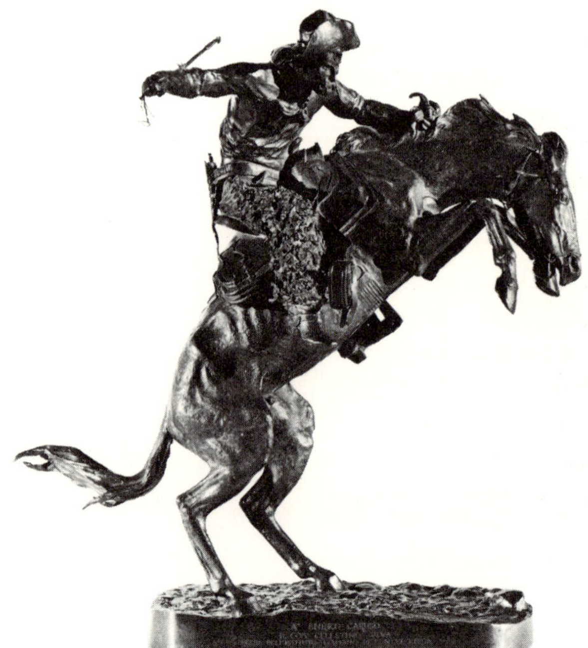

Fredric Remington, *The Bronco Buster,* 1895, 23¼" high bronze. Amon Carter Museum.

Among early twentieth-century works in the collection are a number of interpretations of the Southwestern landscape by artists connected with Alfred Stieglitz's famous American Place Gallery, for example Thomas Marin's *Taos Canyon, New Mexico,* and Stuart Davis' *New Mexican Landscape*, Georgia O'Keeffe's beautiful *Light Coming on the Plains I, II,* and *III,* painted near Amarillo and Canyon, Texas, represent a series of early, near-abstract watercolors in which the artist first achieved the lyrical simplicity that marks her mature work.

Among recent acquisitions by the Amon Carter Museum are a lushly colorful still-life, *The Lobster*, by Arthur G. Dove, another member of the Stieglitz circle; Eastman Johnson's *The Peep,* a charming nineteenth-century genre painting of a mother and child at play; William Merritt Chase's *Idle Hours,* an airy, sunlit view of the beach near that artist's famous summer home at Shinnecock, Long Island; *Mother and Daughter, Both Wearing Large Hats* by Mary Cassatt, the only American welcomed to exhibit alongside the impressionists; and a gilded, six-foot version of Augustus Saint-Gaudens' *Diana,* one of only a few casts of this important nineteenth-century sculpture in existence.

A special attraction of the Amon Carter Museum is its photography collection, one of the largest in the country with more than 120,000 prints and negatives. While many of these are of a documentary nature, the "fine-arts" portion of the collection includes approximately 2,500 prints by masters of American photography from the days of the daguerrotype to the present. This collection includes the entire estate of the late Laura Gilpin documenting that photographer's 65-year career in the American Southwest. The historical photography collection includes several large collections devoted to specific areas of Western American history: nineteenth- and early twentieth-century Colorado, the Plains Indians wars; the Southwest during the 1890s; the history of nineteenth-century Kansas and the West.

Although it is neither by an American nor about the American West, Henry Moore's *Upright Motives I, II,* and *VII* stand in the plaza in front of the museum, framing one of the most spectacular views of Fort Worth's skyline visible anywhere in the city.

The Amon Carter Museum originates a fair number of exhibits, including, most recently, shows of Thomas Moran's watercolors and of works by early Western artist Alfred Jacob Miller, organized jointly with the Walters Art Gallery in Baltimore and the Buffalo Bill History Center in Cody, Wyo. The museum also plays host to traveling exhibits of American art and history. Special recent exhibitions included An American Perspective: Nineteenth-Century Art from the Collection of Joann and Julian Ganz; Cast and Recast: The Sculpture of Frederic Remington; American Photographers and the National Parks: An Exchange

*twentieth
century collection*

photography

exhibitions

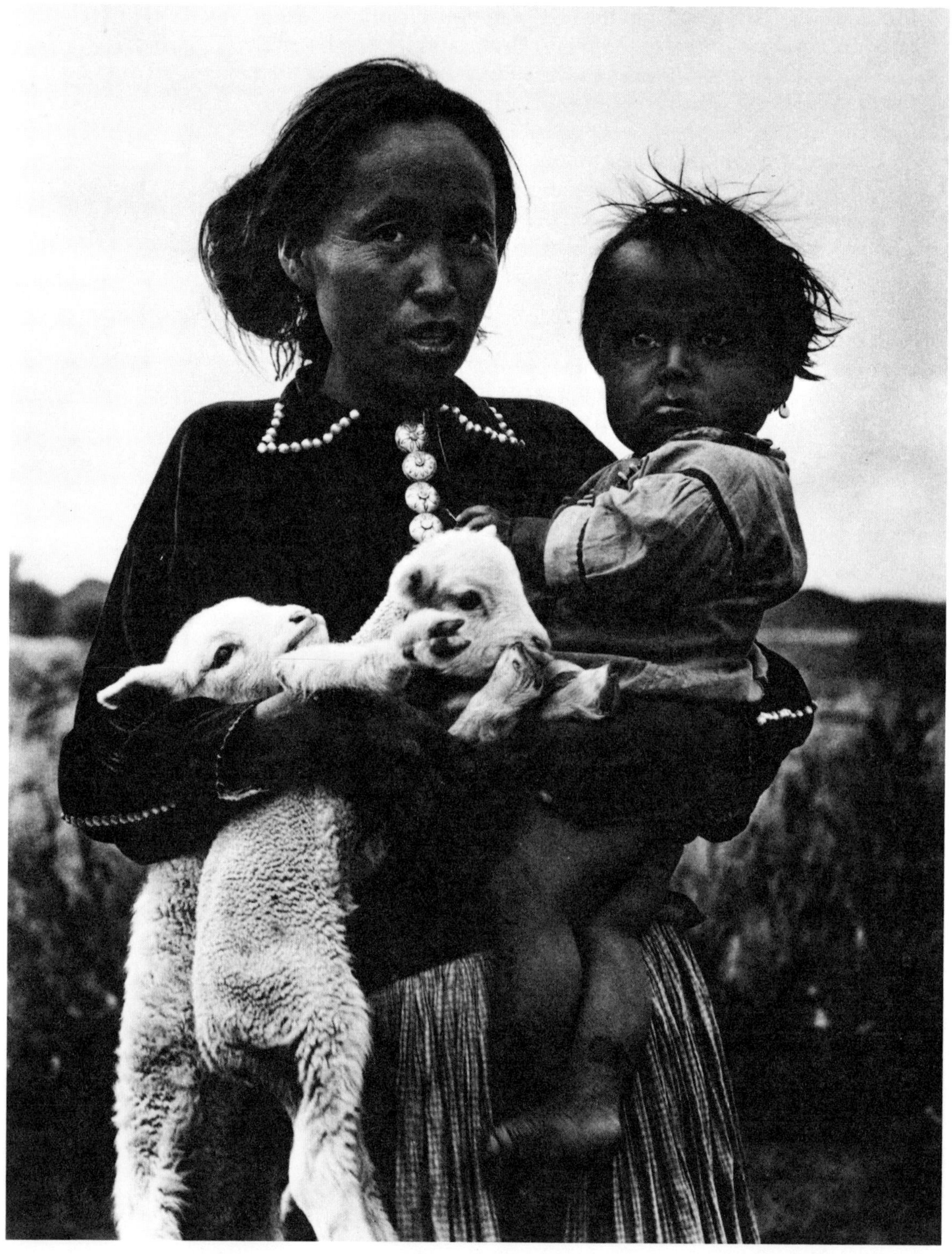

Laura Gilpin, *Navaho Woman, Child and Lambs*, Photograph. Amon Carter Museum.

Exhibit with the Gilcrease Institute of American History and Art in Tulsa; Santos; and American Artists in Brittany and Normandy.

There is a lively schedule of lectures, films, and special programs concerning areas of interest to the museum—the West, American history, and American art, and the book store is well stocked with books on these same subjects. The library, one of the best in its field, is open only by appointment.

To reach the Amon Carter Museum, exit from I-20 at Montgomery and continue north to Lancaster and Camp Bowie Blvd.

Art Center

The Art Center   1300 College Drive   Waco 76708   (817) 752-4371   Tuesday-Saturday: 10-5; Sunday: 1-5

This multifaceted organization was founded in 1972 to provide McLennan County with a permanent visual-arts institution that would encourage the appreciation of art and stimulate creative expression. Established by the Junior League of Waco, with a grant from the Waco Model Cities Agencies, the Art Center has grown in a few years from a small program in a downtown store front to a broad-based, community-supported organization that has become well known throughout Texas for its outstanding exhibitions and activities.

Currently emphasis is on offering the best in changing exhibitions rather than on acquiring a permanent collection. Excellence in a multitude of visual art forms is the aim here: folk art, graphic and industrial design, photography, crafts, and architecture are featured in addition to paintings, drawings, prints, and sculpture.

Classes and workshops are offered in a variety of media. Special events include art tours to other cities, Sunday afternoon "happenings" in the courtyard, "watch and work" sessions with artist/teachers, a series of film classics, or a day-long "Art Affair" designed for family participation.

An innovative docent training course focuses on twentieth-century art forms and prepares volunteers to give tours for schoolchildren and adult groups.

Dallas Museum of Fine Arts

Dallas Museum of Fine Arts   Fair Park   2nd and Parry Aves. Dallas 76226   (214) 421-4133   Tuesday-Saturday: 10-4; Sunday: 1-5   Admission free

In 1962 the Dallas Art Association (which was formed in January 1903) merged with the Dallas Museum of Contemporary Arts to form the Dallas Museum of Fine Arts.

The Dallas Museum of Fine Arts is presently housed in the building that was the original Texas Centennial Building located in Fair Park. It is a simple building with eleven galleries surrounding a large court.

In late 1983, however, the doors will open on a new Dallas Museum of Fine Arts, located on an 8.9-acre site on the northern edge of the city's central business district and designed by Edward Larrabee Barnes. The new $40-million-plus building is unique: half of the costs is being borne by the property owners of Dallas who, in 1979, approved a $25 million bond issue for a new museum. It was the largest such amount ever voted for such a project.

Judging from models and from the building itself, which is now nearing completion, Barnes' design is low-key and functional, yet elegant, a low rambling affair that will be seen to best advantage against the dramatic backdrop of the downtown area. A flowing series of galleries extends along a central circulation corridor with curatorial offices and the museum's education wing located along the opposite side of this corridor. Each of the galleries is pierced by a small courtyard filled with appropriate plantings (bamboo for the Asian gallery, waterlillies for the impressionists). Each gallery is a few steps up from the one before so there is a natural sense of progression. The main, or entrance, gallery will display traveling exhibits. It is topped by a large barrel vault, Barnes' homage to Louis Kahn's Kimbell Art Museum over in Fort Worth. An outdoor sculpture garden will feature waterfalls and reflecting pools.

With the new facility, the Dallas Museum will not just be moving across town; it will be entering a whole new era. Perhaps for the first time in its history, facilities will be adequate for the museum's tasks. Exhibit space is being multiplied three-fold so that the museum will be able to mount a major traveling exhibition and several smaller temporary shows without having to take down any of the permanent collection.

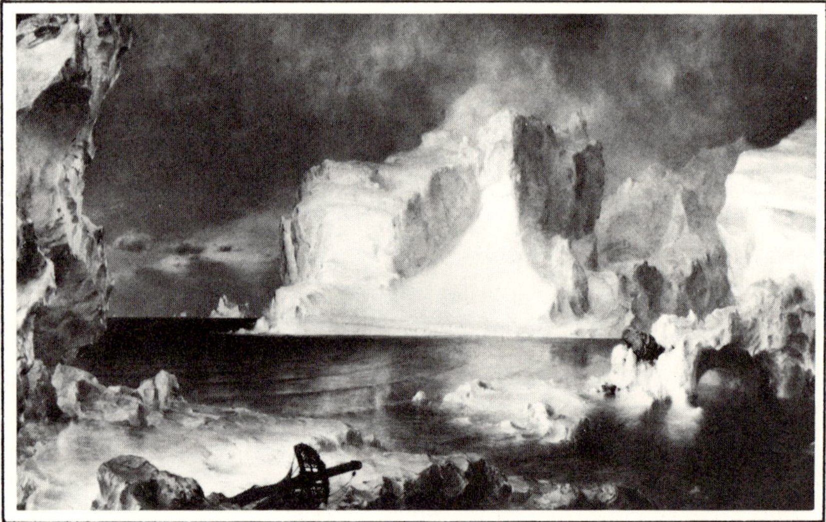

Frederic E. Church, *The Icebergs,* 1861, 64½" x 112½", oil on canvas. Dallas Museum of Fine Arts.

Best of all, when the Dallas Art Association placed the case for a new museum before Dallas voters, one of the most persuasive arguments was an estimated $25 million worth of art, works from some of Dallas' premier collections, that had been promised to a new museum. When the new building opens the permanent collection, which has grown astonishingly during recent years, will be increased by the addition of major impressionist and early modern works and a unique collection of Guatemalan textiles.

In the meantime, some of these works have already arrived at the museum and there is still more than enough in the museum's present facility to occupy an art lover for an extended visit.

The permanent collection includes African sculpture, outstanding pre-Columbian art, Oriental, classical, baroque, nineteenth- and twentieth-century American, Impressionist, modern and contemporary art.

Two main areas of concentration are African sculpture and the pre-Columbian art of central and South America. The heart of the African holdings are the Stillman collection of Congolese sculpture and the Schindler collection of African art, the gift of which immediately catapulted the Dallas Museum into a position of excellence within this field. A huge wooden headdress from Baga, Guinea broods over the gallery entrance. The group of African masks is particularly impressive. The pre-Columbian collection is, if anything, even richer than the African collections. Among the items on display is a chief's ransom in Peruvian gold, including beakers, breastplates and intricate earrings and other ornaments, some so small the museum has placed them behind magnifying glasses. The *Paracas Mantle*, 200-100 B.C., from Peru is one of the most beautifully preserved garments in existence from so early a period. The most important single piece to enter the pre-Columbian gallery, however, is an Aztec mask probably made about 1475 and representing the rain god Tlaloc. Carved of wood and overlaid with turquoise tesserae, the mask was painstakingly restored by the museum and now forms a dramatic centerpiece to the collection.

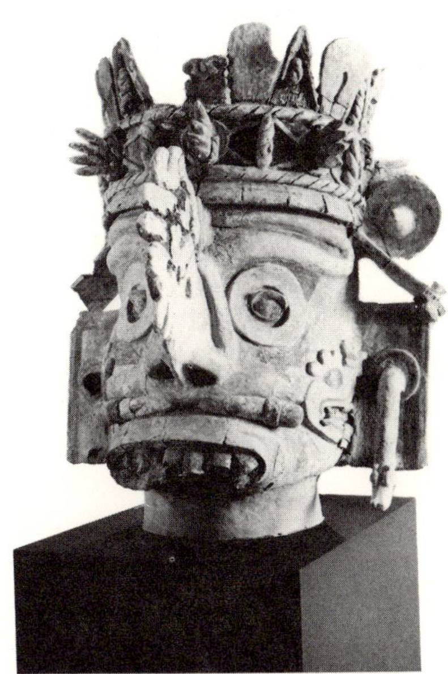

Mixtec (Mexico: Oaxaca, Teotitlan del Camino), *Head of the Rain God, Tlaloc,* (1300-1500 A.D.), polychrome ceramic, 51" high. Dallas Museum of Fine Arts.

Also a recent acquisition, the serene, graceful *Bodhisattva Padmapani* is a twelfth-century gilt bronze statue from Nepal, a region and period not previously represented in the Dallas Museum's collections.

Although the European collection includes a small group of paintings from the Baroque period, main emphasis is upon the nineteenth and twentieth centuries. Gustave Courbet's masterpiece, *Fox in the Snow,* 1860, is a beautiful evocation of an animal in a winter landscape with its contrasting textures of rock, snow, and luxuriant fur, as well as an unflinching vision of the struggle for survival. *Outside the Print-Seller's Shop*, painted about the same time by Honore Daumier, is a richly luminous work, filled with sharp social observation. Edouard Manet's *Portrait of Isabelle Lemonnier* (c. 1879), is one of the small, intimate works this artist painted towards the end of his life, a portrait of an elegant, somewhat cool young woman who reportedly spurned the aging painter's repeated advances. Impressionism is emerging as one of the particular strengths of the Dallas Museum. Claude Monet's *La Seine a Lavacourt* shows off this artist's love of transient lighting effects, captured by the use of short, separate brushstrokes.

The museum's collection of impressionist and modern works was enriched dramatically early in 1982 both in quality and quantity with the presentation of 38 paintings from the collection of the late Algur H. Meadows. The Meadows gift included two more fine Monets, *Blue Mountain* of 1884 and a circular *Waterlilies* of 1908; Berthe Morisot's charming *Woman with Muff*; Camille Pissarro's *Peasant Carrying Hay,* and two intimate interiors, Edouard Vuillard's *Interior* and Pierre Bonnard's *After the Bath.*

The museum's growing collection of nineteenth-century sculpture contains many fine works but few as important and none as dramatic as *Jean d'Aire from the Burghers of Calais,* a full-size bronze cast of one of the figures from Rodin's most celebrated sculpture group.

Centerpiece of the museum's collection of American art is *The Icebergs* painted in 1861 by Frederic Edwin Church, a large, spectacular landscape full of dazzling greens and golds. Long lost and rediscovered only a few years ago hanging in a British orphanage, the work was as celebrated in its own day as it has become again in ours. George Inness's silvery landscape, *View of Rome From Tivoli* (1872) is a softer-focus, more painterly work. The emphasis is upon atmosphere, light and paint-handling rather than upon a dramatic topography. Mary Cassatt's tender *Sleepy Baby* reveals the artist's debt to the impressionist Edgar Degas from whom she learned to handle pastels. The domestic version of impressionism is represented by Childe Hassam's *Flags, Fifth Avenue.* One of the smaller gems in the collection is Winslow Homer's deft little watercolor, *Casting in the Falls.* Its matter-of-fact approach and the brilliant cleansing sunlight also mark Edward Hopper's *Lighthouse Hill* as an essentially American work.

In recent years the Dallas Museum has also developed a growing and increasingly important collection of modern and early modern works. The gift of five paintings by Piet Mondrian from the James H. and Lillian Clark Foundation now means that the museum now has a selection of the Dutch artist's work second to none, one that covers his entire career from early landscapes to the final, geometric abstractions. The Clark gift also includes three important canvases by Bernard Leger.

Other important early modern works in the collection include *Constructed Head No. 2*, a celluloid sculpture by the important Russian modernist Naum Gabo, in which a portrait bust has been rendered as a series of intersecting translucent planes: Rene Magritte's mysterious *Light of Coincidences* (1933), a play on painted versus "real" reality, featuring a picture-within-a-picture of a nude torso lighted by a candle. Henry Moore's *Reclining Mother and Child*, a gift from the artist, is one of the rare plaster originals from which Moore's bronze sculptures are cast.

atrium gallery

The Museum's atrium gallery features a small group of works by the first generation of abstract expressionist painters. These include canvases by Mark Rothko, Franz Kline, and James Brooks, as well as the unusual *Portrait and a Dream*, by Jackson Pollock, in which the artist has juxtaposed a representational image of a young woman's face with the more typical skeins of dripped and splashed paint. Tom Wesselmann's sultry *Mouth #11* hangs high on the wall overlooking this gallery, exhaling smoke. One of the most recent acquisitions is James Rosenquist's *Paper Clip,* a tour-de-force combining a wide variety of images that subtly echo one another.

An adjoining gallery displays even more recent works, such as Al Held's big, colorful *D-C, 1979,* a field of meshing geometric grids and patterns; Carl Andre's sculpture *Pyramid,* a construction of carefully stacked fir planks; Jenifer Bartlett's *Sad and Happy Tidal Wave,* a glossy diptych enameled on steel plates; and *Platform with Stairs,* Richard Shaffer's large painting of his studio interior in which spaces are breathtakingly established by the use of deep shadow and dazzling light.

sculpture gardens

There are a number of important sculptures on the grounds surrounding the museum. Richard Serra's untitled work, in which two massive slabs of steel are deftly balanced against one another, exudes an air of menace. Kenneth Snelson's delicate, airy construction of crane booms and steel cables, another brilliant feat of balancing, stands nearby in the lagoon.

Twelve to 14 temporary exhibits are mounted each year; approximately half of them are generated by the museum itself, and the rest are traveling shows. One of the leading exhibitions of the 1981-1982 season was Impressionism and the Modern Vision: Master Paintings from the Phillips Collection, an unprecedented traveling show of 75 master paintings underwritten by a grant from BATUS Inc.

exhibitions

Some of the other special exhibitions planned in the near future are: Form and Emotion in Photographs: Dallas Collects; Early American Painting; Concentrations VII: Deborah Butterfield; and El Greco of Toledo, a major exhibit organized by the Toledo (Ohio) Museum of Art, the National Gallery of Art, and the Dallas Museum of Fine Arts, to demonstrate El Greco's role as an interpreter of political, economic, and civic concerns through his religious works, myths, and profane subjects. The installation will introduce Toledo, Spain, as depicted in El Greco's art and will show the cultural milieu in which he lived.

The museum also displays a regular series of one-artist exhibitions called "Concentrations." In the past these shows have offered works by a number of important younger artists who are just beginning to receive notice in important art publications.

Educational activities relate closely to current exhibits and also include projects in drama, music, and art. Lectures are given every Wednesday at 11; tours, Tuesday, Thursday, Friday at 11, Wednesday at 1, and Sunday at 2. A Texas Artists Resource File keeps up-to-date information and slides. The library is open Tuesday-Saturday 10-5, Sunday 1-5.

The Dallas Museum's buffet, which has been called the best museum lunch in the U.S., features delicious homemade soups, homebaked bread, salad, dessert, and tea or coffee, all for $5. Wine is available at extra cost.

To reach the Fair Park Building, take I-30 east to Fair Park, 2nd Ave., exit and turn left after the signal light into the parking lot. The new building will be located on a site in the Central Business District bounded by Ross Ave., Woodall Rogers Expressway, St. Paul & Harwood Sts.

Fort Worth Art Museum   1300 Montgomery St.   Fort Worth 76107   (817) 732-9215   Tuesday-Saturday: 10-5; Sunday: 1-5 Admission free

Fort Worth Art Museum

From its beginning in 1901 the Fort Worth Art Museum has steadily evolved into a distinguished museum of contemporary art that complements the collections of its sister institutions, the Kimbell Art Museum, and the Amon Carter Museum.

A growing collection has led to two expansions of the original building built by Herbert Bayer in 1954 to accommodate the collection that was originally housed in the Public Library. The latest renovation in 1974 more than doubled the gallery space and allowed for more extensive exhibitions and continued growth of the permanent collection.

That collection includes a small group of nineteenth- and early twentieth-century paintings, mostly American works acquired in the museum's early days. They include George Inness's *Approaching Storm*, the first painting purchased for the museum, and Thomas Eakins' *The Swimming Hole*, acquired along with two sketch boxes from the artist's window. Early modern works in this group include Arthur B. Davies' semi-abstract *Figures*, 1912; *Continuity*, a precisely rendered painting of factory forms by Charles Sheeler; Milton Avery's *Mando-cello Player*; a John Sloan seascape, *High Tide in Gloucester*, and Georgia O'Keeffe's beautiful floral closeup, *Yellow Cactus Flowers.* These works are usually exhibited together in a small gallery next to the museum's entrance.

Among the few early modern works by European artists are *Beached Boats and Lighthouse,* an airy seascape by the nineteenth-century French artist, Eugene Boudin, usually considered a precursor to the impressionists; *Above and Left,* a geometric abstraction by Wassily Kandinsky; and Picasso's bronze cubist sculpture, *Head of a Woman.*

European collection

The museum has two major paintings by first-generation abstract expressionists, Mark Rothko's *Light Cloud, Dark Cloud,* featuring shimmering fields of red, and an untitled abstract by Clyfford Still in incandescent yellow, orange and black. Three of Josef Alber's spare, geometric *Homage to the Square* paintings were recently presented to the museum by the Joseph Albers Foundation.

Art of the 1960s and '70s, however, is the Fort Worth Art Museum's stock-in-trade. An untitled series of 10 stainless steel and orange plexiglass boxes by minimalist Donald Judd is permanently installed in the museum's stairwell. Other contemporary works in the permanent collection include *Rivers of Ponds IV,* one of Frank Stella's brilliantly colorful "protractor" series of abstract paintings; two lovely acrylic "stain" paintings by Morris Louis, *Beta Mu* and *Picture with Red Stripe*; Claes Oldenburg's *Prop from Massage* (1966): *Tube and Contents,* a large soft sculpture of a tube oozing paint; and Michael Singer's graceful construction of reeds, stones and pine slats, *First Gate Ritual Series 10/78.*

contemporary collections

The Fort Worth Art Museum occasionally commissions artists to create works for its permanent collection. An untitled scrim construction by Robert Irwin has been installed in the museum's stairwell. Robert Rauschenberg's large panel, *Whistle Stop (Spread),* is an homage to the artist's early days in Texas. Red Groom's now-famous *Ruckus Rodeo,* is a bigger-than-life-size comic extravaganza celebrating Fort Worth's annual Fat Stock Show.

The museum's excellent graphics collection includes Picasso's entire *Suite Vollard,* Jasper John's *Figure Series,* and Robert Motherwell's *A La Pintura.* The photography collection is small, but growing. Among the works are a group of seven photographs by Ralph Gibson, selections from Gary Winogrand's *Rodeo Portfolio,* and several photos with a humorous twist by the American, Elliot Erwitt, and by French photographer, Robert Doisneau.

graphics

There is also a small group of large-scale sculpture in the park surrounding the museum: James Surls' big, rough-hewn wood sculpture, *Sticker Woman,* is on long-term loan to the museum. It

sculpture

keeps company with John Henry's large yellow steel work, *Super Fly,* Mac Whitney's *Window,* and an untitled steel sculpture by Harry Geffert.

The museum plays host to a wide range of traveling exhibits emphasizing modern and contemporary art and in addition it has mounted its own excellent "Focus" series of one-artist shows, each spotlighting work by an important contemporary artist. Traveling shows during the past year have included "late entries" to the Chicago Tribune Tower contest, a show of architectural drawings for hypothetical projects; a major retrospective of works by pop artist Roy Lichtenstein; and an exhibit of the tiny clay "civilizations" created by Charles Simonds as dwellings for his imaginary "Little People." Focus exhibits have featured color photographs and a major installation by Sandy Skoglund, paintings by the neo-expressionist Richard Bosman, and Ed Blackburn's black and white paintings of scenes from old grade-B Western movies.

The museum's interests also encompass contemporary architecture, design, photography, film, and the performing arts. Regular gallery talks, a film series, lecture-demonstrations by dancers and other performers, the annual "Critical Comments" lecture series, featuring well-known artists, critics and scholars, children's workshops and special tours fill out the museum's busy schedule of events.

There is a small but well-stocked bookstore in the lobby. The museum publishes an illustrated monthly calendar describing exhibitions and listing special events.

From I-20, take the Montgomery Exit, turn right to Lancaster, and turn right again. The museum is at the corner of Montgomery and Lancaster.

Ralph Gibson, *Untitled,* 20" x 16", Photograph.

Hall of State   Fair Park   Dallas 75226   (214) 421-5136
Monday-Saturday: 9-5; Sunday: 1-5   Admission: Adults 50¢;
children 25¢; Monday afternoon free

The Hall of State of the Dallas Historical Society was regarded as
the architectural centerpiece of the Texas Centennial Exposition in
1936. Even today, this monumental structure is considered by
many to be one of the finest examples of Art Deco architecture in
the United States.

the building

   Faced with Cordova cream limestone quarried in central Texas,
the facade is dominated by a concave entrance flanked by long,
rambling wings. The entrance portal features a heroic bronze and
gold-leaf statue of *The Tejas Warrior* taking aim, with his bow, at
some target high above his head. Inside, the Hall of Heroes is
dedicated to statesmen and soldiers who contributed to the birth
and lasting life of the Republic of Texas. Ensconced on large
marble pedestals are six life-size bronze statues of heroes of the
revolution in which Texas won its independence from Mexico:
Stephen Austin, General Sam Houston, William Barrett Travis,
Mirabeau B. Lamar, Thomas J. Rusk, and Colonel J.W. Fannin.
They were created by Pompeo Coppini. Above the Hall of Heroes,
a frieze by Eugene Savage records various battles of the Texas
Revolution. Bronze plaques explain the significance of the Battle
of the Alamo and of San Jacinto.

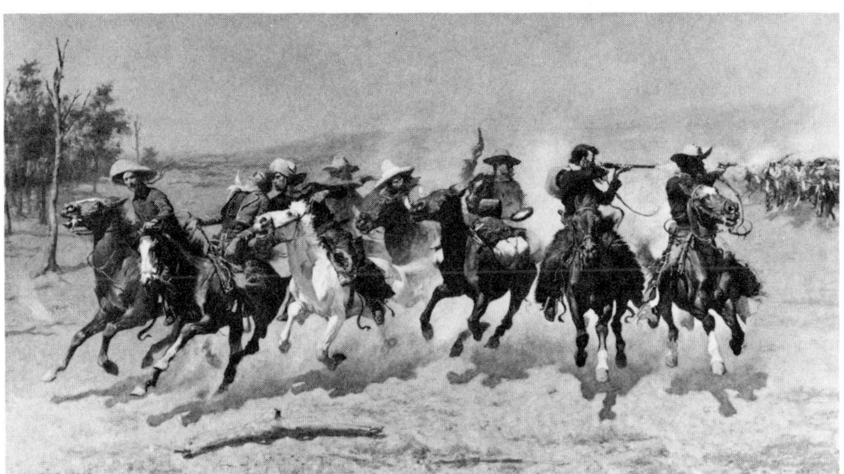

Fredric Remington, *A Dash for the Timber,* 1889, 48¼ x 84¼", oil on
canvas. Amon Carter Museum.

Historical Society

   The Dallas Historical Society has maintained its offices in the
basement of the Hall of State since 1938. The Society serves as a
center for historical research, cares for a large collection of
historical objects that now numbers more than 13,500 items,
maintains exhibits on the main floor of the Hall of State, and
schedules temporary displays, lectures, film series, and other
events.

Among recent exhibitions at the Hall of State have been *Good as Gold: Alternative Materials in American Jewelry*, a show of works by some 90 craftsmen from all over the U.S.; *Visionary Drawings: Architecture and Planning,* a large exhibit of futuristic and utopian plans by architects dating from 1900 through the 1960s; *That Red Head Gal: Fashions and Designs of Gordon Conway, 1916-1936,* a display of work by the Texas-born, internationally known fashion designer; *Mexican Dance Masks*; and *Posters for Victory,* a show of U.S. propaganda posters from the World War II years.

Exhibits during the coming few years will focus on the Texas Sesquicentennial, which will be celebrated in 1986.

To reach the Hall of State from downtown, take I-30 east to the Second Avenue exit, turn right onto Second Avenue and then left at the first signal. Proceed straight through the Fair Park main gate. The Hall of State is about a block due east.

Kimbell Art Museum   Will Rogers Road West   Fort Worth 76107
(817) 332-8451   Tuesday-Saturday: 10-5; Sunday:
1-5   Admission free

Kimbell Art Museum

In 1966 the City of Fort Worth provided space for a building near the Amon Carter Museum and the Fort Worth Art Museum to house the collection of the late Kay Kimbell, a Fort Worth industrialist. The Kimbell collection had its start in the 1930s. On a visit to a Fort Worth Art Association show in the old downtown public library, Kimbell fell under the spell of English eighteenth-century painting. He was later introduced to Mr. Bertram Newhouse of New York, a gallery owner, who helped the Kimbells gather together fine examples of later European Renaissance, French nineteenth-century and American nineteenth-century art, as well as British painting in the grand tradition. It is this magnificent group of paintings that became the nucleus of the Kimbell Art Museum.

When Kimbell died in 1964, he left his art collection together *the building* with the considerable fortune he had accumulated through his various financial enterprises to the Kimbell Art Foundation, along with instructions to provide works of art and a suitable place to display them for the citizens of Fort Worth. Kimbell's wife, Velma, also donated her share of their property to the foundation in return for an annuity. Blessed with this generous endowment, estimated at more than $100 million, and a splendid art collection to build on the foundation hired the late Richard Brown, former director of the Los Angeles County Museum. Shortly after arriving in Fort Worth, Ric Brown turned to his old friend, architect Louis I. Kahn, to design the museum that would house the collection.

The innovative building is a work of art in itself. Considered Kahn's masterpiece, it was the last design completed before his death in March 1974 and has won numerous national awards for architecture. The main entrance to the museum is a tree-filled plaza, flanked by two open cycloid vaults which face reflecting pools. Slits to admit natural light run the length of the vaults of post-tensioned concrete that comprise the building.

The core of the Kimbell collection is European painting from the Middle Ages to the early twentieth century, with smaller concentrations of works from South Asia, China, and Japan. The museum also has what are, in effect, mini-collections of Greek and Roman antiquities, African sculpture and pre-Columbian objects.

British art is especially well represented. The *Barnabas Altarpiece* dates from about 1250-60 and is the earliest surviving English painting on wood panel. Kay Kimbell was fond of eighteenth-century British portraiture and the collection is rich in Gainsboroughs, Reynolds, Romneys, Raeburns, and Lawrences. There is also a fine example of Gainsborough's early painting, *Suffolk Landscape.*

Rembrandt's *Portrait of a Young Jew,* from the artist's mature years, combines deep sympathy with the sitter with subtle modulations of color and dramatic lighting. In contrast, *Henry III, Count of Nassau-Breda,* one of the finest portraits by Jan Gossaert, called Mabuse, is elegantly formal, a study of courtly dignity and luxuriant costume.

Among Spanish works, too, portraits dominate the collection. El Greco's *Giacomo Biso* is particularly imposing, with its restrained use of color and the solemn, ascetic bearing of its subject. Francisco de Goya's portrait of *The Matador Pedro Romero,* depicts one of the early superstars of bullfighting in a moment of relaxation, at ease but alert and supremely self-confident.

The early Italian Renaissance is represented by *Triptych of the Madonna and Child with Saints,* by the Sienese master Giovanni di Paolo. The three panels were acquired by the museum over a period of several years and reunited only in 1978 with the addition of the central panel's pinnacle depicting God the Father.

French art is another of the Kimbell's strengths. Four large, sumptuous paintings by Francois Boucher celebrating the power of love may have been intended as tapestry designs. Marie Louise Elizabeth Vigee-Lebrun, who painted members of the French aristocracy in the years before the Revolution, is represented by no less than four charming portraits. *Roedeer at a Stream* by Gustave Courbet is one of the artist's thickly painted, luminously colorful landscapes. *Peasant in Blue Blouse*, painted during Cezanne's last decade, when the artist made a number of breakthroughs that eventually led to the cubism of Picasso and Braque, is modeled in chiseled planes of robust color.

Thanks to an informal agreement of long standing, the Kimbell and Fort Worth's other two art museums, the Fort Worth Art

British collections

European collections

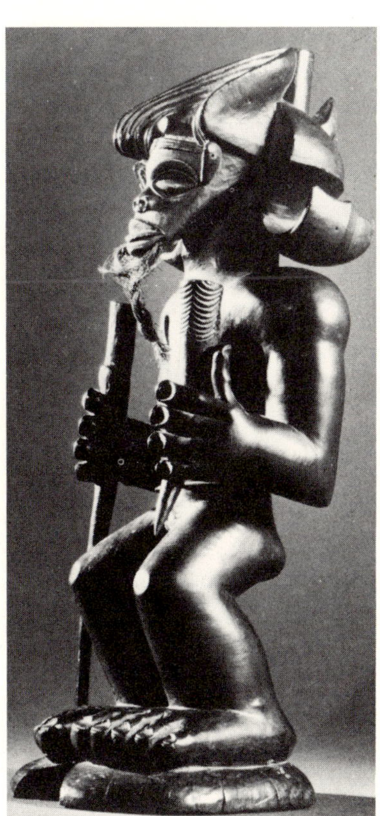

Chokwe (Northeastern Angola), *Chibinda (The Hunter) Ilunga Katele,* wood. Kimbell Art Museum.

Museum and the Amon Carter Museum, have very carefully divided the territory to avoid duplicating each other's collections. Under this arrangement the Kimbell's collection includes several important works from the early twentieth century. Picasso's *Man with a Pipe* is a prime example of analytical cubism at its high tide, an oval composition in which the very language of painting is taken apart and splayed across the flat canvas surface. Henri Matisse's *Odalisque with Green Shawl* features the elegant contours, the vibrant colors and patterned surface of that artist's work at its most decorative.

The Kimbell Museum remains one of the few art museums in the country with the financial muscle to go out and buy the very best. Under its new director, Dr. Edmund P. Pillsbury, a museum man very much in the same scholar-connoisseur mold as Ric Brown, the museum has embarked on an acquisition binge, adding a number of major new works to its collection within the past two years. A late Cezanne landscape, *Maison Maria with a View of Chateau Noir,* neatly supplements the Cezanne portrait. Its new Velazquez (1559-1660), *Don Pedro de Barberana*, is one of the best examples of that artist's works now in the United States. The renowned *Cheat with the Ace of Clubs*, painted by the great French master, Georges de la Tour (1593-1652), is a rare example of that artist's "daylight" genre scenes. "Skeletons Warming Themselves," by the Belgian expressionist James Ensor continues the Kimbell's commitment to early twentieth-century art. Works by Manet, David, Stubbs, Watteau, Carracci, Claude Lorrain, and Benjamin West have also been recently added, as well as sculptures by Canova and Banbaia, a pair of ancient Assyrian reliefs, and other objects.

major acquisitions

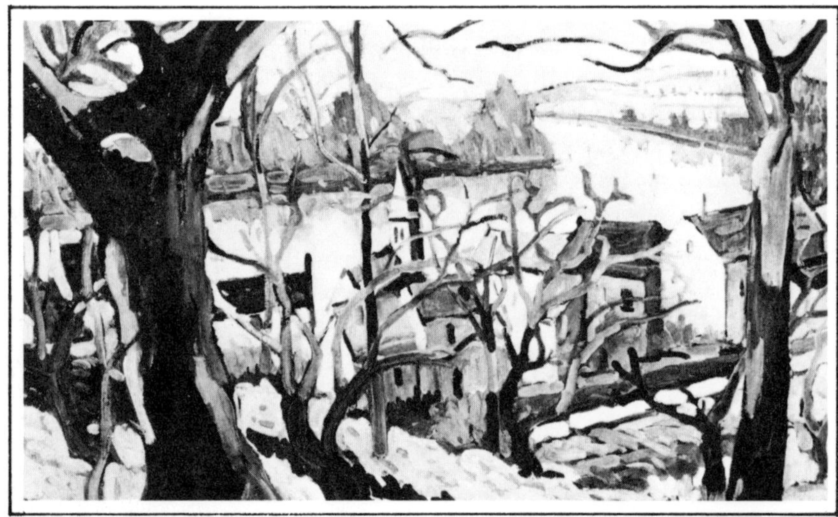

Andre Derain, *The River Seine at Chatou,* 1905, oil on canvas. Kimbell Art Museum.

The Kimbell has been committed to collecting Asian art since its *Oriental arts* opening. The permanent collection includes several outstanding objects from the entire Asian continent, particularly Near Eastern Silver, Indian and Southeast Asian sculpture, Chinese ceramics and painting, and Japanese painting, ceramics, and lacquerwares.

One of the rarest objects among the new acquisitions in this area is *Hachiman in the Guise of a Buddhist Priest,* a tenth-century wood sculpture of the Japanese god of war. Among the new paintings are two landscapes that present contrasting examples of the literati tradition of scholar-artists in China and Japan. A pair of six-fold screens dating to about 1800, and a red lacquer wine flask dating to the late fourteenth century give an indication of the breadth of the collection.

Ramesses II as the God Osiris is the first monumental piece of Egyptian sculpture acquired by the Kimbell, and it is no doubt a sign of new directions.

Perhaps another sign of new directions is the recent re-installation of the Kimbell's permanent collection under Dr. Pillsbury. The works are now arranged by school, in roughly chronological order, and the central bay of the south galleries has been transformed into a large sculpture court in order to show off the museum's growing collection of sculpture. The drawing and print collection has been retired to storage for the time being, freeing the north galleries to house temporary exhibitions.

The Kimbell maintains a busy exhibition schedule, with the emphasis upon masterpieces of European and Oriental art. In the past year, the museum has hosted major traveling exhibits of sculpture and drawings by Bernini, treasures from Japan's famed Idemitsu Collection, ballet costumes from Diaghilev to Balanchine, old master paintings from the Collection of Baron Thyssen-Bornemisza, and sculpture and paintings depicting the Indian god, Shiva.

The year 1982 marks the Kimbell Art Museum's Tenth *exhibitions* Anniversary. A number of exhibitions are planned for late 1982 and early 1983 to celebrate the occasion: Elisabeth Louise Vigee Le Brun (1755-1842), one of the foremost female painters of all time, who did major portraits of figures in the French court before the Revolution; The English Miniature; The Votive Tradition: Treasures of Buddhist Sculpture from Japan, and The Paintings of Jusepe de Ribera (1591-1652), a great Neapolitan painter.

For its anniversary year the museum has also issued a "Handbook to the Collection," a well-written, well-illustrated guide with more than 285 pictures, 14 in color. It is available from the museum shop for $9.75. The Kimbell has also begun to issue a handsomely printed semi-annual Calendar, featuring short features on current and forthcoming exhibits, and listing special events at the museum. These include special lectures by visiting scholars, a film program, a subscription concert series, tours, gallery talks, and workshops. Except for the concert series, all programs are open to the public on a first-come, first-serve basis.

The museum buffet serves homemade soup, salad, bread and desert, with coffee, tea, or lemonade for $5 from 11:30 a.m. to 2 p.m. Tuesdays through Saturdays.

To reach the Museum take the I-20 to University Dr. exit and travel north; turn west on Lancaster one block; then go right onto Camp Bowie. From downtown Fort Worth go out W. 7th St. which becomes Camp Bowie Blvd., proceed south to the Park.

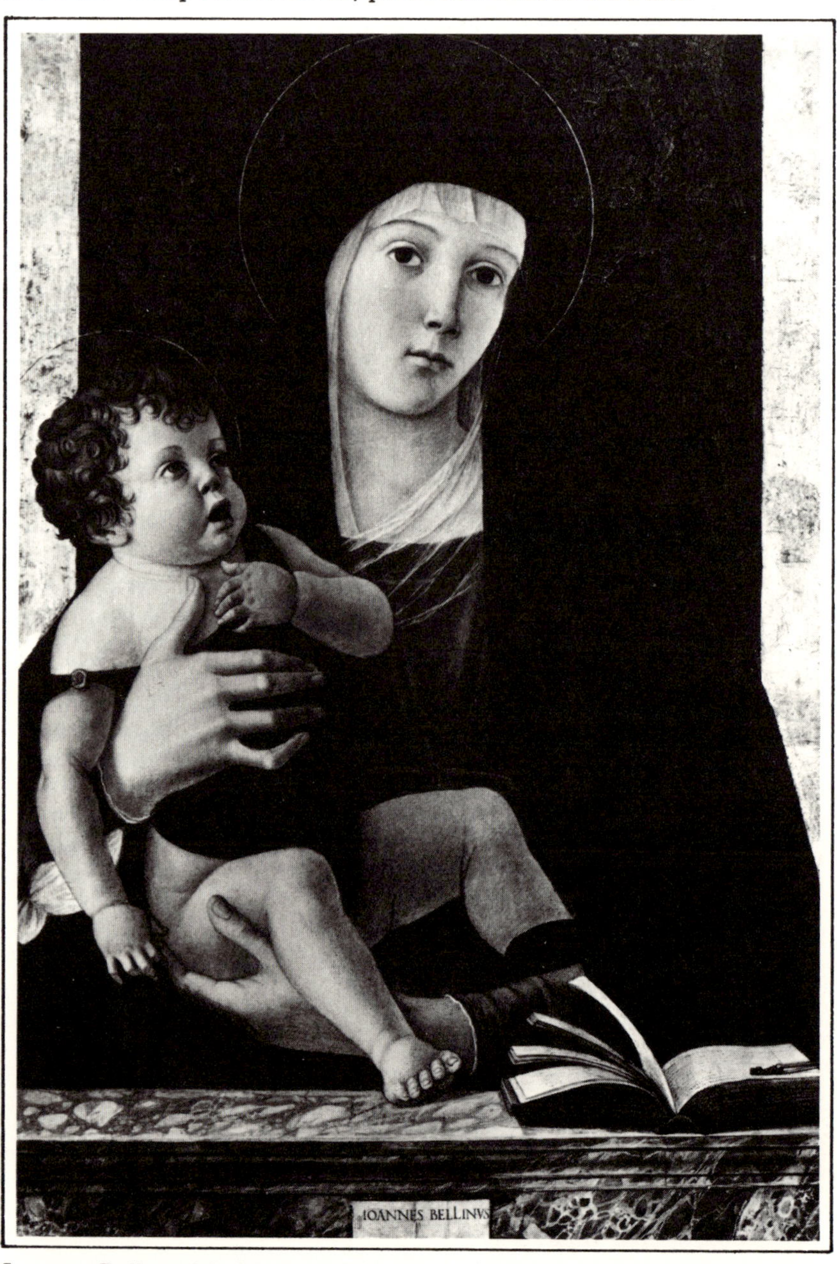

Ioannes Bellini, *Madonna and Child,* (c. 1470-75), tempera and oil on panel. Kimbell Art Museum.

The Longview Museum and Arts Center   102 W. College
Longview 75606   (214) 753-8103   Monday-Friday: 9-5; Sunday:
1-3

The Longview
Museum

In the spring of 1976 the Board of Trustees of the Longview
Museum voted to take advantage of an opportunity to purchase the
old Northcutt Furniture building as a permanent home for the
Longview Museum. The museum opened formally in 1977.

The permanent collection consists of paintings, drawings,
prints, and sculpture by leading artists of the Southwest, who
represent a cross-section of a major sampling of innovations and
styles in traditional and contemporary American art. A small print
collection has not yet been catalogued.

The 60 or so works included in the collection have been
executed by Southwest painters who are represented in many
private and public collections throughout the country: Peter Hurd,
Merritt Mauzey, Ronald Thomason, John Guerin, Wayne
Amerine, and Otis Dozier, to name just a few.

Fall Fest, an annual event at Longview, exhibits sculptures,
paintings, graphics, and handcrafted items made by local artists.

Special exhibitions planned for the summer of 1982 are the
Citation Show of the East Texas Fine Arts Association, and Works
by Women.

Ruby Laura Hooper Martin Museum of Art   Hooper-Schaefer
Fine Arts Center   Baylor University   Waco 76703   (817)
755-1867   Tuesday-Sunday: 1-5

Martin Museum

For the most part the Martin Museum exhibits works from Baylor's
own collection. Special strengths are in primitive African art,
German porcelain, and in painting. Included in the painting
collection are works by Inness and Constable.

Special exhibits and works on loan are occasionally displayed.

The University Art Gallery is opened from 8-5 Tuesday-
Saturday and from 1-5 on Sunday. It exhibits works of prominent
artists, faculty, and students, and presents traveling exhibitions
and group shows, local and otherwise.

Meadows Museum and University Gallery   Southern Methodist
University   Dallas 75275   (214) 692-2727   Monday-Saturday:
10-5; Sunday: 1-5

Meadows
Museum

The Meadows Museum may be Dallas' best-kept art secret.
Certainly few casual visitors to this city have even heard of the
museum. And yet wise is the art lover who schedules a visit to the
Meadows Musem during his stay in Dallas. This small university
museum houses one of the finest collections of Spanish art outside
Madrid's famous Prado.

The Meadows Museum was founded in 1965 with the gift of a

collector of pictures, mostly Spanish, acquired during the previous decade by Mr. Algur Meadows. The story of that collection and how it came to be assembled has entered into local folklore and forms a fascinating bit of background for any visit to this surprising museum.

The late Algur Meadows was a highly successful oilman when he began collecting art—mostly School of Paris works by Chagall, Matisse, Manet, Picasso, Modigliani, Utrillo, Renoir and the like. Gradually, however, a Dallas art dealer became suspicious of the collection. He notified Mr. Meadows of his doubts, and a panel of national experts was called in to examine the collection. Almost every painting turned out to be fake.

history

Although Mr. Meadows could have absorbed the loss and kept his silence, he did not. Instead, he pressed for the prosecution of the Paris dealer who sold him the phony works and then with the help of an art scholar, Dr. William Jordan, began to assemble another collection, this one of unquestioned masterpieces. Dr. Jordan's specialty is Spanish art and it was the Spanish works in Mr. Meadows' second collection that, in 1965, formed the nucleus of the new Meadows Museum. The continued patronage of Mr. and Mrs. Meadows over the years and, today, of the Meadows Foundation has built the museum into a splendid repository of Spanish art containing more than 100 paintings spanning five centuries, more than 300 original prints by Ribera, Goya and Picasso, and a small group of twentieth-century Latin American works.

Before he died in 1978, Mr. Meadows also presented SMU with the Elizabeth Meadows Sculpture Garden. Located on the grounds in front of the Meadows Museum, the garden offers a small but choice collection of sculpture by some of the pivotal artists of the twentieth century. Just inside the lobby of the building, which also houses SMU's Meadows School of the Arts, is Rodin's large white marble, *Eve in Despair*. A lead cast of Aristide Maillol's *Three Graces* has been installed in the entrance courtyard. Isamu Noguchi's tall, graceful black basalt monolith, *Spirit's Flight,* stands in front of the building. Nearby are Jacques Lipschitz's *Le joie de vivre,* Henry Moore's *Three Part Reclining Figure,* David Smith's burnished, stainless steel *Cubi VIII,* Claes Oldenburg's rather sinister *Geometric Mouse,* as well as works by Marino Marini and Giacomo Manzu.

Sculpture Garden

But the Meadows Museum, located just to the right of the entrance courtyard, is the major attraction here. The Spanish collection begins with a remarkable group of panels, one dating from the fifteenth century and several from the sixteenth. Fernando Gallego's powerful *Acacius and the Ten Thousand Martyrs,* painted about 1490 and once part of an altarpiece, reveals the continuing influence of Northern European artists upon

Spanish collection

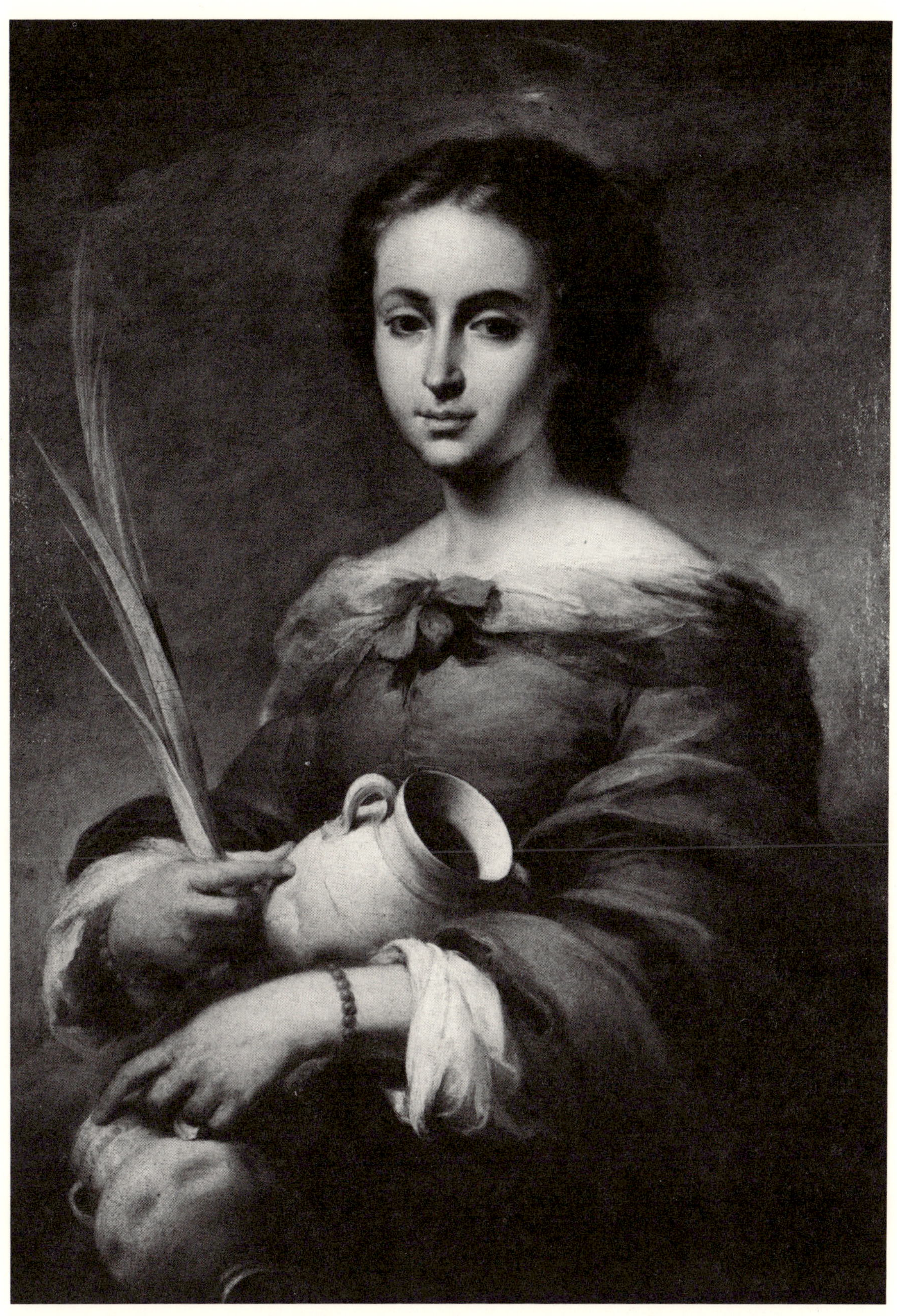

Bartolome Esteban Murillo, *St. Rufina,* 36¾" x 26¼", oil on canvas. Meadows Museum.

Spanish painters even at this late date. The huge *Investiture of St. Ildefonso,* painted about 20 years later (c. 1508-1510) by Juan de Borgona, displays the impact of the Italian Renaissance. It is one of the most important Spanish works of its period. Fernando Yanez de la Almeddina's *St. Sebastian* (c. 1506) gives further evidence of the Italian influence in Spain.

Velazquez's lyrical *Sibyl with Tabula Rasa* is accompanied by the artist's early *Portrait of King Philip IV* and his late portrait of the king's second wife, *Mariana of Austria.* Only the Metropolitan Museum of Art in New York, among American museums, possesses a greater number of authentic works by Velazquez. De Ribera is represented by his early *St. Paul the Hermit* and the *Portrait of a Knight of Santiago.*

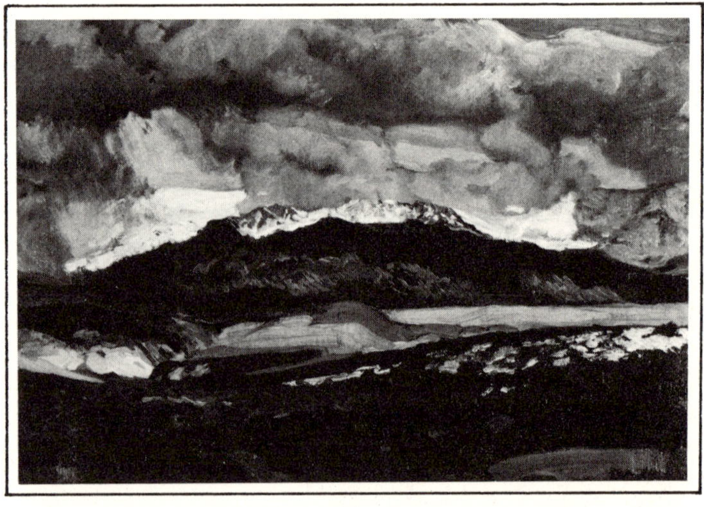

Joaquin Sorolla y Bastida, *View of La Pedriza from El Pardo,* 1907, 24½″ x 35¾″, oil on canvas. Meadows Museum.

Bartolome Esteban Murillo's glowing *Immaculate Conception* is one of the finest versions of this oft-repeated subject. This Baroque master is especially represented in the Meadows collection. His paired paintings of *Saints Justina and Rufina* are sweet, rather than profoundly spiritual, but his *Jacob Laying the Peeled Rods Before the Flocks of Laban* is one of the masterpieces of the artist's career.

There are six oils and more than 200 first edition prints by Francisco de Goya in the Meadows Museum. Included are all four of his major series, *Los Caprichos* (1799), *La Tauromaquia* (1816), *Los Desastres de la Guerre* (1863), and *Los Disparates* (1864). The most important Goya in the museum collection, however, is the famous painting *Madhouse at Saragossa,* an eerily lit, nightmarish vision based upon the artist's actual observations. Even more unusual is the artist's *Still-life with Woodcocks,* a grim, dark picture that has reminded at least some scholars of the heaped-up bodies depicted in some of the prints in the artist's *Los Desastres de la Guerre.*

The Meadows Museum is almost unique in collecting and displaying works by artists of the later nineteenth and early twentieth century who are little known outside of Spain, for example the academician Antonio Maria Esquivel whose frank *Girl Removing Her Garter* seems unusually voluptuous for a Spanish work; the fashionable portraitist Raimundo de Madrazo (1841-1920); and landscapist Joaquin Sorolla y Bastide, a famous painter in his own times whose *View of Las Pedrizas From El Pardo* is a piece of virtuoso painting, brisk, vigorous and fluid.

Finally, the museum has a small but very good collection of works by Picasso, Gris, and Miro, Spanish artists who stand at the very wellsprings of modern art. Picasso's *Still-Life in a Landscape,* painted in 1915, with its severely flattened planes, represents the waning years of "synthetic" cubism while Miro's *Queen Louise of Prussia,* 1929, is a bright, witty picture in which the form of the queen has been reduced almost to an abstract sign. Two works by the famed Mexican muralist, Diego Rivera, are also in the museum's collection: *Portrait of Ilya Ehrenburg,* painted in 1915, and *La Canoa Enflorada* of 1931.

Modernists

The Meadows Museum has recently acquired its first sculpture, a rare seventeenth-century polychrome wood *St. John the Baptist* by the master carver Juan Martinez Montanes. Only one other work by Montanes in the U.S. is in the collection of New York's Metropolitan Museum of Art.

The University Gallery, which adjoins the museum, provides the SMU student body and the community of Dallas with an active and varied series of temporary exhibits throughout the year. Recent exhibitions of note have included: Paintings and Drawings of Cy Twombley; Complete Etchings of Canaletto; Livres d'Artiste by Braque, Matisse, and Picasso; Joseph Cornell: Collages; Milton Avery Paintings; and Mel Bochner: Twenty-Five Drawings.

University Gallery

The gallery also serves as a showcase for faculty and student work.

Guided tours may be scheduled through the Meadows Museum office.

To reach the museum from downtown Dallas, take the 21-SMU bus eastbound on Main Street and get off at Hillcrest and Grenada.

Milam County Historical Museum   Main & Fannin Sts.   Cameron 76520   (817) 697-9223   Tuesday-Saturday: 9-12, 1-5; Sunday: 1-5

Milam County Historical Museum

The museum building is an official Recorded Texas Historic Landmark and is on the National Register for Landmark Buildings. It was constructed in 1895 by the Pauly Jail Manufacturing Company of St. Louis. The families of many sheriffs have lived in the family rooms which now contain exhibits from many communities of Milam County.

Left as permanent artifacts in the building are the cast-iron tub in the bathroom, the built-in cabinet in the kitchen, and the woodburning heater in the stairwell of the jail area.

The collections include farm tools, household utensils, guns, handcrafted items of needlework, items of clothing, a doll collection, and photographs of buildings, site locations, and early settlers. Items used by early settlers, such as spinning wheel, side saddle, and copies of documents and newspapers, are also in the museum.

The oldest item is a pewter plate used in colonial times in North Carolina brought from Ireland before the American Revolution and then brought to Texas from North Carolina in the early 1870s by John Bickett, who became sheriff of Milam County in 1895.

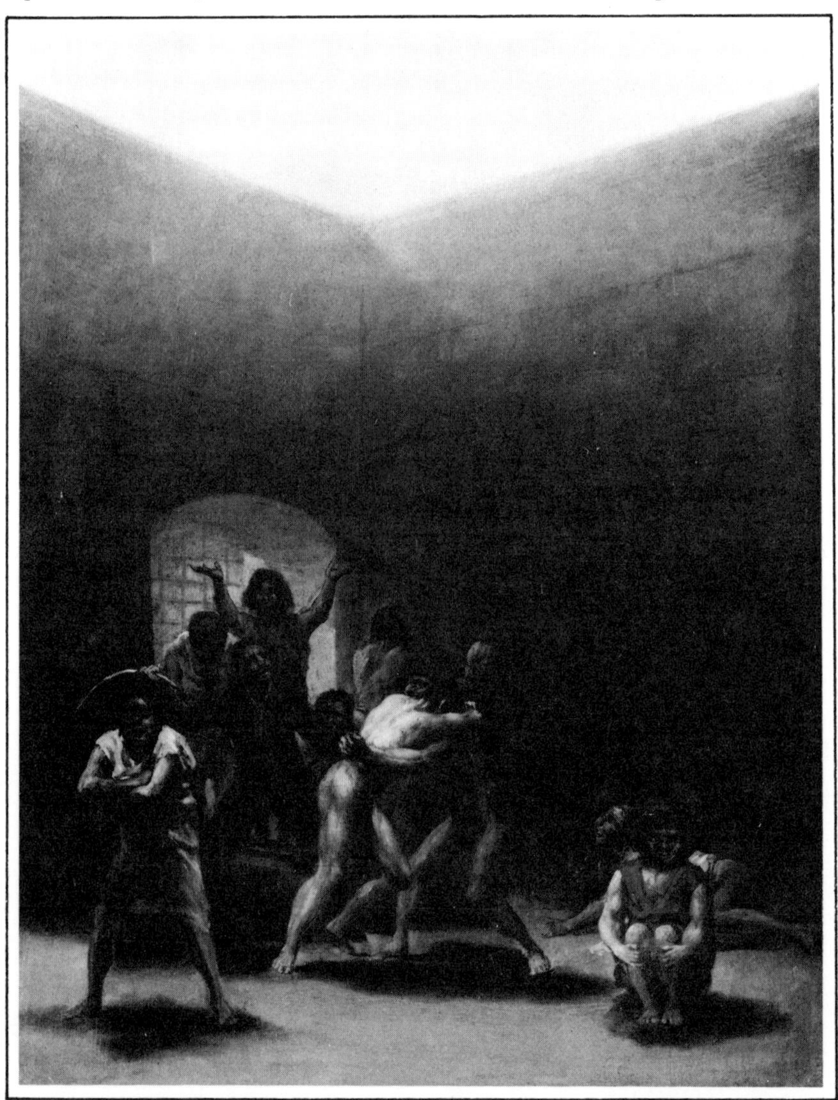

Francisco de Goya, *The Madhouse at Saragossa,* 1974, 17¾" x 12¾", oil on tin. Meadows Museum.

North Texas State University Art Gallery   Corner Ave. A and
Mulberry   P.O. Box 5063   Denton 76203   (817) 788-2855
Monday-Friday: 12-5; or by appointment

This handsome 1600-square-foot gallery is connected to one of the
university buildings by an attractive atrium. The permanent
collection consists of about 500 objects, many of which are
displayed in other campus buildings since storage space is at a
premium.

The collection consists mainly of gifts and student work. In
addition to a sizable number of prints, there is a growing collection
of handmade books. On extended loan is a bronze sculpture by
Jacques Lipschitz entitled *The Sacrifice*, on loan from Owen
Weiner of Fort Worth. Paintings by Jim Dine, Kenneth Noland,
and other contemporary painters are on loan from Regent Lucille
Murchison.

Exhibits change frequently. Each spring there is an exhibit of
award-winning works by students which have included the work of
Toni Lasalle, a student of Hans Hofmann; works in clay by NTSU
graduates; selections from the print collections; in early October,
four major photographers in an exhibit in conjunction with the
Society for Photographic Education; in December, a faculty exhibit; and, early in 1983, a Japanese metals exhibit and a major
traveling exhibit funded by the National Endowment for the Arts.

Every year or two pieces on loan from the Dallas Fashion
Museum (a research facility for students and designers) are on
display. The Dallas Fashion Museum, though housed in the same
building, is not open to the public.

The Texas Christian University Galleries: Brown Lupton and
Moudy Building   Fort Worth 76129   (817) 921-7926   Monday-
Friday: 11-4; Saturday-Sunday: 1-4

Texas Christian University has two art galleries worth a visit.

The Brown-Lupton Gallery, located in the university's student
center and operated by the center's exhibit committee, offers a
schedule of regularly changing shows featuring works by
important Texas and Southwestern artists as well as occasional
exhibits by TCU students. In addition the gallery hosts small
traveling shows and an annual arts festival. During the past year
the gallery has shown ceramics and watercolors by Fort Worth
artist Linda Blackburn, small sculptures by Nancy Chambers of
Dallas, Nic Nicosia's color photographs of scenes he has altered
with paper and paint, and the glitter-encrusted constructions of
New York artist Gilda Pervin. The Brown-Lupton Gallery has also
mounted several imaginative group exhibitions such as, "Keep
Those Cards and Letters Coming," an international exhibition of

North Texas State University Art Gallery

The Texas Christian University Galleries

postcard and other mail art, and "A Sense of Spirit," featuring a
group of Houston artists whose works tend toward the visionary
and mystical. This exhibit later traveled to the University of
Houston.

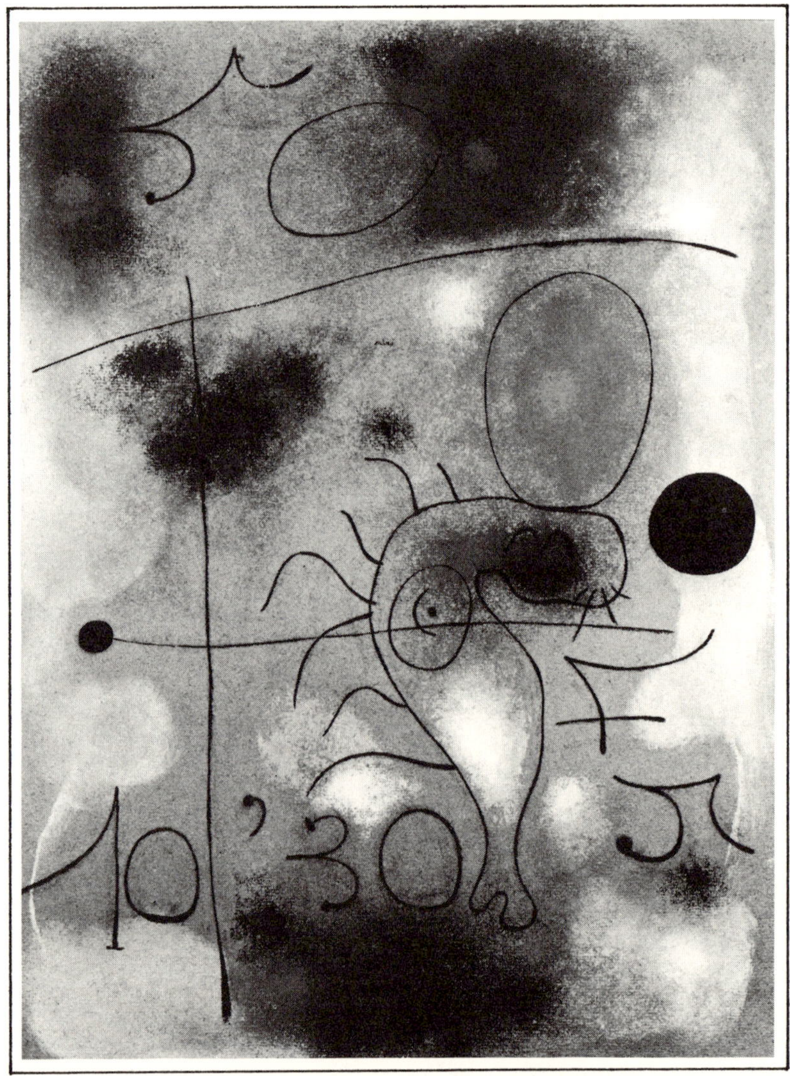

Joan Miro, *The Circus,* 1937, 47¼" x 35½", tempera and oil on celotex.
Meadows Museum.

The Brown-Lupton Gallery schedules a free, weekly brown-bag
series of lectures and illustrated talks. Visitors are encouraged to
bring their lunches, and the gallery provides free beverages.
Speakers include visiting artists, artists whose works are on view in
the gallery, art historians, critics, and local museum officials.

TCU's other gallery is located in the beautiful new J.M. Moudy
Building for Visual Arts and Communications, designed by Roche
and Dinkeloo. The Moudy Gallery opened in 1982 with a TCU
faculty show. The Moudy Gallery has a small permanent

*Brown-Lupton
Gallery*

collection, mostly drawings and prints, including works by
important contemporary artists such as Richard Diebenkorn. One
of the plans of the gallery's director, Ronald Watson, who is also
chairman of the university's art department, is to put some portion
of this seldom-exhibited collection on display.

Both the Brown-Lupton and the new Moudy galleries have
occasionally coordinated exhibit plans with the Fort Worth Art
Museum, the museum showing an exhibit of recent work by some
artist, for example, while one of the university galleries offers a
small retrospective of the artist's past works.

Tyler Museum of Art

Tyler Museum of Art   1300 S. Mahon Ave.   Tyler 75701
(214) 595-1001   Tuesday-Saturday: 10-5; Sunday: 1-5

Construction of the museum was begun in February 1970. The
building contains two major temporary exhibition galleries of
approximately 5,000 square feet and a third gallery on the upper
level which was designed for display of the museum's permanent
collection, but is well suited for small temporary exhibitions or as a
lecture room. The exterior facade of the building is dominated by
two large cantilevered decks which overlook a reflecting pool with
fountains.

The museum is dedicated to showing work of artists in East
Texas, an area that does not include major population centers but
covers a wide region from Dallas to Houston. Artists who live in
this area are somewhat isolated, and for this reason are able to
work with distinct expression unspoiled by outside influences.

A recently mounted exhibit, Recent Works, from East Texas,
showed a variety of works from fifteen artists of this region:
painting, printmaking, sculpture, ceramics, handmade and cast
paper, and mixed-media installations.

University Art Gallery

University Art Gallery   University of Texas at Arlington
Arlington 76019   (817) 273-2891   Monday-Friday: 9-4; Sunday:
1-4

The University Art Gallery, located in the Fine Arts Building,
serves the university community through a program of exhibitions,
public lectures, films, workshops, and special events. Exhibitions
draw on all cultures and all periods.

The gallery mounts cooperative exhibitions with neighboring
colleges and universities, as well as with the Amon Carter Museum
of Western Art, the Dallas Museum of Fine Arts, the Fort Worth Art
Museum, and the Kimbell Art Museum.

The exhibit of etchings by Goya from the collection of the Sarah
Campbell Blaffer Foundation—*The Disasters of War*—was
recently on view as part of its tour of museums throughout the
state.

Dallas-Forth Worth
Gallery Specializations

Many of the galleries found below exhibit a wide variety of art styles and mediums. The following list represents concentrations of a particular artistic mode and not necessarily the individual focus of the gallery. Thus, some galleries which exhibit many styles may be found in several listings. Some, but not all, of the galleries which are listed under a specialization are classified on the basis of excellence in that respective area, rather than for the size of their collections.

American:
contemporary: Adams-Middleton, American Fine Arts, Arthellos, Carlin, Carr, Contemporary Gallery, D-ART, Gallery Downtown, Delahunty, DW, 500 Exposition Gallery, Hall, Mattingly Baker, MJS, Nimbus, Gallery One, Paige, Pruitt, Ps, Reminisce, SL, Southwest Art Center, Southwest II Gallery, The Studio, Taylor, Gallery 13, Upstairs Gallery, Valley House

periods: Hall, Sundance, Valley House

European & other continents:
contemporary: Contemporary Gallery, Hall, Houshang, Paige, Phillips, SL, Valley House

periods: Hall, Valley House

Graphics:
contemporary: Adams-Middleton, Berger, Clifford, Mattingly Baker, MJS, Nimbus, Southwest Art Center, Southwest II Gallery, The Studio

Sculpture: Adams-Middleton, Alterman, Gallery One, Valley House

Photography: Afterimage, Coldwell, Delahunty

Primitive/Ancient: Herling, Shango

Crafts: Human Arts

Western & Native American: Adams-Middleton, Alterman, Carr, McCulley, Pruitt, Reminisce, Texas Art Gallery

Dallas-Fort Worth
The Galleries by Location

Dallas

Oak Lawn Area:
   Cedar Springs Blvd: Alterman, SL Galleries, Carol Taylor
   Fairmont: Phillips, Ps Gallery, Shango
   McKinney: DW Gallery, Mattingly Baker
   Quadrangle Mall (2800 Routh): Afterimage, Contemporary
     Gallery, Herling, Human Arts
   Other: Adams-Middleton, Southwest II Gallery

Central: Clifford, D-ART, Nimbus, The Studio, Gallery 13

Downtown: Texas Art Gallery

East Dallas: Delahunty, 500 Exposition Gallery

North: Houshang, McCulley, Paige, Southwest Art Center,
   Valley House

South: Arthello's

Suburban:
   Arlington: Upstairs Gallery
   Irving: American Fine Arts

Fort Worth

Downtown: Downtown Gallery, Hall, Pruitt, Sundance
Camp Bowie Blvd: Berger, Coldwell, MJS Gallery One,
   Reminisce
Central: Carlin, Carr

Adams-Middleton Gallery   3000 Maple Ave. Dallas 75201
(214)742-3682   Tuesday-Friday: 10-6; Saturday: 11-5

Adams-Middleton

Terry Adams and Anita Middleton opened the gallery several
years ago in a marvelous converted mansion now occupied by a
variety of businesses. Still intact are the Victorian galleries, sitting
rooms and stairways. Though the gallery essentially consists of one
room, it is mammoth in its proportions and artfully spaced-out by
wallways and sculptures, giving it more the look of a museum
gallery than a commercial space.

The works shown are all by contemporary artists, many from the
Southwest. Selections include paintings, sculpture and graphics of
high quality. Many tend to be figurative or deal with what Director
Middleton calls "abstract expressionism." Most noticeable are the
sculptures of Francisco Zuniga; many are life-size and depict the
people of his native Mexico. A good selection of his drawings and
prints are also available. Another Southwest artist, Veloy Vigil,
also shows his abstract works which, though soft in their colors, are
strong in their imagery, tending toward representationalism.
A hint of the Southwest, its people and landscapes can be drawn as
one views Vigil's large-scale drawings.

Consistent with the gallery's emphasis on the Southwest are the
works of Ed Singer and R.C. Gorman, both Navajo Indians living
in New Mexico. Teodulo Romulo's mixographic works may also be
seen along with the figurative sculptures of Shirley Thomson Smith
who depicts American Indians.

Marcia Meyers shows her large abstract oils, bold in color and
powerful in presentation. Meyers works with colorfields and
successfully adds a "third dimension" to the canvas. Noted New
York painter Paul Jenkins also shows his colorful works from time to
time.

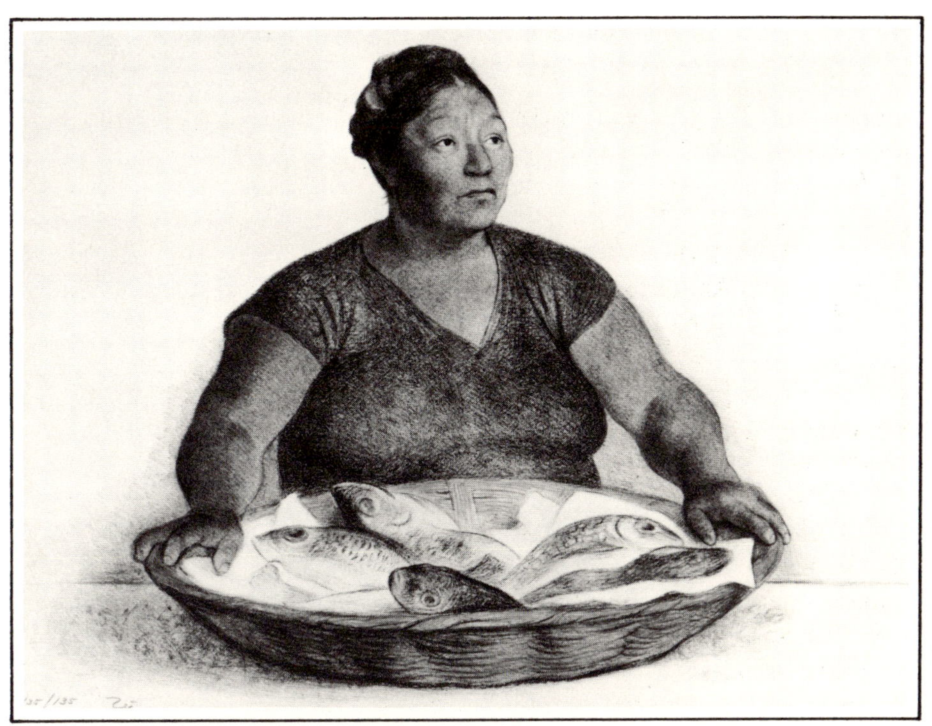

Francisco Zuniga, *Mujer con Pescados,* 22″ x 30″, stone lithograph in 9 colors. Adams Middleton Gallery.

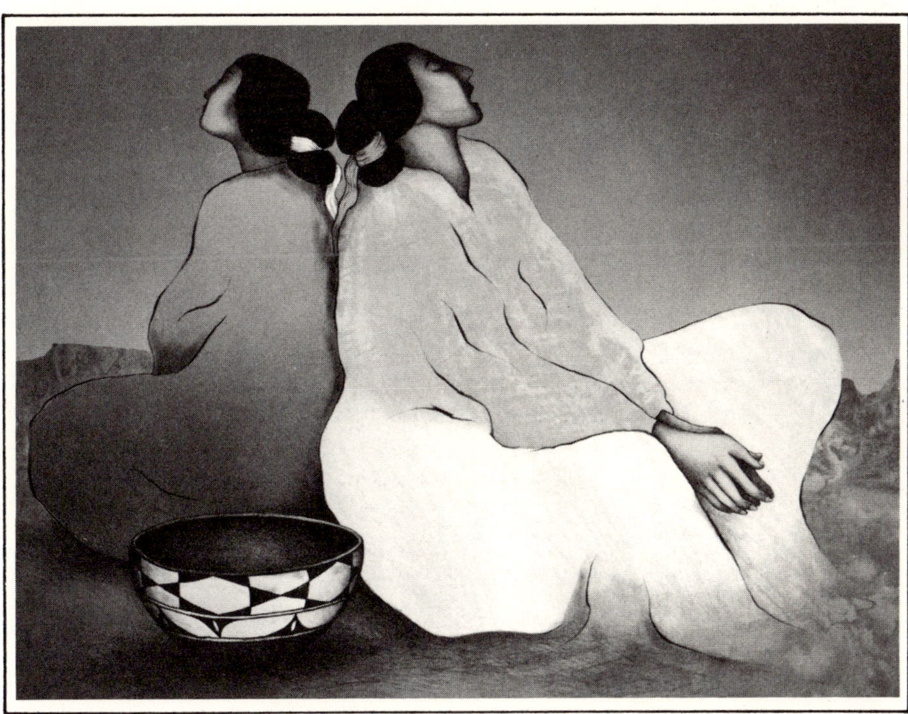

R. C. Gorman, *Santo Domingo,* 29″ x 38″, stone lithograph. Adams Middleton Gallery.

The Afterimage   No. 151, The Quadrangle, 2800 Routh St.   **Afterimage**
Dallas, 75201   (214) 748-2521   Monday-Saturday: 10-5:30

When Ben Breard opened in 1971, this was one of the only
photographic galleries between New York and San Francisco.
And it remains Dallas's only gallery devoted exclusively to
photography.

Breard's taste runs to the well-made photograph. The gallery
regularly stocks images by such American masters as Ansel
Adams, Harry Callahan, and Edward Weston, as well as
occasional works by notable Europeans including Cartier-
Bresson and Brassai. The visitor is also likely to find works by a
number of other important twenteith-century photographers on the
walls, such as Walker Evans, George Tice, Robert Frank, Yousuf
Karsh, Eva Rubenstein, and Ruth Orkin.

The Afterimage, which is located in Dallas's most charming
shopping center, offers a regular schedule of changing exhibits.
Typical shows have featured the unusual architectural
photographs of Harry Wilkes, eerie long-exposure nighttime color
photographs by Eric Staller, Elliott McDowell's humorous
photographs, and Texas landscapes by Jim Bones, a former printer
for Eliot Porter. Breard recently purchased and is now selling a
large collection of prints and collotypes by L.A. Huffman,
a photographer in turn-of-the-century Montana.

One of the pleasanter things about the gallery is the bins of
photographs by talented but lesser-known artists. There is also an
exceptionally fine selection of in-print photographic books.

Altermann Art Gallery   2504 Cedar Springs Rd.   Dallas 75201   **Altermann**
(214) 745-1266   Monday-Friday: 9-5; Saturday: By appointment

Director Tony Altermann is concerned with the acquisition and
sale of fine Western, wildlife, and American art. Featured are both
paintings and bronzes from significant contemporary and
deceased artists.

Included are Western bronzes by Harry Jackson, Truman
Bolinger, Joe Beeler, Peter Fillerup, and Ken Ottinger; wildlife
bronzes by Bob Wolf and Clark Bronson; and Western and
American oils, watercolors, gouaches, by James Boren, Nick
Eggenhofer, G. Harvey, Frank McCarthy, Chuck Ren, Don Ricks,
Douglas Ricks, Gordon Snidow, Robert Summers, Mark Swanson,
Loretta Taylor, Olaf Wieghorst, David Wright, P. Salinas, O.C.
Seltzer, J.H. Sharp, and Robert Wood.

The gallery, small but attractive, only displays a sampling of the
many works which are available. Those interested in a more
complete picture of the works available will want to ask for the
gallery's catalogue, an annually published and extensive
presentation of Altermann's area of interest.

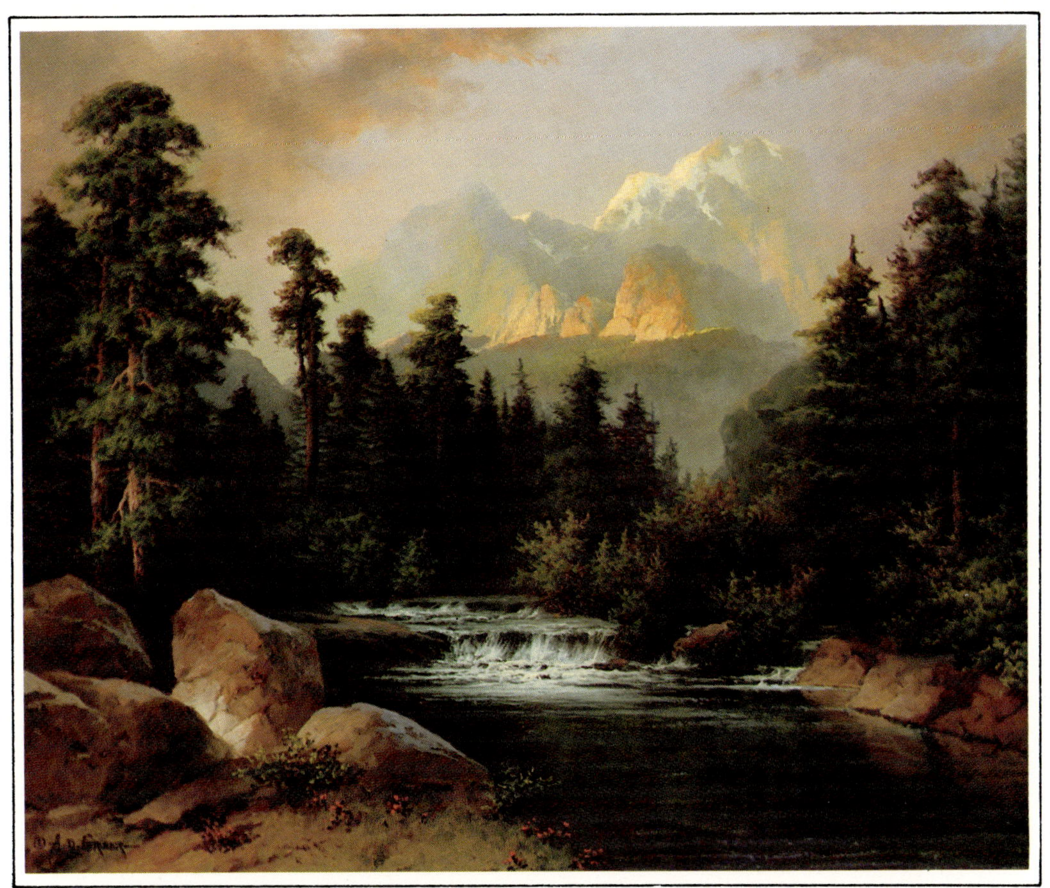

A. D. Greer, *First Light in the Rockies,* 24″ x 30″, oil on canvas. American Fine Arts.

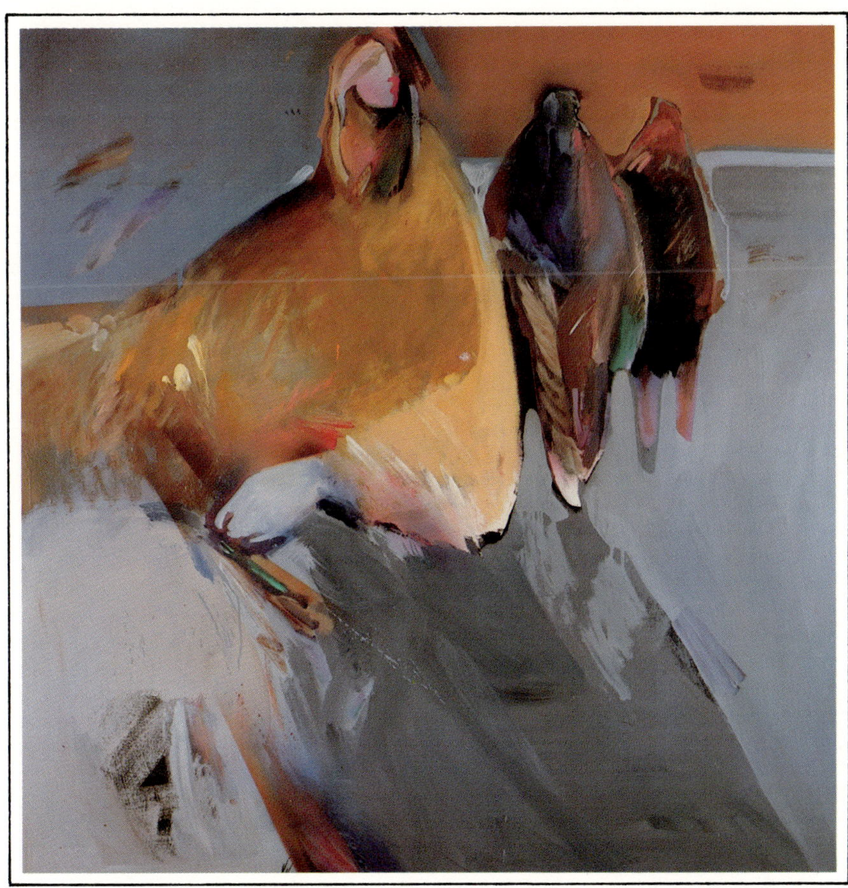

Veloy Vigil, *Autumn,* 60″ x 60″, acrylic on canvas. Adams-Middleton
Gallery.

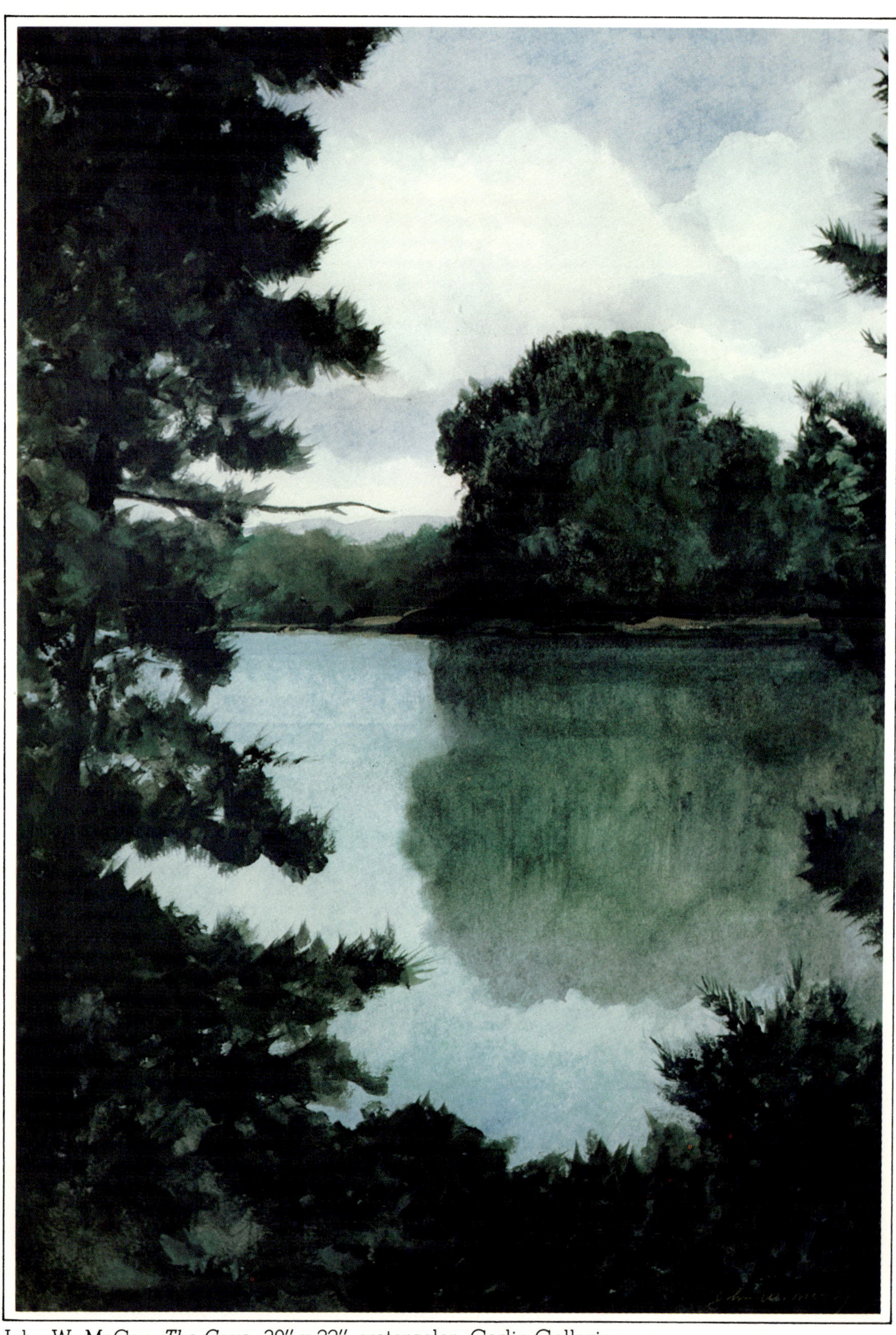

John W. McCoy, *The Cove,* 30″ x 22″, watercolor. Carlin Galleries.

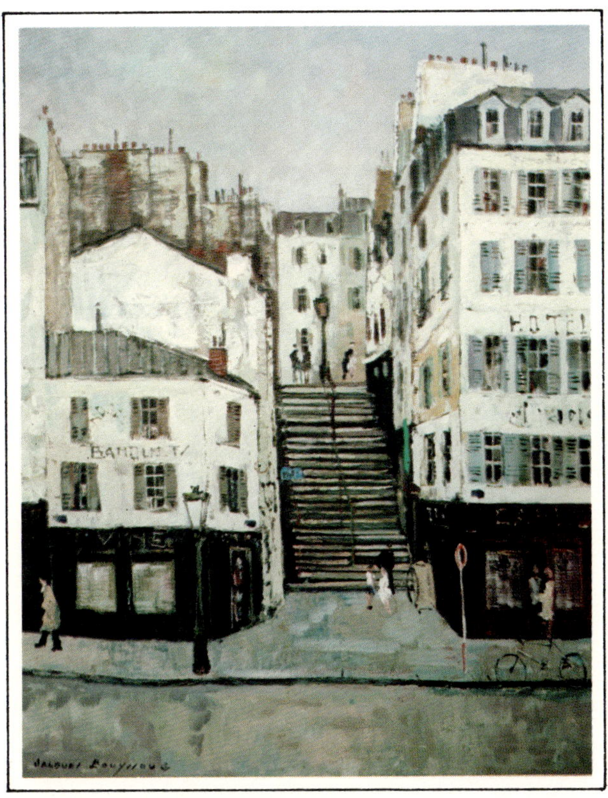

Jacques Bouyssou, *Street Scene,* oil on canvas.
Phillips Galleries.

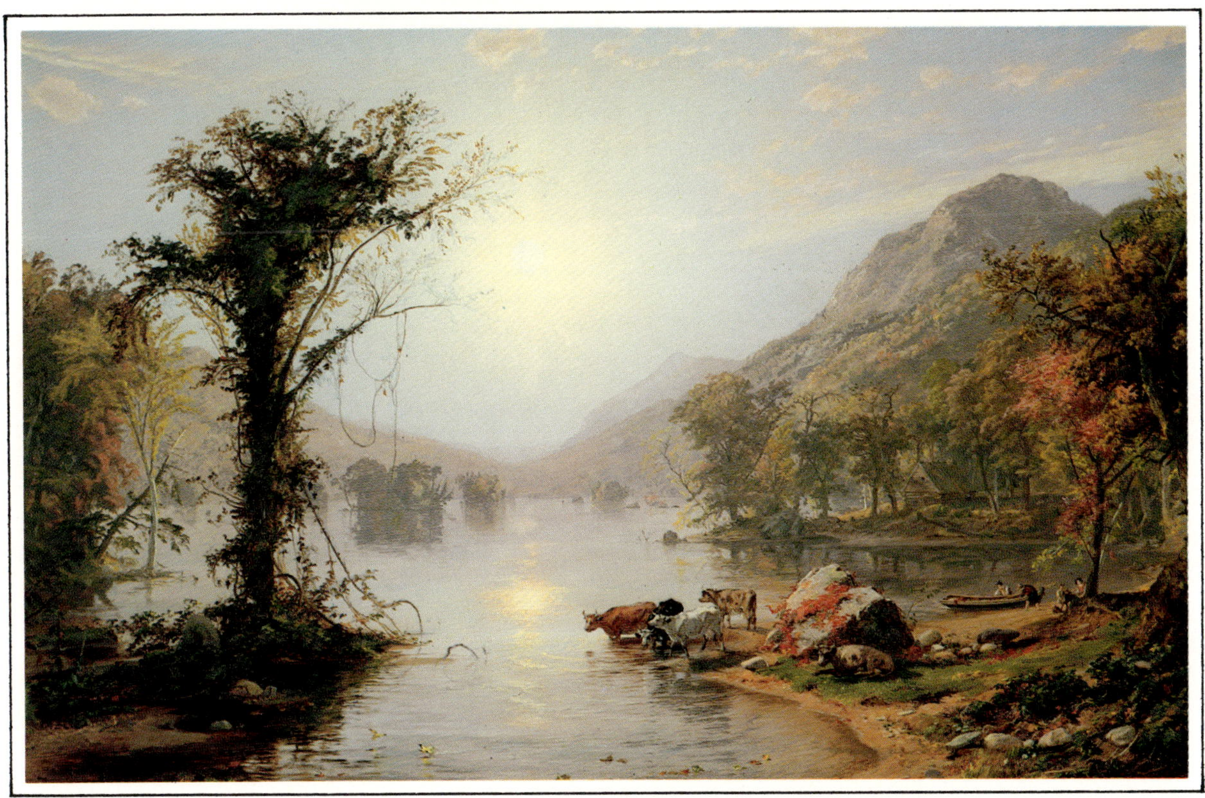

Jasper Cropsey, *Autumn on Greenwood Lake,* 24″ x 38″, oil on canvas. Ron Hall
Galleries.

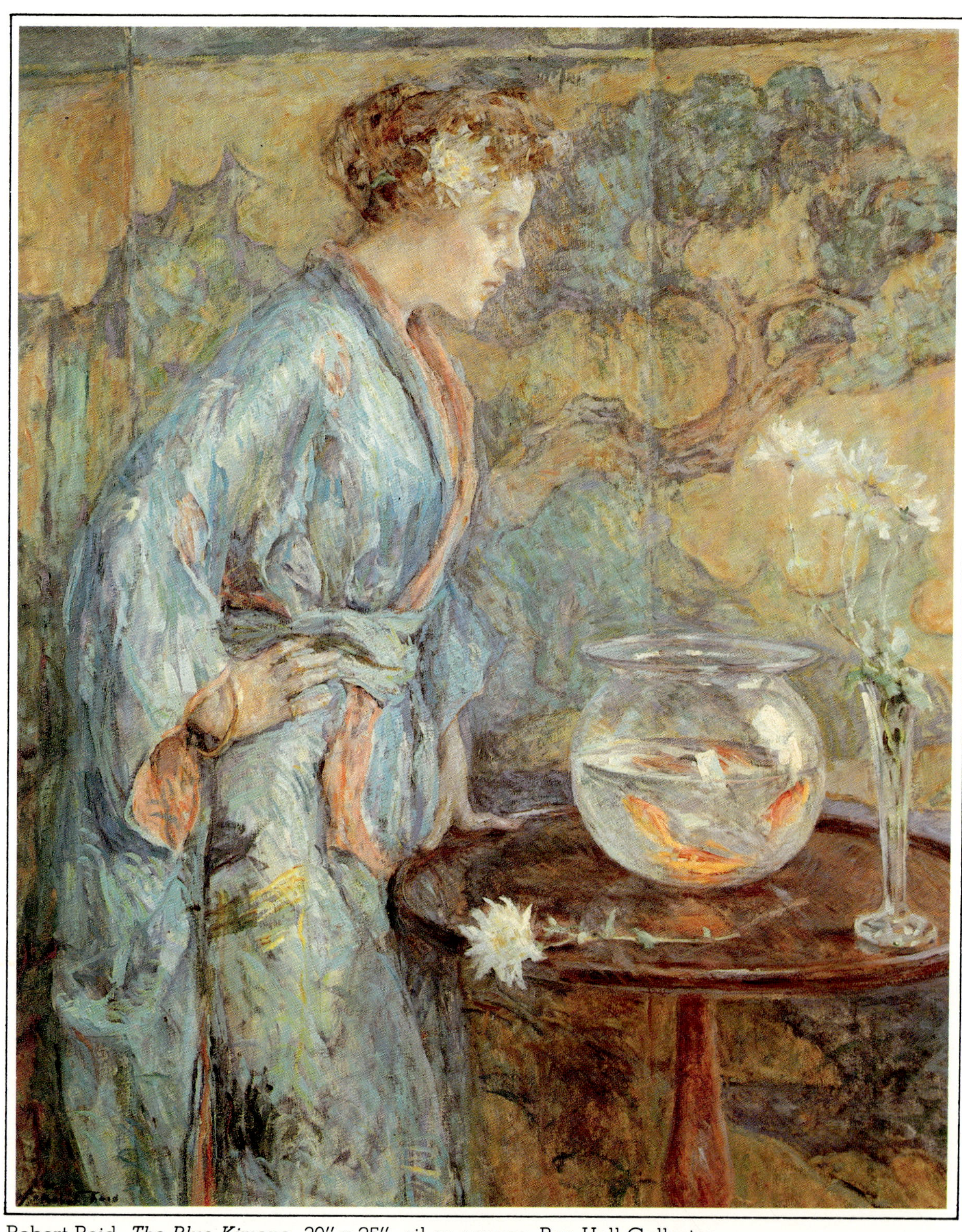

Robert Reid, *The Blue Kimono*, 30″ x 25″, oil on canvas. Ron Hall Galleries.

American Fine Arts

By opening her gallery in 1968 Addie White was expanding her lifelong interest in painting. Her interests reflect her origins in the Southwest ranch-land. The gallery displays mostly realistic and impressionistic paintings.

Featured is A.D. Greer (1904-) who has been painting for more than fifty years. His work depicts mountain, canyon, and landscape scenes as well as florals, orientals, and still-lifes. Mostly self-taught by studying nineteenth- and early-twentieth-century painters, he developed his own style and techniques. Raul Gutierrez uses watercolor and oils to bring out the Southwest landscape with wildlife, horses, and Western figures as his subjects. His colors are soft and subtle, employing many tones of one color in a painting. Also shown are the color and impressionistic works of international artists Eva and Americo Makk.

David Nicholas paints still-lifes of many subjects in oil. Whether he is painting an old saddle, a rope, a silver bowl and vase, fruit, or pottery, his rich colors and minute detail dominate his work.

Clinton Baermann's Western and wildlife subjects and Larry Prellop's seascapes and hill-country scenes are always popular. Baermann does many large murals for commercial establishments.

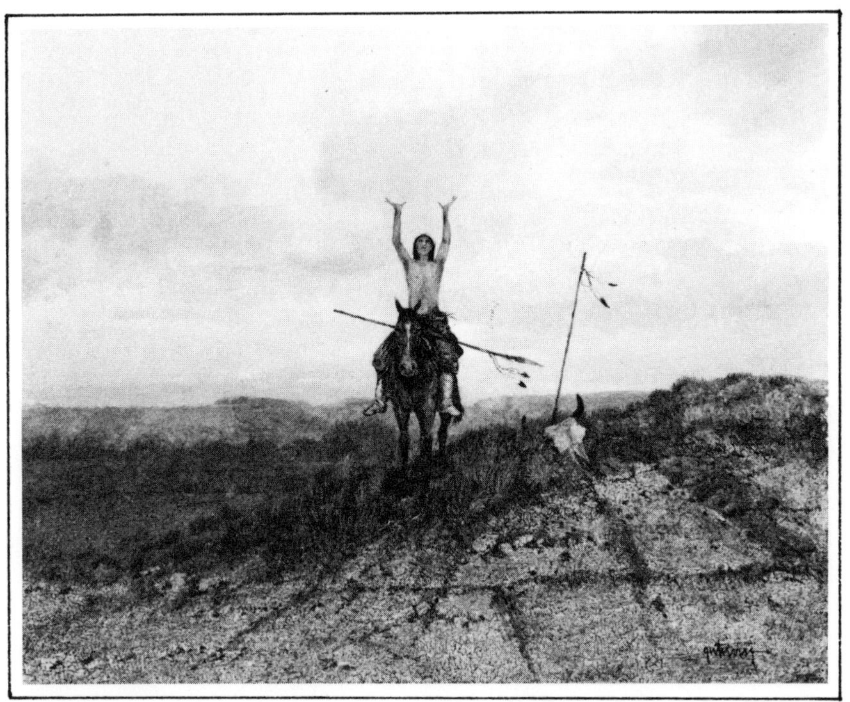

Raul Gutierrez, *No Man's Land,* 11' x 14" watercolor. American Fine Arts Gallery.

Arthello's Gallery   1922 S. Peckley Ave.   Dallas 75224
(214) 941-2276   Monday-Friday: 10-5:30; Saturday, Sunday: by
appointment

Arthello's

Occupying both floors of a converted apartment building about 20
minutes from downtown Dallas, Arthello's is the only gallery in the
Dallas area devoted exclusively to work by black artists.

The paintings, drawings and prints that crowd the walls are
invariably representational, stressing such black themes as family
and children, scenes of everyday life, village scenes in Africa. The
gallery regularly exhibits the meticulously detailed pencil
drawings of Nathan Jones; oils, watercolors and prints by Arthello
Peck, Jr., who, together with his wife, founded the gallery three
years ago; and two-dimensional works by James Dunn, Burl
Washington, Taylor Gurley, and Carl Sidle, who are all from the
Dallas area.

Arthello's also has a selection of inexpensive prints and
reproductions by gallery artists. A few sculptures and photographs
are also displayed. If planning a visit, it is best to phone first.
Arthello's is a one-man operation and occasionally that one man,
who also operates a printing company, is out.

Marie Berger Art Gallery   4916 Camp Bowie   Fort Worth 76107
(817) 737-6062   Monday-Saturday: 10-5

Berger

Marie Berger opened her gallery in 1971. The gallery specializes
in graphics by contemporary artists including Chagall, Miro,
Rockwell, Calder, Neiman, and Tobaisse.

Graphics by Marie Berger herself are also featured. She works
in all media—oils, acrylic, watercolor, and original etchings,
lithographs, and callographs. Ms. Berger, whose work is
published nationally, described her own style by saying: "I work
from realism to surrealism to impressionism and what I call
fantism." She has had a one-woman show at the Oklahoma Art
Museum, and has participated in group shows at the Oklahoma Art
Museum in Oklahoma City and the Laguna Gloria Museum in
Austin.

Carlin Galleries   710 Montgomery   Fort Worth 76107
(817) 733-6921   Monday-Friday: 10-5

Carlin
Galleries

Electra Carlin opened the Carlin Galleries in September 1959.
The gallery represents American painters, printmakers, and
craftsmen and Canadian Eskimo prints and sculpture.

Among the painters represented are landscape artists Peter
Hurd, John McCoy, George Harkins, and Emily Guthrie Smith.
Henriette Wyeth, the well-known still life and portrait painter, and
John Guerine, whose landscapes tend toward an abstract style, are
also in stock. James R. Blake, Bill Bomar, and Luis Eades defy a

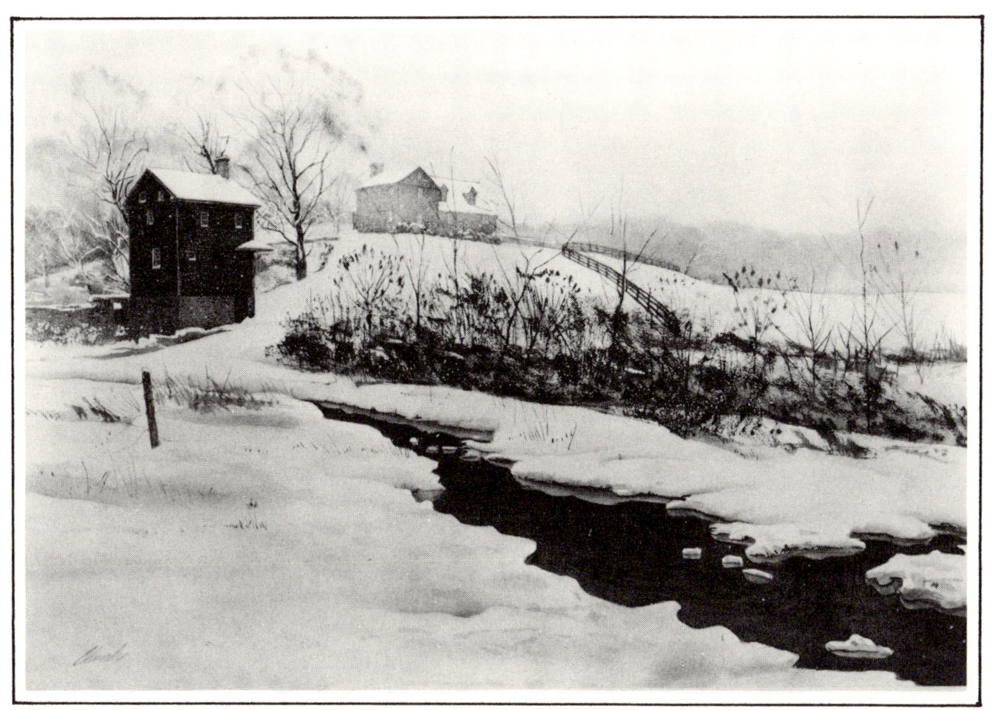

John Chumley, *Below the Mill,* 20″ x 30″ watercolor. Carlin Galleries.

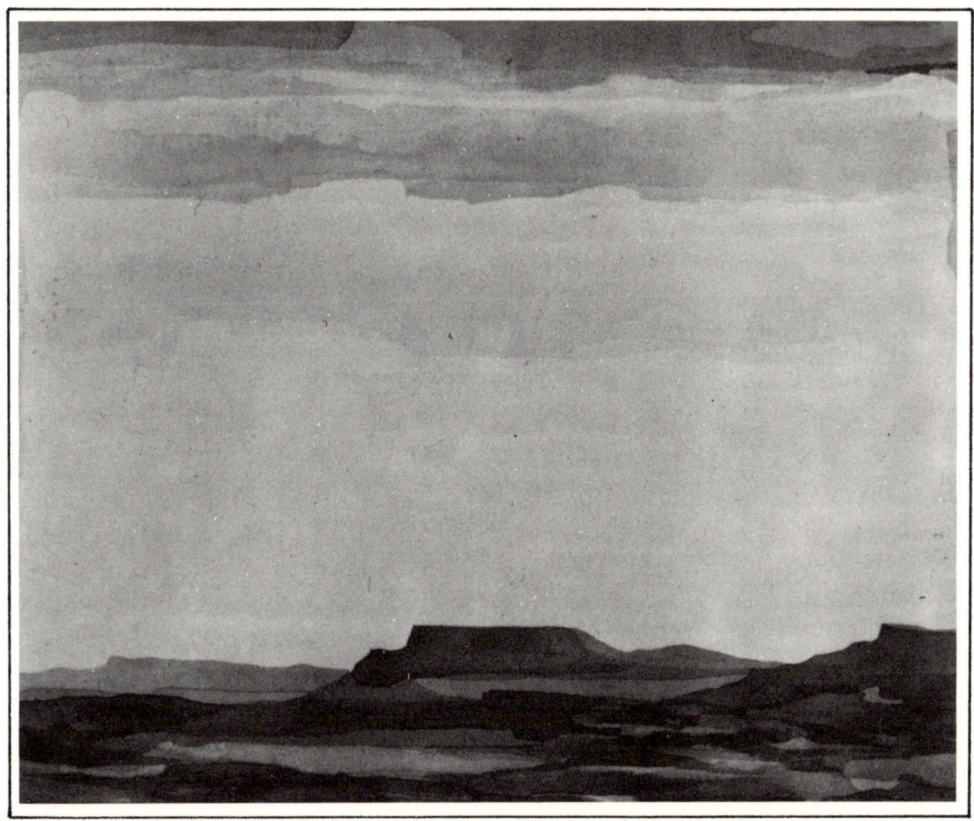

Cobie Russel, *New Mexico #3,* 42″ x 33″ acrylic on canvas. Contemporary
Gallery.

descriptive category; their work is very individual and highly
personal.

The Canadian Eskimo sculpture complements the contemporary
painters and printmakers in an unusual and interesting way. The
Eskimo prints, because of their unique and strong images, are
usually shown as a group in a separate gallery room.

Carlin represents ten nationally known printmakers, including
Clare Romano, Will Barnet, John Ross, and Beatrice Berlin.

Among the craftsmen shown here are potters Richard M.
Lincoln and Elmer Taylor, who have shown in national and international crafts exhibitions.

The annual schedule includes five special exhibitions including
an Eskimo art show and a gallery artists' and craftsmen show each
fall. There are three one-man shows of artists represented by the
gallery scheduled each spring. Informal gallery exhibitions are on
view from time to time.

Carr Gallery

Carr Gallery   907 University Dr.   Fort Worth 76107   (817)
336-0251   Tuesday-Friday: 9:30-5; Saturday: 10-2

Carr Gallery is associated with the Gallery of the Southwest in
Taos, N.M., and shows many of the same artists. There are always
a fair number of Western landscapes, especially works displaying
the influence of the Taos school, on exhibit.

In addition, the gallery's regularly changing shows have
featured works by Gene Ravinger, an Oklahoma artist who paints
large acrylic abstracts; Anne Cofrin, painter of landscapes and of
children; and the painting Blagg brothers from Fort Worth:
Woodrow, who specializes in traditional Western subjects, Dennis,
a painter of Southwestern landscapes, Daniel, who paints urban
landscapes, and Doug who draws and paints oilfield scenes.

The gallery has a small selection of sculpture, particularly
Western bronzes. There is also a large number of prints,
representing, according to co-owner Ralph Carr, "a little bit of
everything," which includes LeRoy Neiman sporting prints, Frank
Stella lithographs, and prints by Red Grooms, Peter Hurd, Allan
D'Arcangelo, Josef Albers, and others.

Clifford

Clifford Gallery   6610 Snider Plaza   Dallas 75205   (214)
363-8223   Tuesday-Saturday: 10-5:30

Jutta Clifford opened her gallery in 1974. She is a foremost print
appraiser and lecturer and a member of the Dallas Print and
Drawing Society. Emphasis is on Texas regional artists, including
painters, printmakers, and sculptors within the contemporary arts
community.

Both representational and Abstract Expressionist color-field
painters are shown here. Outstanding examples of the
representational group are James Dowell, Jane T. Goldman, and

John Evans. Leah Goren, Wayne Toepp, and Hans Schiebold do Abstract Expressionist work.

Betsy Muller has shown her print and drawing collages at area museums along with Peter Nickel, a notable lithographer.

The rear of the gallery is devoted to corporate work with prints from publishers of national and international artists.

Perry Coldwell   4727 Camp Bowie Blvd.   Fort Worth 75107
(817) 731-1801   Wednesday-Saturday: 2-7

Coldwell

Fort Worth's only gallery devoted exclusively to photography is found in a onetime clinic and dentist's office. Presided over by Perry Coldwell, a longtime amateur photographer, the gallery so far has featured mainly local talent.

Among the works exhibited have been Cirrus Bonneau's beautiful prints of the byways and back alleys of Fort Worth, Larry Sanders's prints of cowboy subjects, George Jara's photos of Old Mexico, Jana Walker's close-up Cibachrome prints emphasizing the texture of everyday objects, and June Van Cleef's prints on homemade paper.

The most unusual show was of the work of the extraordinary Byrd Williams family, five generations of Fort Worth photographers, ranging from great-great grandfather Byrd Williams's photo of an old coal stove, made in 1893, to Byrd Williams IV's picture of his father at work at the enlarger.

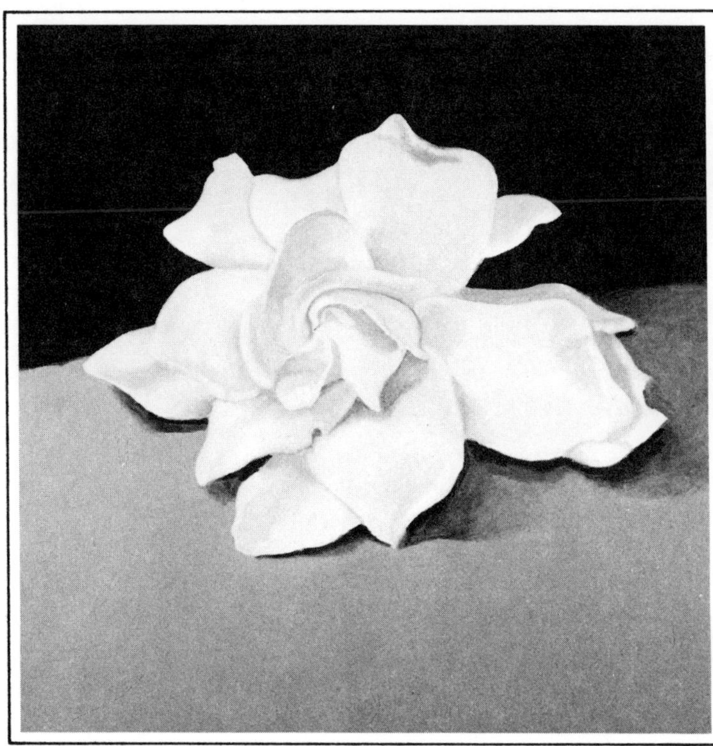

James R. Blake, *Gardenia on Black Beige Background,* 30″ x 30″, oil. Carlin Galleries.

Contemporary Gallery   2800 Routh St.   Dallas 75201   (214)
747-0141   5100 Beltline Rd.   Dallas 75240   (214) 934-2323
Monday-Saturday: 10:30-4

Contemporary
Gallery

Twentieth-century painters are exhibited at Contemporary Gallery
in one-artist monthly shows. Graphics by artists such as Picasso,
Miro, Chagall, Dine, and Motherwell are always on hand.

Twentieth-century sculpture is a secondary area of
concentration here.

In addition recent shows have included the work of: painters
Cobie Russell, Carole Scholder, and Jeanne Koch, and sculptor
Joe Orlando, from Dallas; Joan Brams, Florida; paintings and
graphics by Skynear, Prescott, Arizona; country landscapes by
Pat Thomas of Milwaukee; drawings, sculpture, and graphics by
Bruno Brumi, an Italian artist now living in Germany; and new
works by California artist Martin Stoelzel.

D-ART Visual Arts Center for Dallas   2917 Swiss Ave.   Dallas
75204   (214) 821-4553   Monday-Saturday: 9-5

D-ART

Intended as a multi-purpose art center like the Torpedo factory in
Alexandria, Va., D-ART opened its doors in a onetime warehouse
and chemical factory a little over a year ago. Since then, there is
almost always something going on at D-ART: an exhibit or two,
painting classes, workshops, demonstrations and other special
events.

The space is spartan, with bare walls and vast empty floors, but
volunteers are working to correct that with the help of a few
generous grants. Studio space may soon be available for rental.

Most of the shows are by artist-members (membership in D-ART
is $35 a year), or by special groups such as the Texas Fine Arts
Association that rent space in the facility for specific shows.
Exhibits have included a Businessman's Art Show, a Law
Enforcement Officer's Art Show, Texas Area Artists Membership
Show, a display of John Lennon's lithographs, and numerous one-
artist exhibits by predominantly local talents who have not yet
received exposure or recognition elsewhere. As one might expect,
quality of the art on display varies, and emphasis is apt to be on
more traditional styles. Nevertheless, D-ART is a valuable addition
to the community.

Since D-ART is not a commercial gallery, work is not kept on
hand for sale.

Gallery Downtown   815 Houston St.   Fort Worth 76102
(817) 332-8891   Monday-Friday: 10-5

Gallery
Downtown

Gallery Downtown specializes in works by Mexican and South
American artists as well as those from New York and the
Southwest.

In addition to the work of Ramayo, Morales, and others, Maria
Luiso Pacdeco from Bolivia and Christina Fournier from Costa
Rica are well represented. Amado Pena's works are beautifully
executed silkscreens of figures and scenes of Indian women.
Jerome Schurr's almost surrealistic landscapes are haunting, and
the colors are exquisite.

Sculpture in steel by Joyce of Guatemala, and marbles and
bronzes by Castenada round out Gallery Downtown's inventory.

The gallery also carries new investment-quality prints by up-
and-coming contemporary artists.

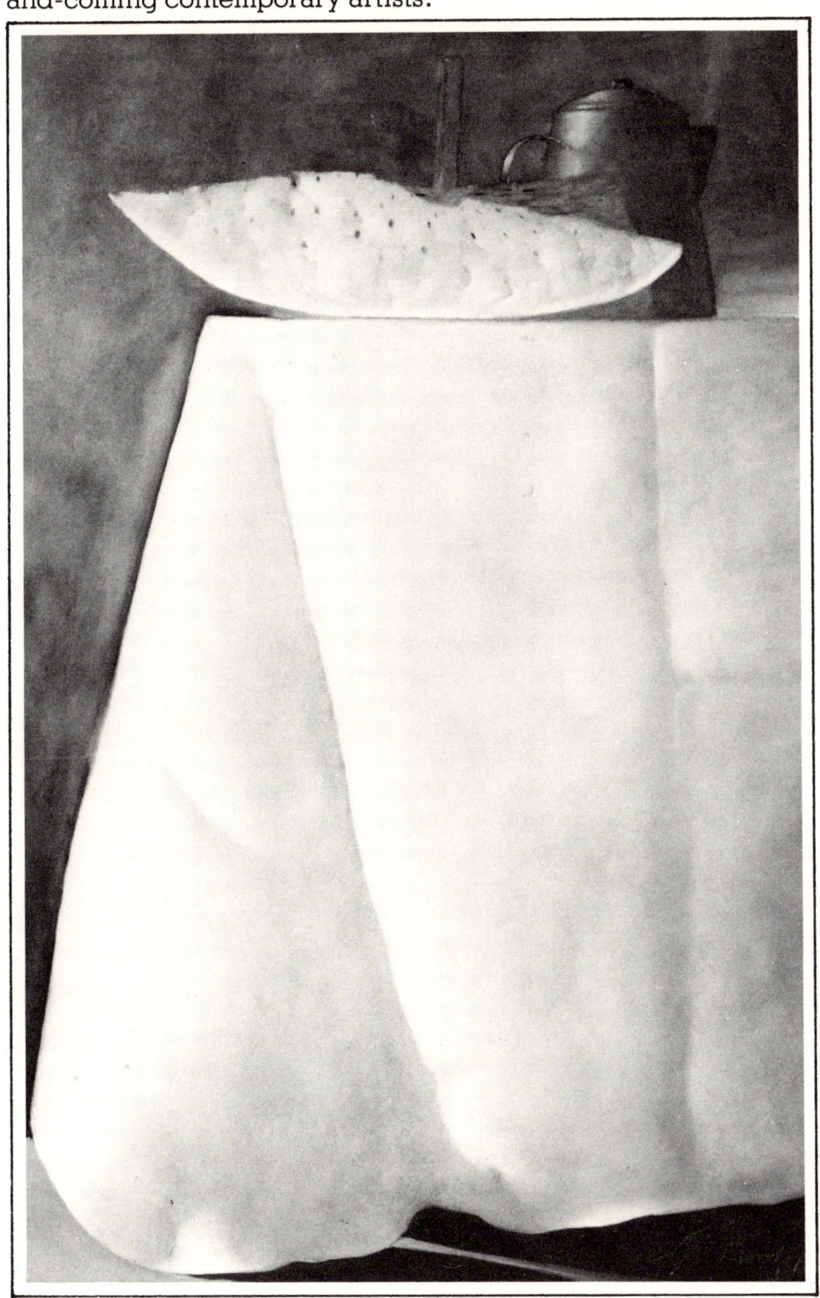

Julio Larraz, *The Fortress*,
60" x 40", oil on canvas.
Hall Gallery.

Delahunty Gallery   2701 Canton St.   Dallas   75226
(214) 744-1346   Tuesday-Saturday: 11-5

Delahunty recently moved from the location it had occupied for
the past seven years into a newly refurbished two-story warehouse
on the edge of downtown Dallas. One of Dallas's oldest and most
important galleries, it traces its lineage back to two earlier
galleries operated by Murray Smither, a 20-year veteran of the
Dallas gallery scene. Smither remains the Delahunty's co-owner
and under the collective guidance of Smither, co-owner Laura
Carpenter and director Barry Whistler, the gallery regularly
exhibits paintings, prints, ceramics, sculpture, and photography
by mostly Texas artists, a number of whom have started to receive
national recognition.

James Surls's spiky, rough-hewn wood sculptures and Vernon
Fisher's narrative works combining imagery and a written text,
which have been widely exhibited and favorably reviewed, are
regularly seen at the Delahunty. Also in the Delahunty stable are
ceramic sculptors Clyde Connell and Nick Wood, collagist-painter
Dan Rizzie, printmaker Juergen Strurck, assemblagist David
McManaway; Roger Winter, Stephen Lorber, Nancy Chambers,
Peter Bodnar, Robert Gordy, Danny Williams, Nick Wood and
John Ross. Photographers represented by the gallery include
Debora Hunter, Al Souza, Nico Nicosia, John Pfehl, Mark
McFadden, Wanda Hammerback, Judy Fiskin, Lee Friedlander,
and Gail Skoff.

The Delahunty also has a print section featuring the works of
such nationally important artists as Jim Dine, Robert
Rauschenberg and Frank Stella. There is also an extensive and
busy framing operation on the premises. The gallery has recently
inaugurated a photography department with its own curator and
also opened a New York branch.

DW Gallery   3305 McKinney Ave.   Dallas 75204   (214)
526-3240   Tuesday-Saturday: 11-5

DW started life seven years ago as a co-operative gallery,
organized by a group of women artists for the exhibition of works
by women artists. Since then the gallery has expanded its program
and its horizons. No longer a co-op, DW now shows the work of
some of the most interesting and important North Texas artists of
both sexes.

Among those artists are Ellen Soderquist, known for large pencil
"paintings" of the nude; Lee Smith III, who paints haunting scenes
of boyhood; sculptor Linnea Glatt, who constructs large-scale
works in wood, cement, sand, and similar materials; and Martin
Delabano, whose paintings and tableaux reflect the religious folk
art of the American Southwest and Mexico. Other gallery artists

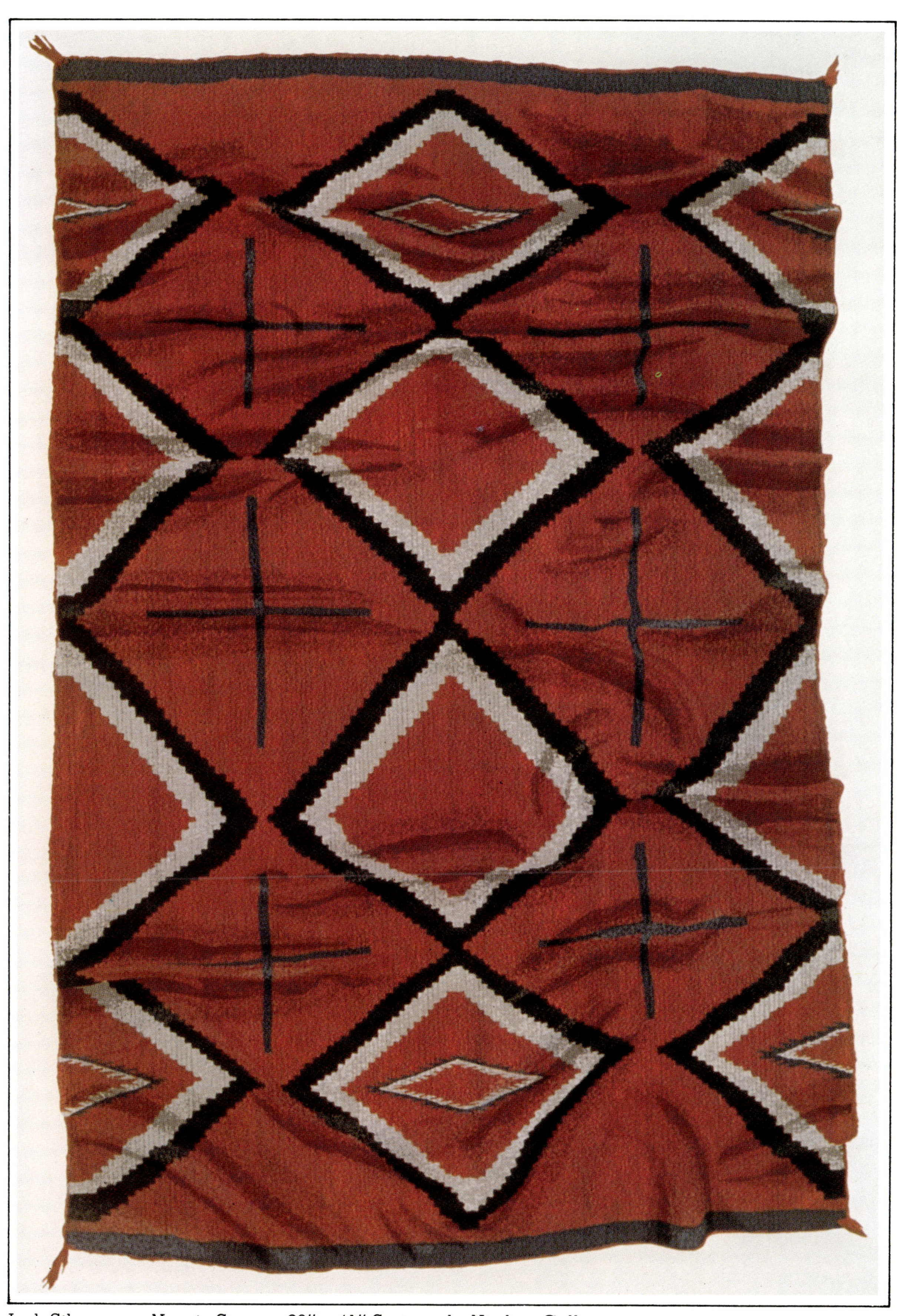

Jack Silverman, *Navajo Serape*, 30″ x 41″ Serigraph. Nimbus Gallery.

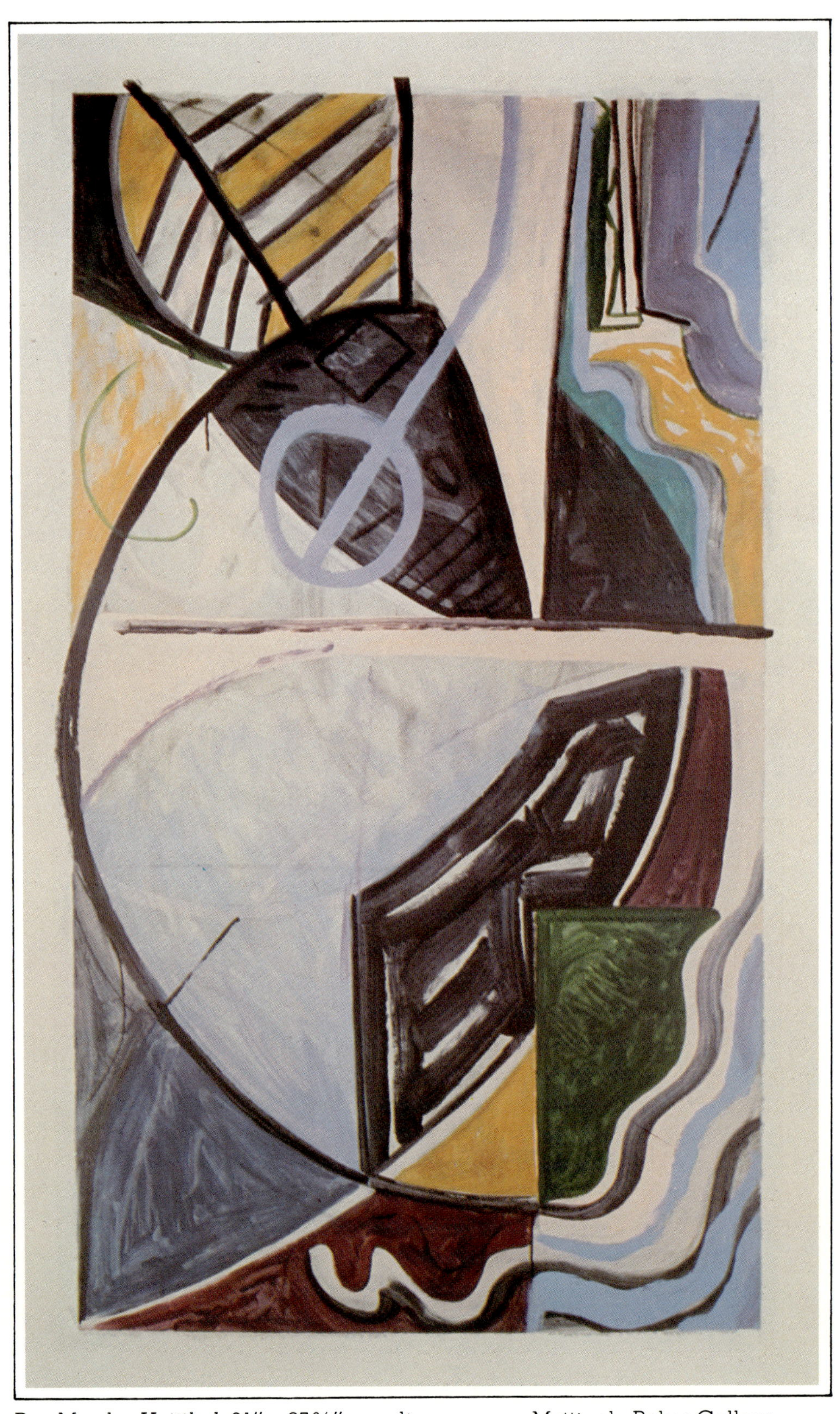

Ron Moody, *Untitled,* 61″ x 35¾″, acrylic on paper. Mattingly Baker Gallery.

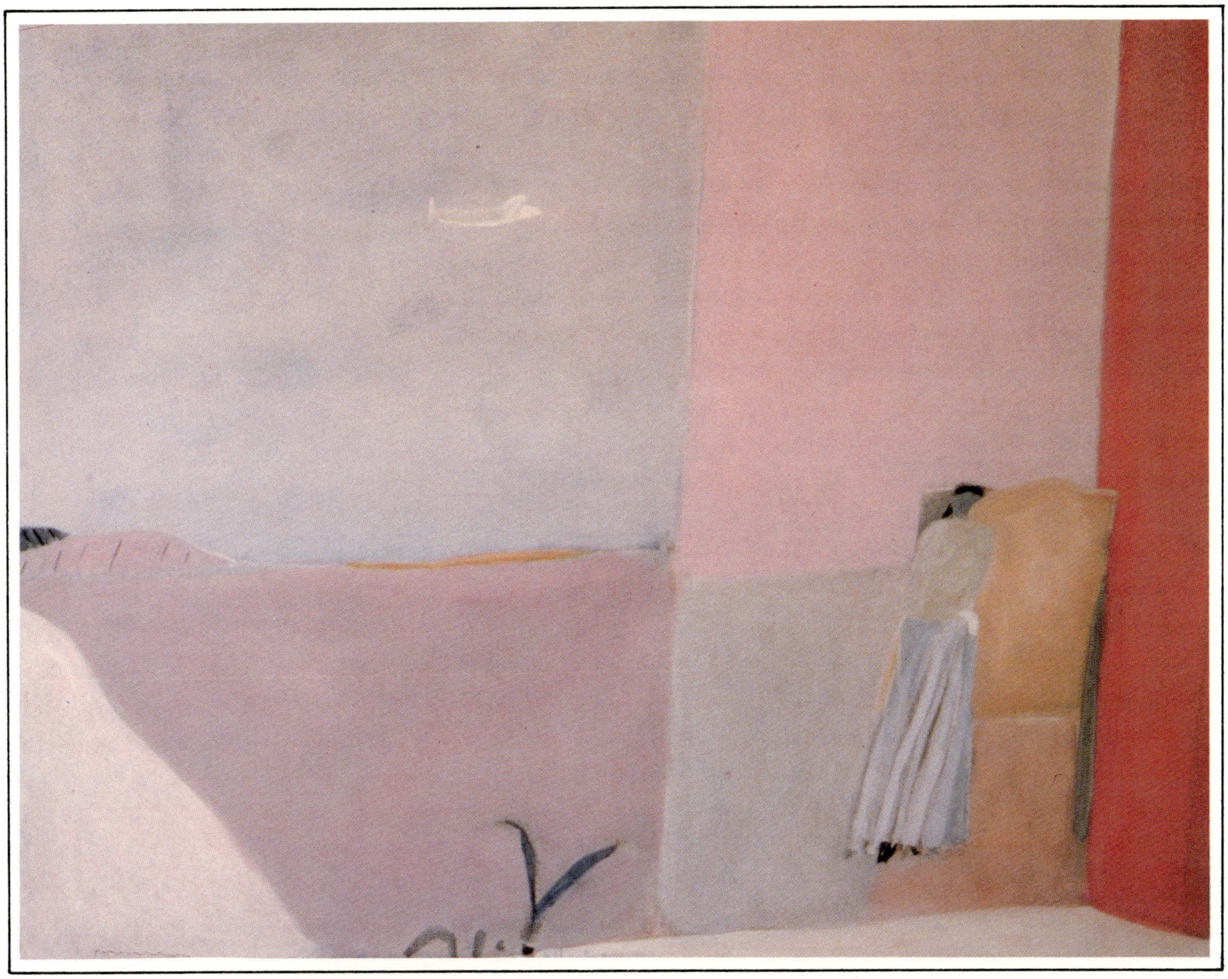

Joy Laville, *Anunciation II,* 89″ x 116″, acrylic on canvas. Nimbus Gallery.

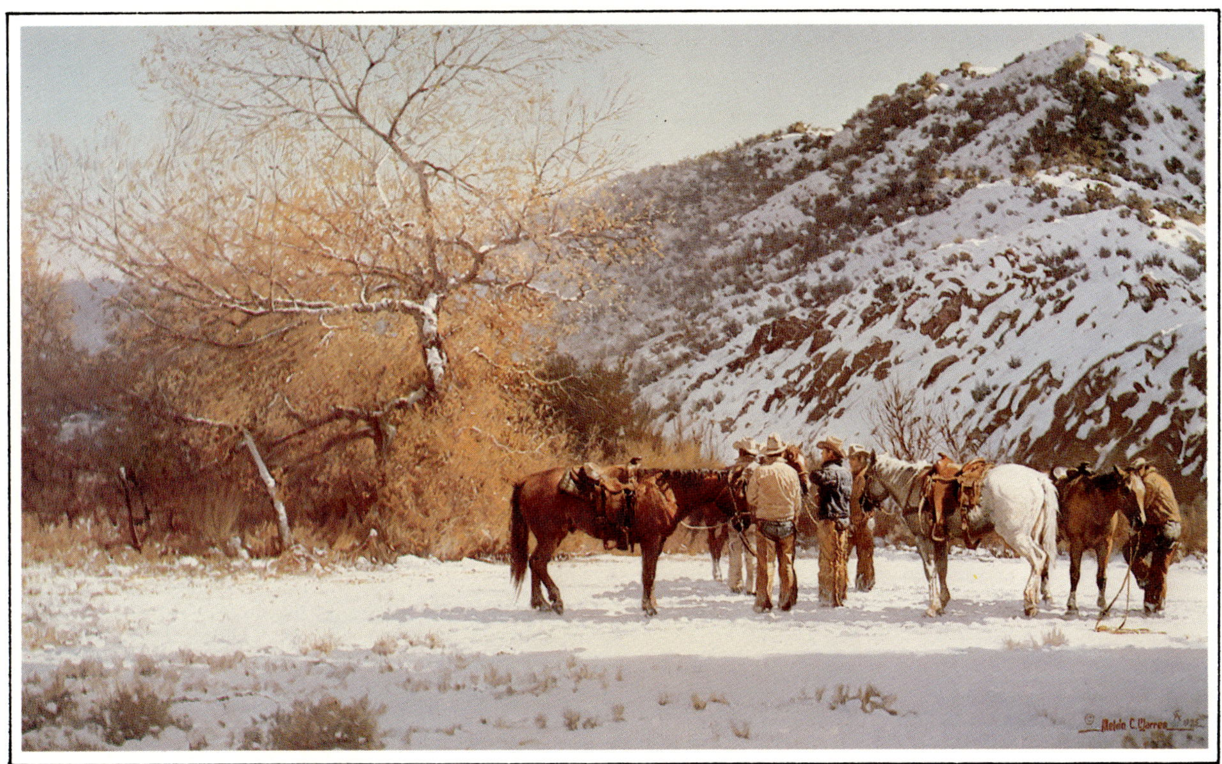

Melvin C. Warren, *Cowboy Rendezvous,* 36″ x 60″, oil on canvas. Reminisce Gallery.

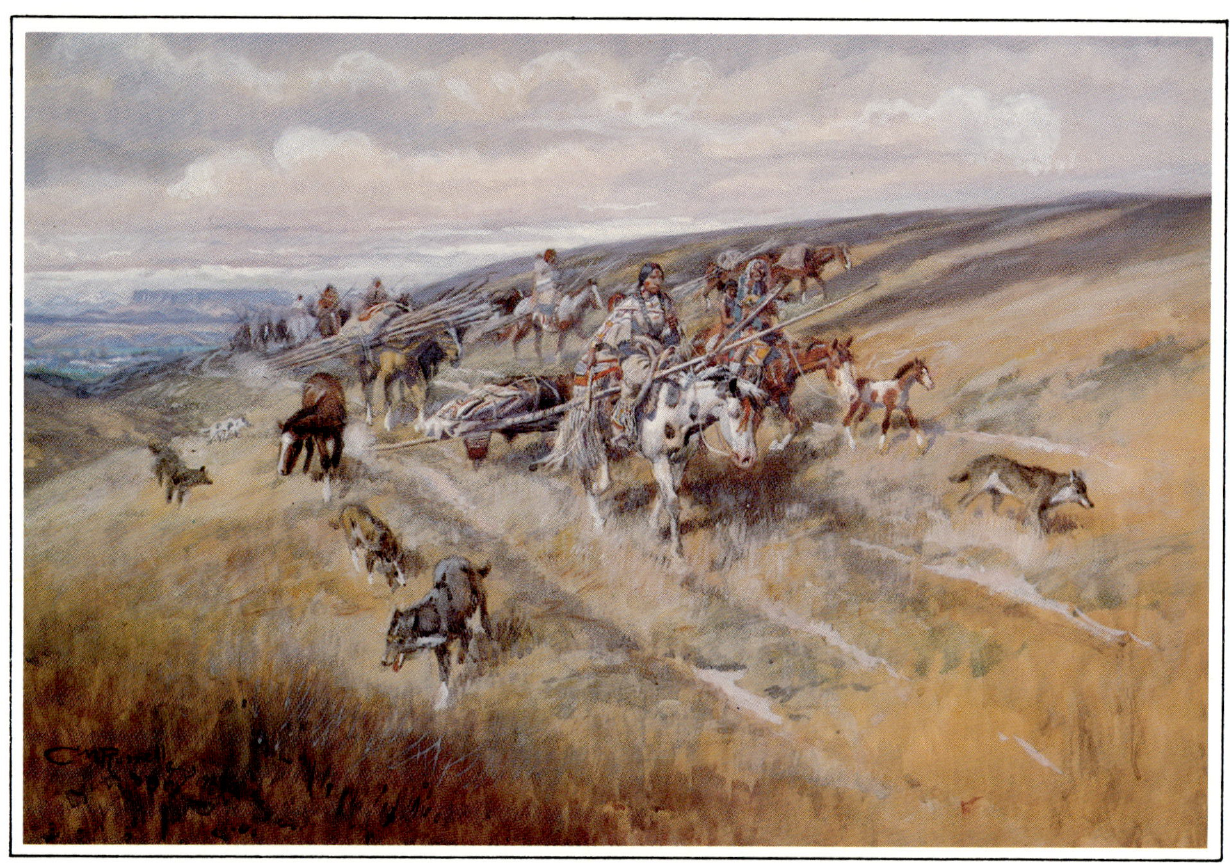

Charles Russell, *Women of America,* 20″ x 30″ watercolor. Ron Hall Galleries.

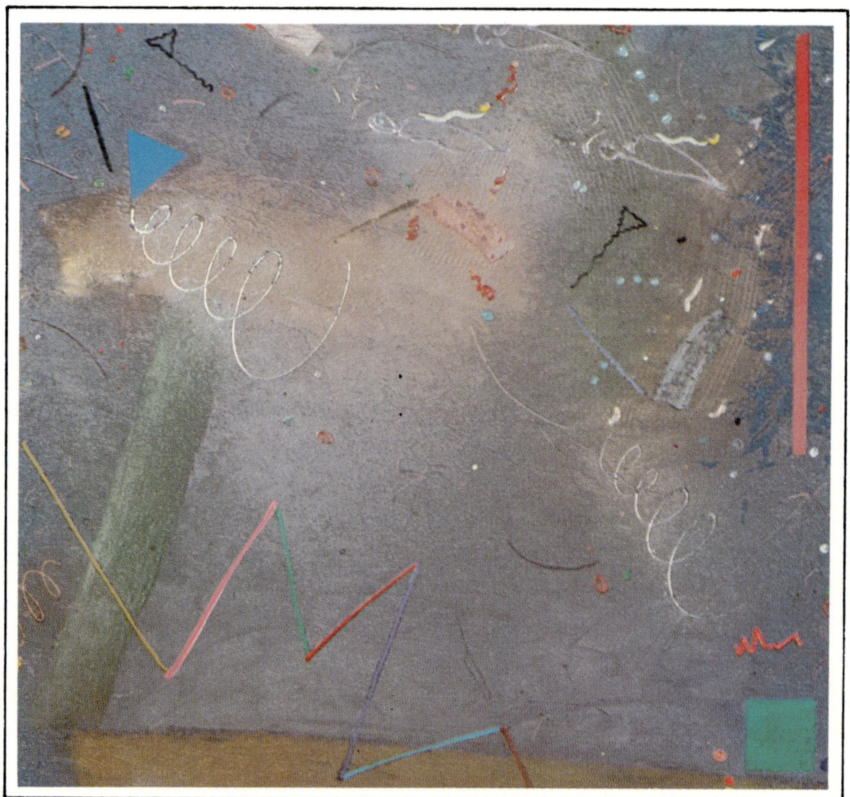

David McCullough, *Flying in Eye Formation,* 74″ x 80″, acrylic on canvas. Nimbus Gallery.

whose work appears regularly include Linda Ridgeway Taylor,
Anne Lee Stautberg, Francis X. Tolbert, Richard Bates, Rebecca
Best, and Herb Rogalla. In addition there are occasional shows of
works by out-of-state artists, a recent example being the work of
San Francisco photographer Jack Wellpott.

Under its new director, Diana Block, DW Galleries continues to
hold regular "theme" shows. Within the past year the gallery has
held exhibits of artists' self-portraits, of artists' books, and a Young
Collectors' Christmas Show. The gallery also hosts artist's
performances and poetry readings.

500 Exposition Gallery   500 Exposition Ave.   Dallas 75226
(214) 828-1111   Tuesday-Saturday: 1-5

500 Exposition Gallery

Blessed with one of the largest and most flexible exhibition spaces
among Dallas galleries, 500 Exposition has endeared itself to art
lovers by making its walls available to serious but struggling local
artists. It is also famous for its opening-night parties, which are
well-attended, lively, and a good place to meet and exchange
gossip.

Sharing a two-story onetime air-conditioning warehouse with a
number of artist's studios, 500 Exposition emphasizes works by
young Texas artists, with occasional looks at what young artists are
doing in other parts of the country. All media are represented in
the regularly changing shows, and works on view range from
photography and abstract paintings to frankly experimental
multimedia installations and video in the gallery's two "project"
rooms.

The gallery is managed by a committee of artists, which selects
gallery shows. Among the artists exhibited more or less regularly
at 500 Exposition Gallery are Will Hipps, one of the founders of the
gallery and formerly owner of the building, Frances Bagley,
Linnea Glatt, Georgia Stafford, Scott Madison, Cyd Romeo, Bruce
Stiglich, Kathy Drake, and Gilda Pervin. Every so often, however,
the walls of 500 Exposition are simply thrown open to all comers.
The result is some of the most uneven, but liveliest, exhibits in
town.

Hall Galleries   312 Main St.   Fort Worth 76102   (817) 332-3773
Monday-Saturday: 10-5:30

Hall Galleries

Ron Hall, an established Fort Worth dealer in museum-quality
nineteenth- and twentieth-century art, has recently moved his
gallery to the renovated Conn building in Sundance Square in
downtown Fort Worth. The architecture of the turn-of-the-
century brownstone-type structure provides a dramatic setting for
Hall's changing inventory of master paintings by American and
French artists. Hall personally collects and selects works from the

Hudson River School, the Luminist movement, the Western
landscape genre, the American Impressionists, and the French
Post Impressionists. He has sold major works by Charles Russell,
Thomas Moran, Mary Cassatt, George Inness, Robert Reid,
Frank Benson, Georgia O'Keeffe, and Peter Hurd.

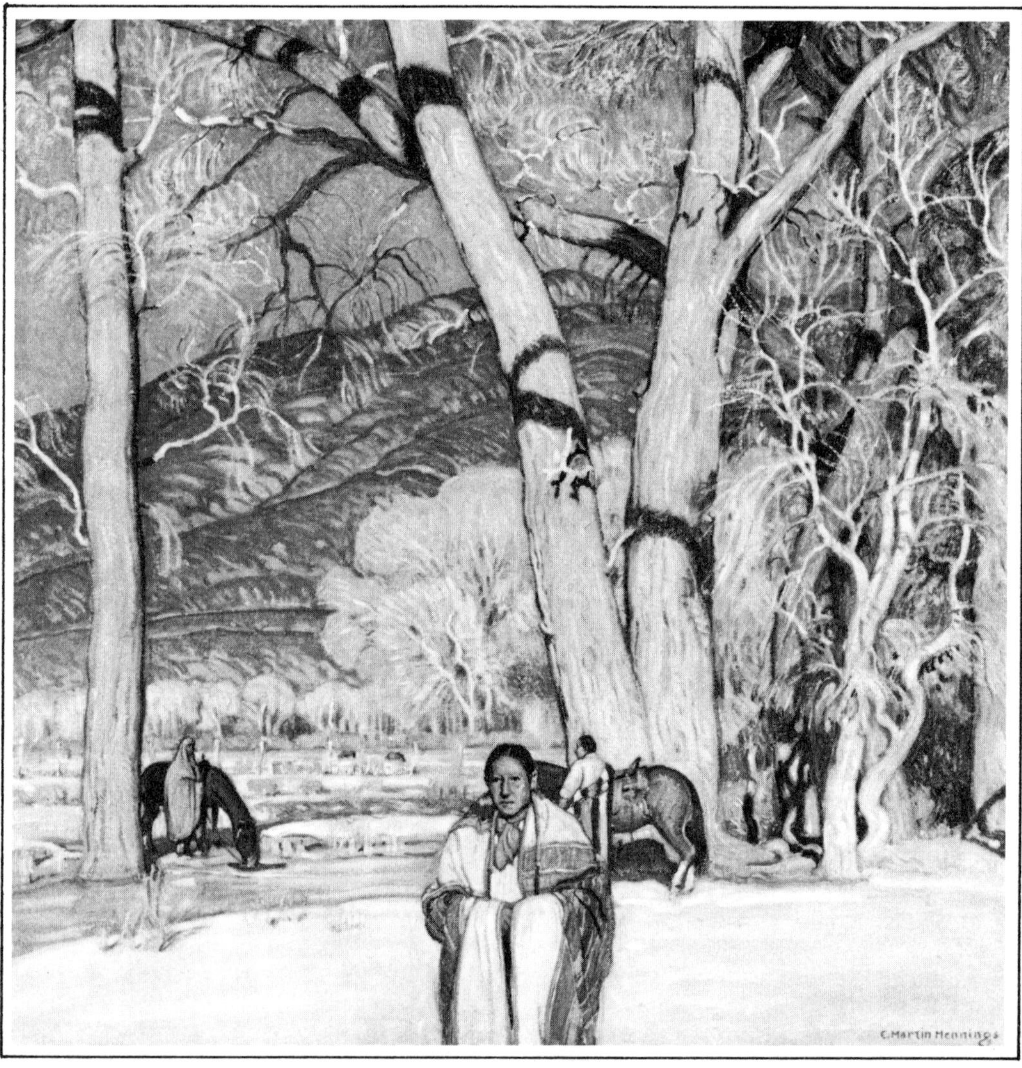

E. Martin Hennings, *Navajos at the Stream,* 30¼" x 30¼", oil on canvas. Hall Gallery.

In addition to his continually changing selection of nineteenth-
century art, the gallery does several contemporary exhibits each
year. Hall has been known to mount ambitious exhibitions which
include an inaugural show for Cuban American realist Julio Larraz
and Californian David Ligare. Both artists prefer working with
large canvases and vivid images that hang beautifully in
contemporary homes, or, as in the case of Hall Galleries, in an
older setting with high ceilings and large windows.

Michele Herling Galleries   Suite 260, The Quadrangle, 2800
Routh St.   Dallas 75201   (214) 748-2924   Tuesday-Saturday:
12-5:30

Herling

For 16 years, Michele Herling has dealt in Pre-Columbian
African and Oceanic art to discriminating collectors in the Dallas
area. For 13 of those years she has been in the same location, a
suite of rooms and a terrace on the second floor of The
Quadrangle, a charming small shopping center near the
downtown area.

Statuettes, masks, fetish objects, vases, figures, pots and
carvings crowd every available inch of wall and shelf space in the
gallery's five rooms, and objects have started to spill out into the
hallway. "And you should see the closets," says the owner.

In addition to primitive art, the gallery has jewelry from
Afghanistan and India. In a back room there are piles of rugs from
Afghanistan, Russia, and—though they are getting difficult to
obtain—from Iran. Occasionally the gallery also has a few Roman
or Egyptian antiquities on view.

Once each year Mrs. Herling travels to San Blas Island off the
coast of Panama to acquire the colorful applique blouses or
"molas," made by the native Cuna Indians. These inexpensive
examples of folk art have become very popular with local
collectors.

Michele Herling Galleries has a selection of books on primitive
and ethnic art for sale. The gallery also has its own well-stocked
reference library on those subjects.

Houshang's Gallery   9820 N. Central   Dallas 75231
Sakowitz Village   Dallas 75240   1901 Commerce   Dallas
75231   (214) 363-5300   Monday-Wednesday, Friday-Saturday:
10-6; Thursday: 10-9

Houshang's

Houshang's Gallery, now in three Dallas locations, has been
operating since 1970. The gallery features the work of John Nieto
and Amado Pena, but also carries the work of 60 major artists from
all over the world, including Zuniga, Alvar, Delacroix, Boulanger,
Agam, Simbari, and Tamayo.

Nieto's works carry strong contemporary imagery with bright
coloration and Indian influence. Pena's work is warm, flowing, and
romantic, with a strong dedication to form. The work of Alvar is a
cross between traditional and contemporary with an emphasis on
lithographic quality.

The original works of Simbari include a number of silkscreens,
which are gorgeous impressions from Italy. McGuire and
Atkinson, sculptor and painter of the Southwest, are also
represented here. Bruno Bruni, Italian detailist, and sculptors Bill
Carr and Klugman are part of Houshang's stable of artists.

One-man shows are given every couple of months.

Human Arts   Suite 150, The Quadrangle, 2800 Routh St.
Dallas 75201   (214) 748-3948 Monday-Saturday: 10-5:30

Opened in 1975 under a different name and expanded in 1979,
Human Arts now offers fine contemporary glass, pottery, and
jewelry. Also shown on a limited basis are works in fiber and wood.
Fine crafts range from the work of the well-known to the work of the
emerging artist. The criteria used for selecting work are excellence in craftsmanship and creativity.

Leaning more toward the "art in crafts" than toward the
functions, the gallery has been seeking more and more artists with
a national reputation such as Harvey Sadow in pottery, Harvey
Littleton and Dale Chihuly in glass, and Ronald Pearson in
jewelry.

Important also are the emerging artists whose works may have
not yet attracted national attention, such as Jim Bowman of Dallas
who works with fused glass, Lucinda Malin who executes
handbuilt pottery, and Dallas's Charlene Biesele who creates
repousse silver jewelry.

In the fibers area are wearables and some fiber art, wall pieces
such as the batik silk paintings of Geneva Moore of Austin, Texas.
In wood are the works of such artists as Bob McKeown of California
who does acrylic resin inlay into hardwoods, and Bill and Nan
Bolstad, also Californians, who do fine one-of-a-kind and
limited-edition boxes.

Mattingly Baker Gallery   3000 McKinney Ave.   Dallas 75204
(214) 526-0031   Tuesday-Friday: 10-6; Saturday: 11-5

The gallery, located not far from the Dallas Museum of Fine Arts, is
spacious, with both natural and artificial lighting. Divided into two
viewing areas, the front gallery is designed for works on paper and
installations, while the main exhibit area accommodates painting,
sculpture and group shows. The gallery specializes in living,
established and lesser known artists from New York and the
Southwest who work in a contemporary vein.

In the area of painting and drawing is Peter Julian's figurative
German Expressionist style, Mark Lavatelli's shaped canvases
which are a combination of geometry and layers of color-field, and
the colorful, open abstractions of Susan Crile. Narrative
expressionism in bold color is the work of Wendy Edwards, while
Polly Little and Don Shields concern their art with landscapes, and
the relationship of the landscape to the human figure in brilliant
colors usually worked with oil on canvas.

Ron Moody's paintings are of the Abstract Expressionist style,
while Vincent Falsetta uses expressionism in a geometric "new
wave" fashion. Aaron Karp paints strata-like vestiges of thick
colorful layered acrylic, while Gary Wiley creates animal-like

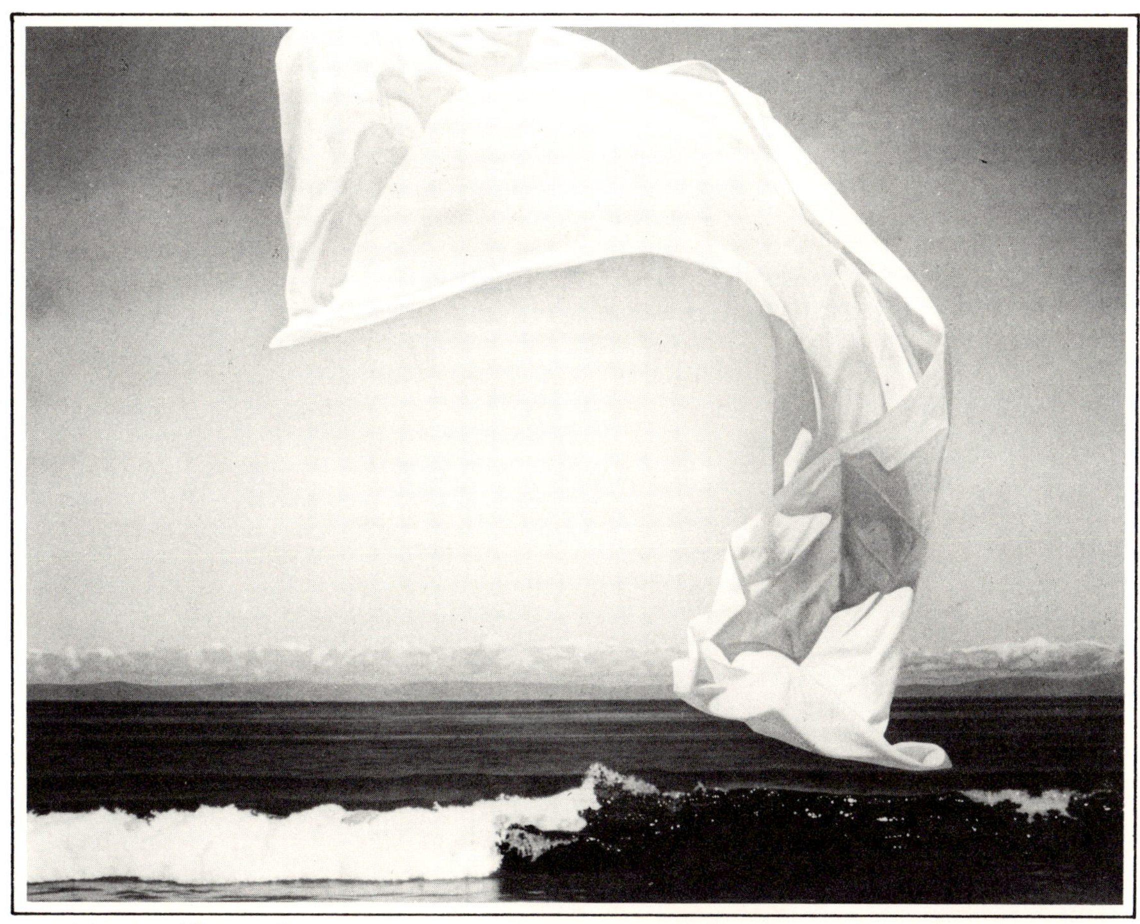

David Ligare, *Thrown Drapery,* 72″ x 96″, oil on canvas. Hall Gallery.

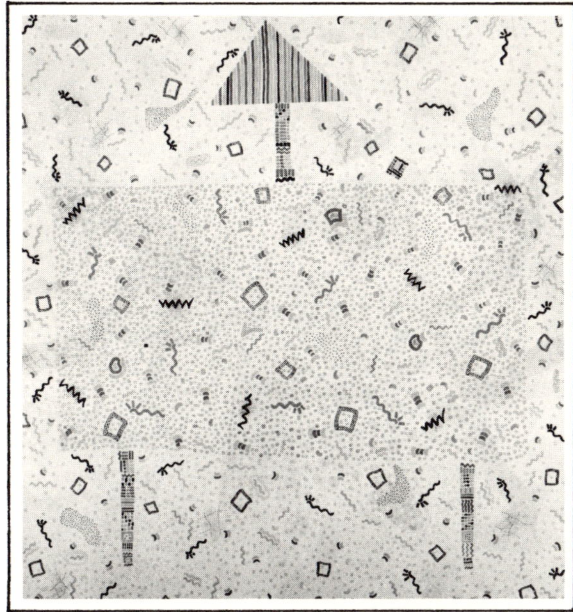

Vincent Falsetta, Untitled, 75″ x 70″, acrylic/ irredescent paint on canvas. Mattingly Baker Gallery.

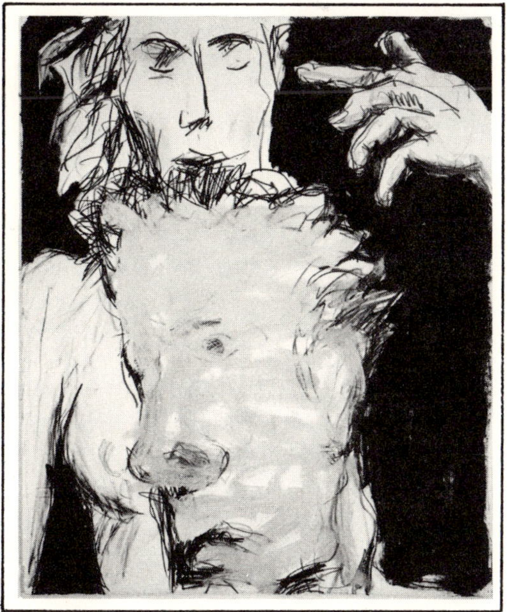

Peter Julian, *Magic,* 31″ x 26″, oil/ graphite on paper. Mattingly Baker Gallery.

creatures of various media that hang in relief off the wall. Philip Van Keuren and Timothy App work in a romantic tradition of pure form and color, while Van Keuren makes paintings, and App makes anodized aluminum wall reliefs and drypoint prints. James Malone presents floral images in a representational manner.

Artists working in other media include Linda Blackburn's whimsical and creative potteryware and watercolors, Roberto Munguia's mixed-media paper collage-paintings with encaustic, powdered pigments, and color xeroxes, Jesus Bautista Moroles' small-scale and public-scale granite sculptures which are softly geometric, and Jana Vander Lee's tapestries of silk, wool and linen with Bauhaus geometric designs.

Prints by such stellar names in printmaking as Jasper Johns, Roy Lichtenstein and Robert Rauschenberg are shown, as well as prints by less established artists. Photography by Dallas artist Philip Lamb who uses his own home-made camera to produce polaroids in color as well as nationally known photographers such as Joel Meyerowitz and Eliot Porter are also in Mattingly Baker's cabinets.

McCulley Fine Arts Gallery, Inc.   5440 Harvest Hill Rd., No. 125   **McCulley**
Dallas 75230   (214) 386-9194   Monday-Friday: 8-4

Western paintings and bronzes, mostly contemporary but with an occasional work dating from the last century, are the stock in-trade of this gallery which caters mostly to the serious collector.

Western action and landscapes predominate, and the emphasis is upon realism. The gallery regularly carries Frank McCarthy's meticulously researched canvases depicting clashes between cavalry and Indians, and the bronze Indian portraits by his son, Kevin. Tom Lovell's paintings of Indian life, Ray Swanson's contemporary Indian subjects, and David Blossom's cowboy and Indian scenes are also carried by the gallery. Although he is not represented by McCulley, Clark Huling's landscapes and genre scenes are also usually on view.

Perhaps the most unusual works in the gallery are the loosely painted and lively works of Bob Peak, the highly successful illustrator who created the first Marlboro Man ads. McCulley also carries a selection of limited-edition graphics, including a full line of Frank McCarthy prints.

MJS International   6333 Camp Bowie Blvd.   Fort Worth 76116   **MJS**
(817) 732-5713   Tuesday-Saturday: 11-5   **International**

Owner/Director Susan Roth opened her gallery five years ago. Although during that time the gallery has shown work drawn from all media, the selective emphasis has been placed on emerging painters and sculptors.

Over the years a close relationship has developed between the gallery and several important artists such as Bob Wade, a Texas

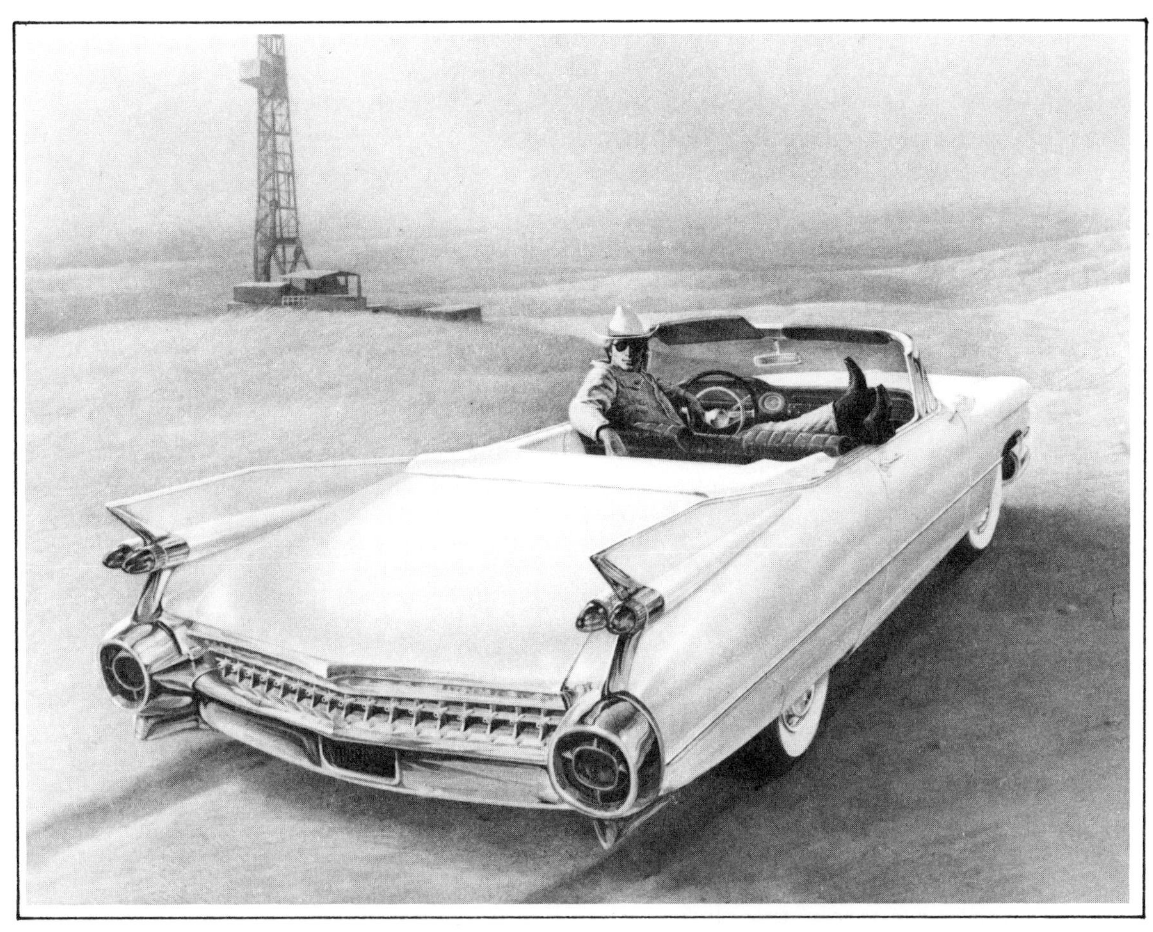

Don Ivan Punchatz, *Fantasia Americana* (*detail*), acrylic on board. MJS International.

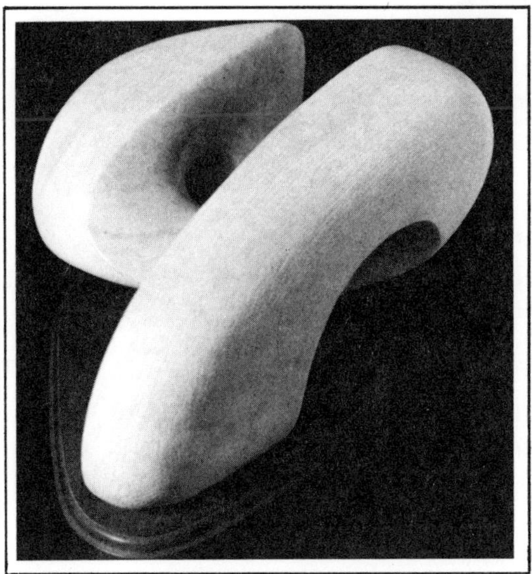

Pat Stone, *Segment IV,* 13″ x
15″ x 10″, white alabaster.
Nimbus Gallery.

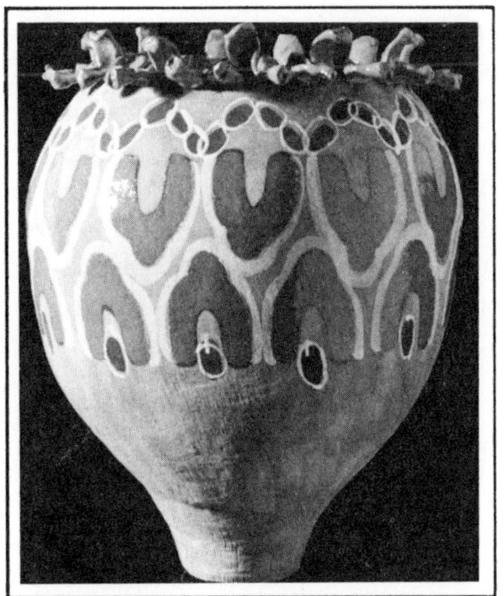

Kathleen Smith-Schooley,
Untitled, 21″ diameter x 26″,
painted terracotta. Nimbus
Gallery.

painter, photographer, and sculptor; Don Ivan Punchatz, an illustrator; Carole Feuerman, a New York artist who works in polyester resin; printmaker Susan Harrington; Larry Harmon, who uses metal and stone; Sandy Sussman, a Los Angeles Expressionist; Todd Christensen, and ceramicist Roscoe West.

The gallery prides itself on its involvement with regional artists whose work deserves a wider audience, as well as its fine selection of contemporary limited-edition lithographs, etchings, and serigraphs.

The increasing interest in ceramics is reflected in the exhibition of such prominent artists as Christensen and West. Once a year the gallery is devoted to a major show of contemporary and master photographers.

Nimbus Gallery   1135 Dragon St.   Dallas 75207   (214) 742-1348   **Nimbus**
Monday-Saturday: 9-5

Located in a near-downtown neighborhood of warehouses and distributing companies where the art lover might least expect to find a gallery, Nimbus successfully cultivates a clientele of designers, interior decorators and private collectors with a mixture of contemporary painting, both abstract and representational, sculpture in a variety of media, prints, and fiber works.

The large, L-shaped exhibition area offers regularly changing shows, and two other, smaller, galleries feature works by Nimbus's regulars. They include the large, nonfunctional ceramic vessels of Kathleen Smith-Schooly, marble travertine carvings by Pat Stone, stainless steel and wood sculpture by Ken Drew, pastel landscapes by Joy LaVille, aquatints of Navajo rugs by Jack Silverman, and the large, richly textured abstract acrylics of David McCullough. Also shown are some notable fiber and cast paper works. Almost always on hand are Dana Romeis's hand-woven silk modules and Lesley Shearer's large wall hangings. Flat-weave pieces of Lois Isenburg and Dandy Kinnee's hand-cast paper kimonos and fans are also on display.

Those interested in an eclectic selection of prints of all kinds will also find the gallery to be an excellent source. Custom framing at the gallery is also available.

Gallery One, Inc.   4715 Camp Bowie Blvd.   Fort Worth 76107   **Gallery One**
(817) 737-9566   Tuesday-Friday: 10-5; Saturday: 10-2

Gallery One was opened seven years ago by owner Bill Campbell. The work shown is contemporary, representing primarily painters and printmakers. A very select amount of photography, acrylic sculpture, and fine crafts concentrating on nonfunctional ceramics are also exhibited. The painters and printmakers represented are both regional and nationally recognized—mostly American, with a sprinkling of contemporary European representation.

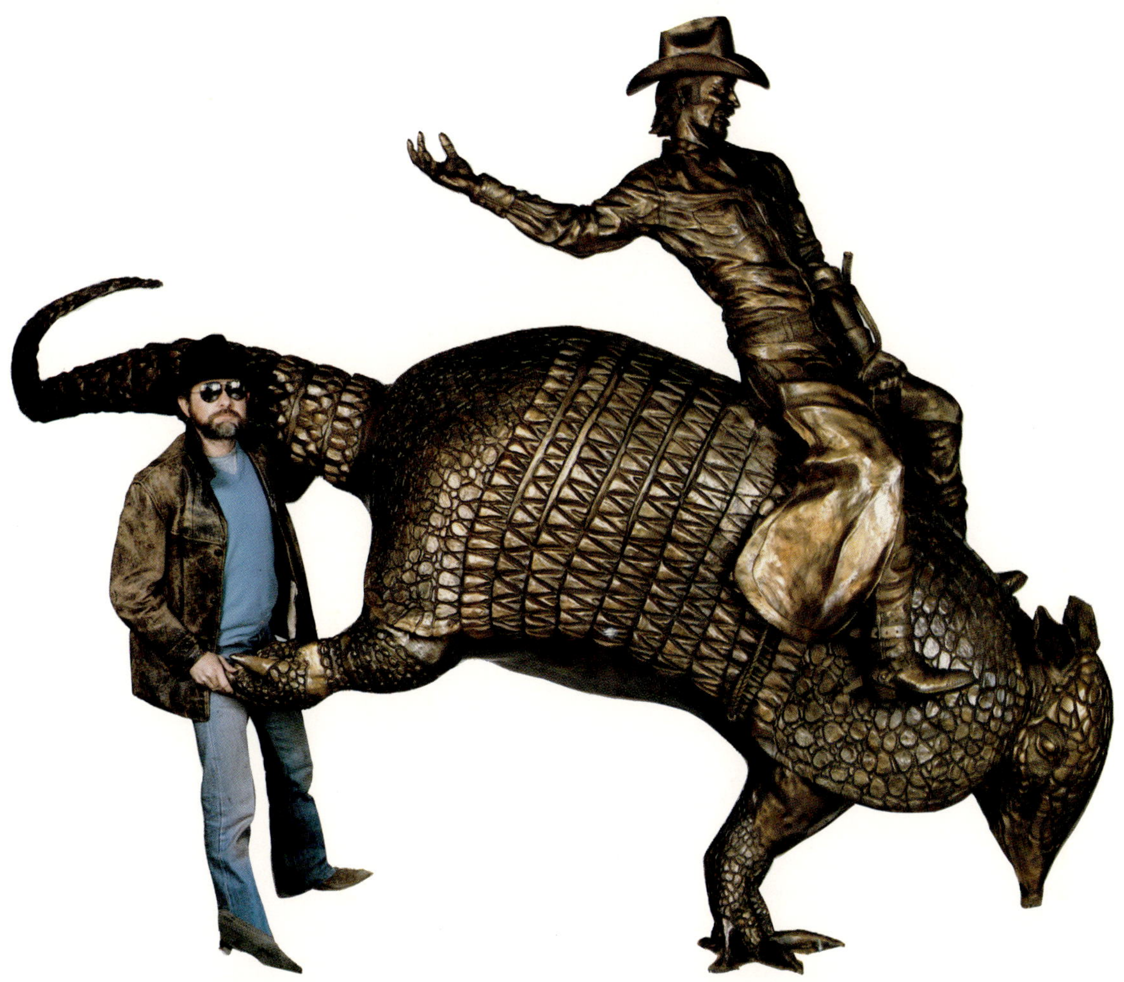

Bob Wade, *Bucking Armadillo with Rider,* 8′ x 12′, bronze. (Collection—Pasadena Town Square, Texas) MJS International.

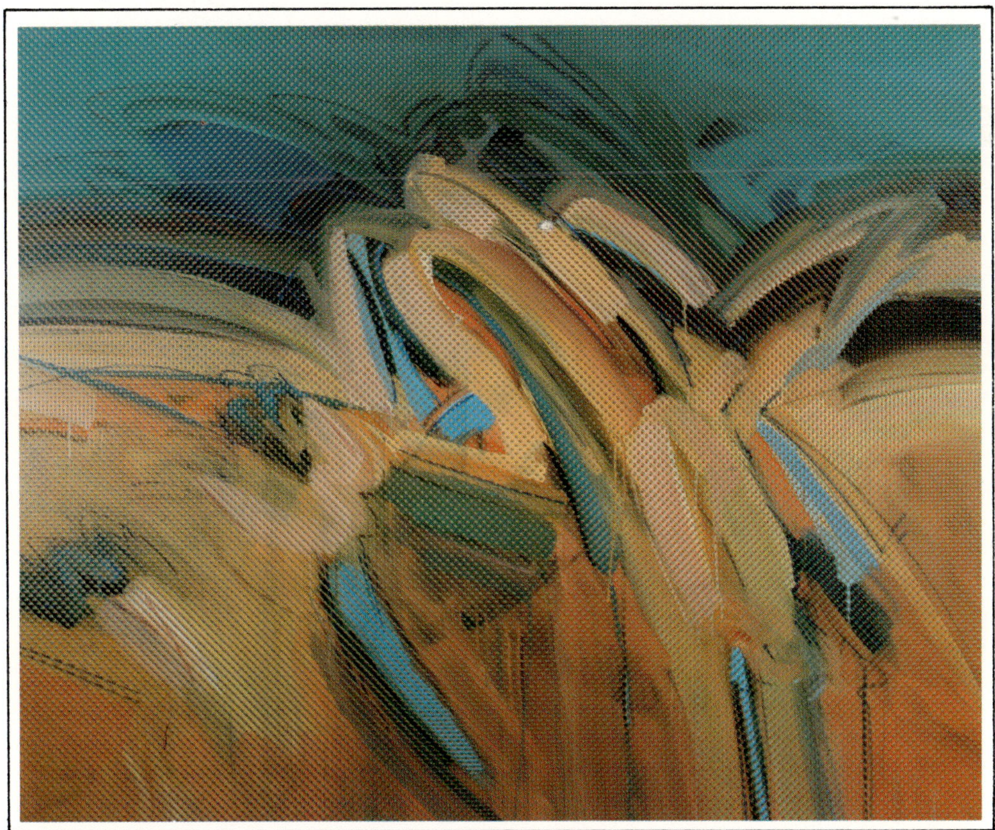

Sandra Leveson-Meares, *The Devil's Marbles,* 48″ x 60″, acrylic with screenpoint on canvas. Gallery One.

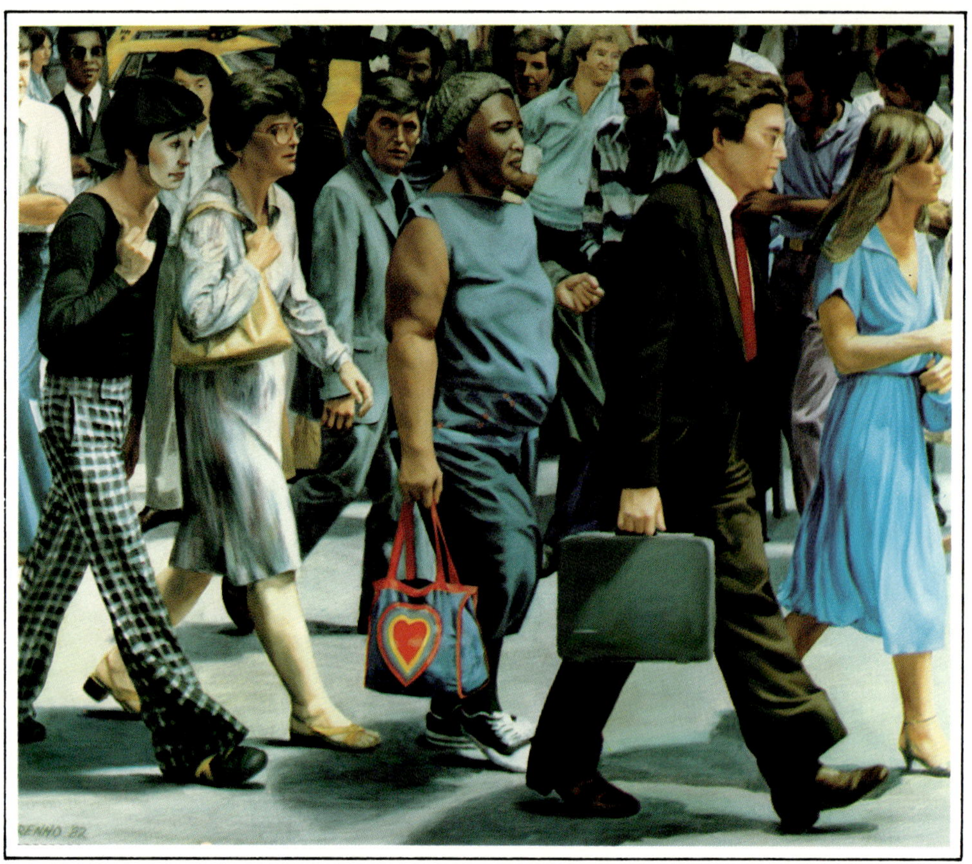

Vonnie Brenno, *Dying Slave,* 42″ x 50″, oil on canvas. Ps Galleries.

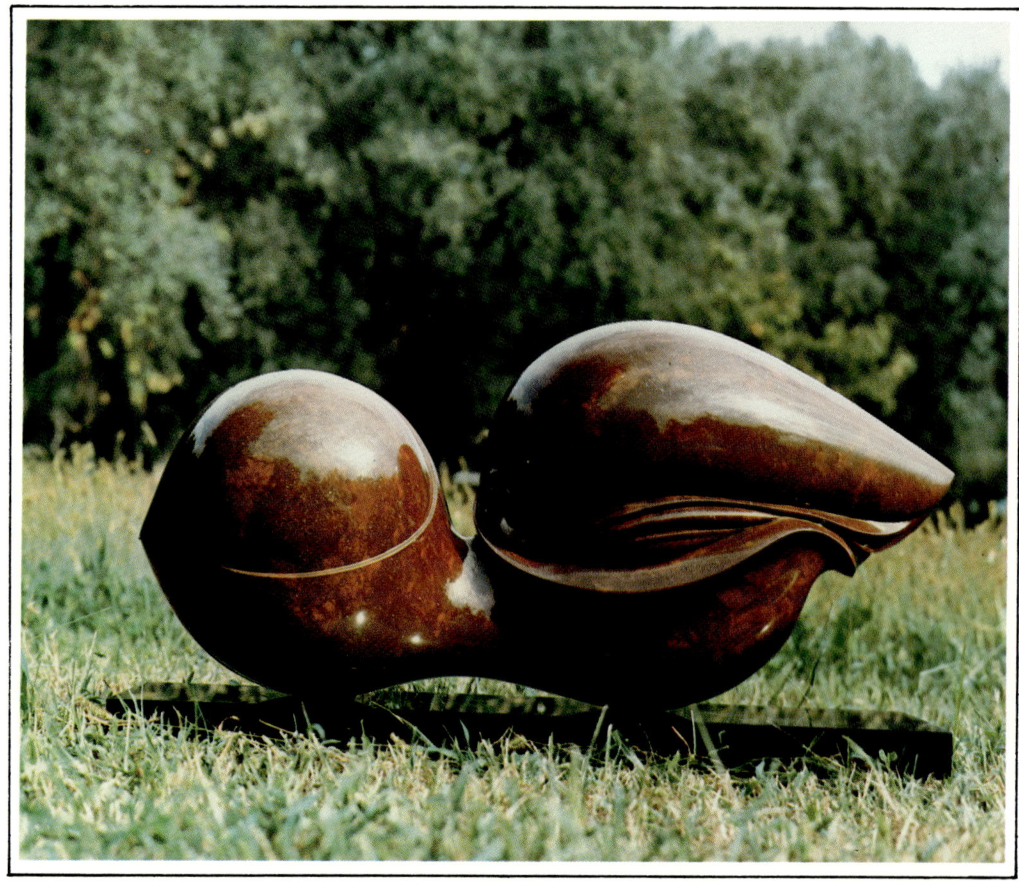

Tarabella, *Douce,* 28″ x 13″ x 16″, red marble. SL Art Gallery.

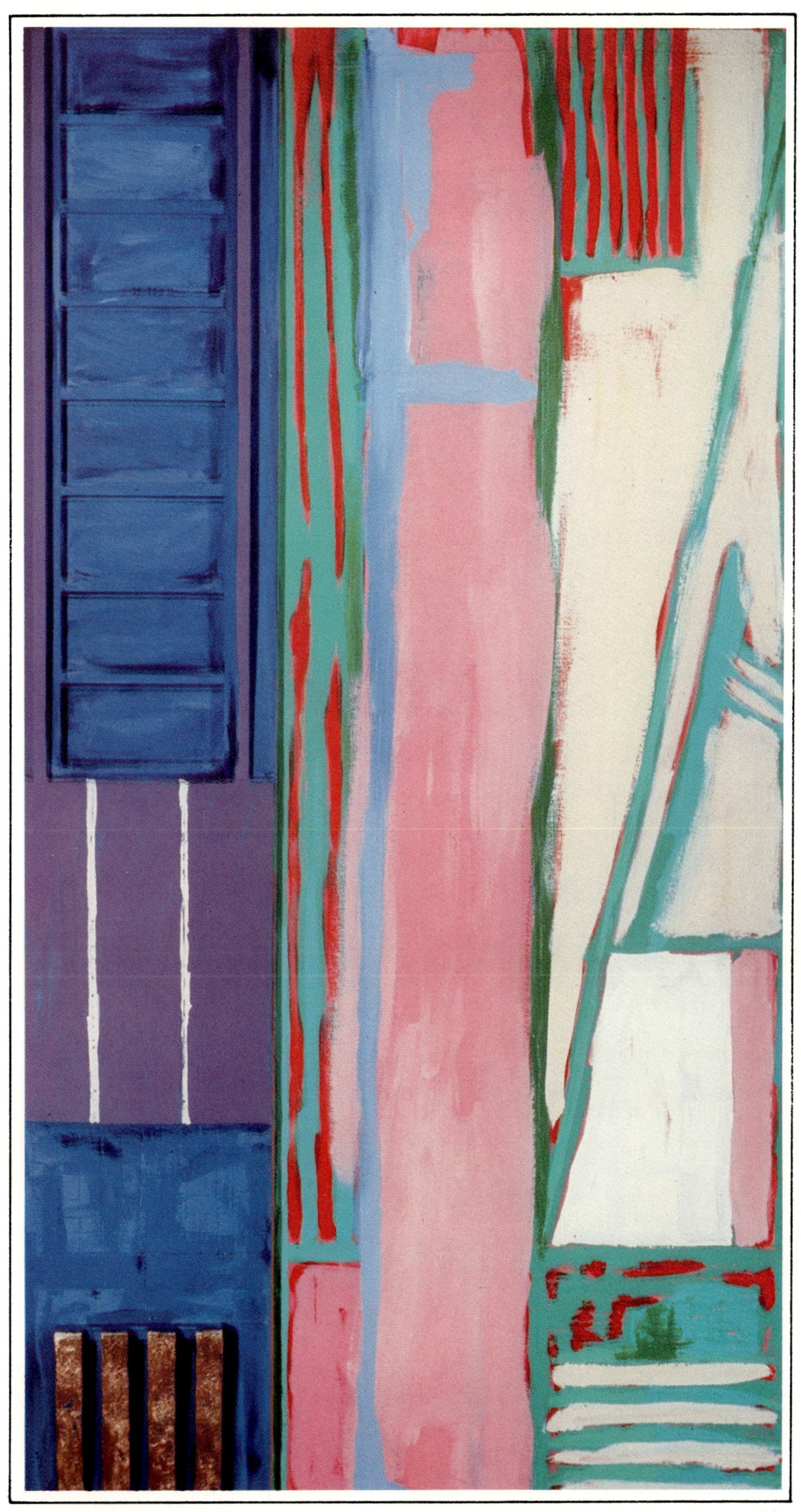

Bruce Robbins, *UR III,* 1981, 88″ x 48″ x 5″, acrylic on wood with copper leaf. Carol Taylor, Art.

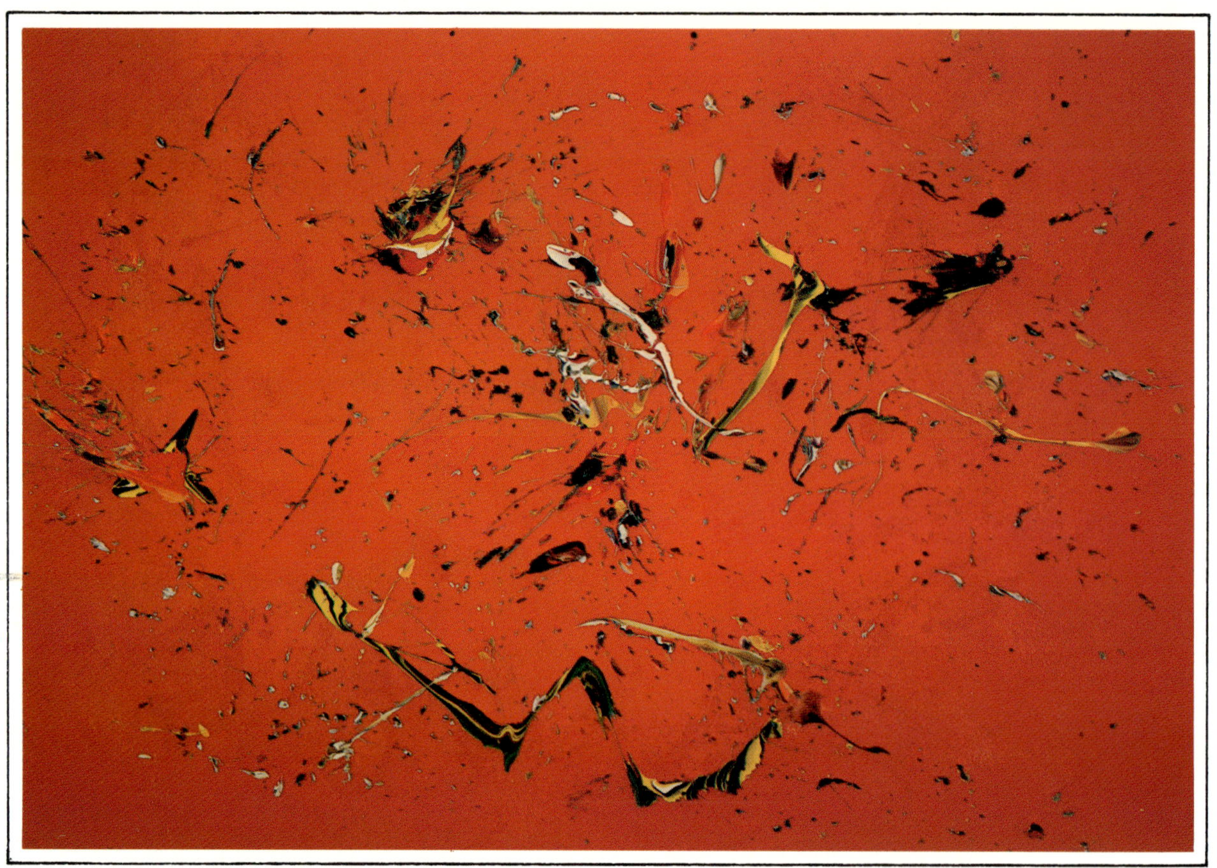

Richard Childers, *Star Dance,* 24' x 9½', acrylic on canvas. SL Art Gallery.

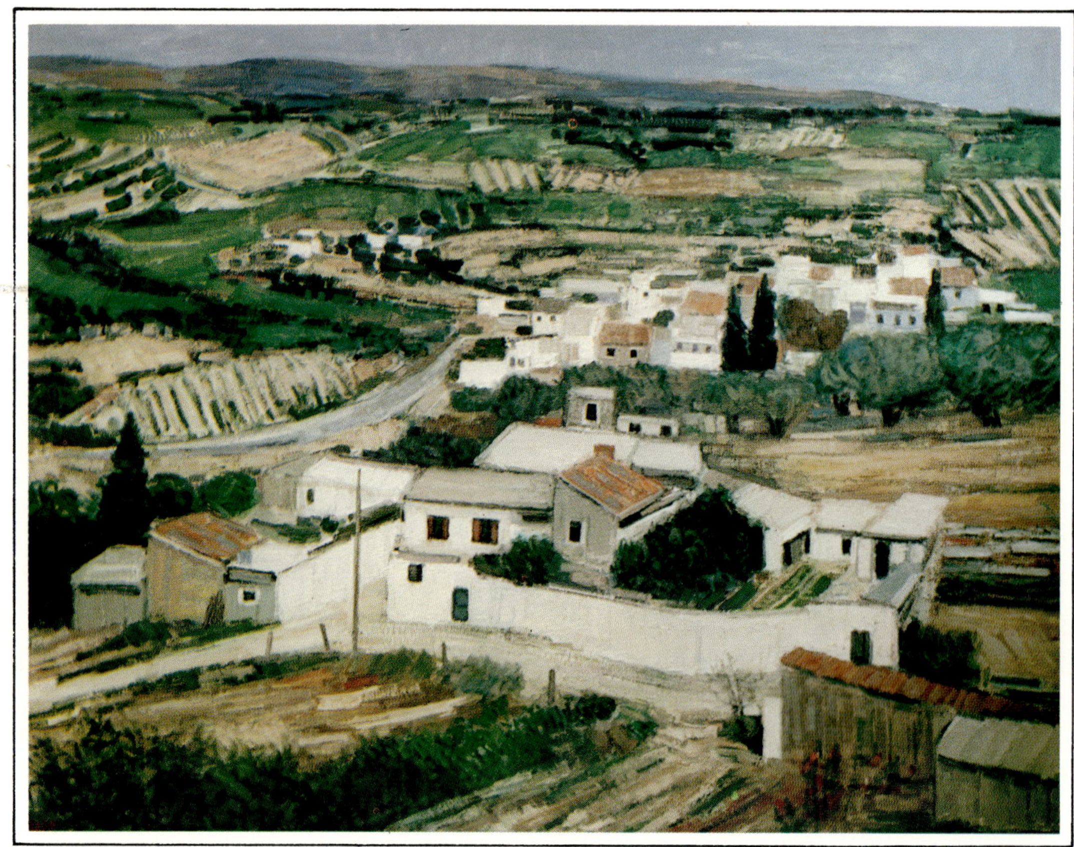

Ginnette Rapp, *Paysage Cretois,* 44¾" x 57½", oil on canvas. Phillips Galleries.

Lamar Briggs's paintings and prints deal with flowing areas of color interpreting the wind and the sea. Len Agrella paints very contemporary, but figurative, images of Indians. Other painters shown are Sandra Leveson-Meares, David McCullough, Jack Boynton, Michelle DeManche, Luanne Standish, and Bette Kohlberg. The prints of Richard Smith, Jim Dine, Ellsworth Kelly, Joe Goode, Stella, and Robert Rauschenberg are also in the Gallery One collection.

The sculptural works of New York artist Dorothy Gillespie are outstanding. Her aluminum pieces are curved and curled, and are then painted with brightly colored enamel geometric shapes.

Crafts include the raku work of Dennis Gabbard; Bill Wilhelmi's nonfunctional pieces, such as his air-brushed ceramic cowboy boots; the high-gloss glazes on small vessels and plates done by California Harvey Brody, large vessels with iridescent glazes done by Curt Brill; acrylic pieces by Vasa and James Norman.

Six to eight major openings each season begin with a group show. During the summer exhibits change monthly.

Clark Harrah and Larry Flukinger, neon sculptors who work jointly, create high-tech, powerful works which study light as a medium. These "light studies", as Campbell refers to them, are extraordinary exercises in both sculptural treatments of glass as well as visual imagery.

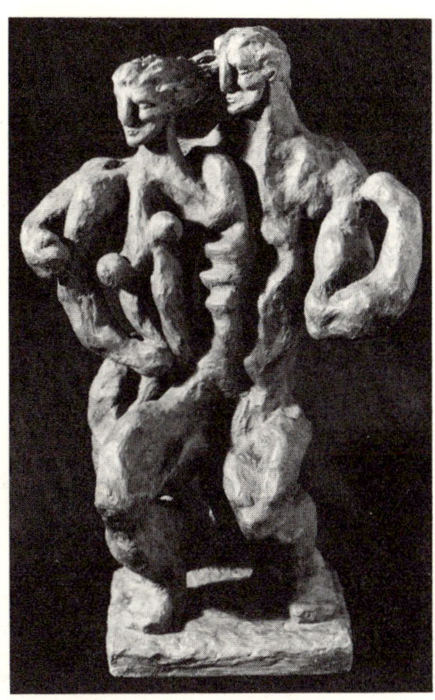

David Newman, *Adam and Eve*, 20" high, cast bronze. Nimbus Gallery.

Paige Gallery   1519 Hi Line Dr.   Dallas 75207   (214) 742-8483   **Paige**
Monday-Saturday: 9:30-5:30

Established in 1980 by Howard Crow, Michael Crow and Gus Dubinsky, Paige occupies another one of those vast former warehouses where anything seems possible. Director Bobette Bird describes Paige as a "commercial gallery" which shows both contemporary realism and abstract work. Clientele consists mainly of designers and decorators, but the gallery is making an effort to cultivate private collectors by changing exhibitions each six weeks.

The gallery opened with all-European art but it has lately accepted a number of Americans including one or two local artists. Recent shows have featured landscapes by British artists Michael D'Aguilar and Hugh Boycott-Brown; landscapes of Texas and Northeastern states by Jean Johnson; steel and bronze sculpture by Joseph Anthony McDonnell, whose *Triple Cube* stands in front of the gallery; the bone-like bronzes of David Burt; and contemporary religious icon paintings by Dallas artist Bobbi Winborn. Paige Gallery also exhibits the work of a number of fiber artists.

The colorful work of the naive painters of Yugoslavia and Eastern Europe is a gallery specialty. Ivan Generalic, "Father of Naive Art in Eastern Europe," Ivan Rabuzin, who paints pastel-

colored fantasy-landscapes; Ivan Lackovic, painter of winter
scenes, and Milan Madj, whose paintings on glass, with their
gem-like colors, are especially brilliant, are just a few of the naive
artists represented.

Phillips Galleries   2517 Fairmount   Dallas 75201   (214)
748-7888   Monday-Saturday: 10-5

Founded by Ray Phillips in 1970 and still in the same location, a
magnificent mansion, this is one of Dallas's best housed galleries.
Phillips describes his gallery's specialization as "school of Paris"
and the 5,700-square-foot, two-floor exhibit area is filled with
impressionistic landscapes and still lifes by such artists as Monique
Journoi, Renee Theobald, Ginette Rapp, Jacques Bouyssou and
Paul Jean Anderbouhr.

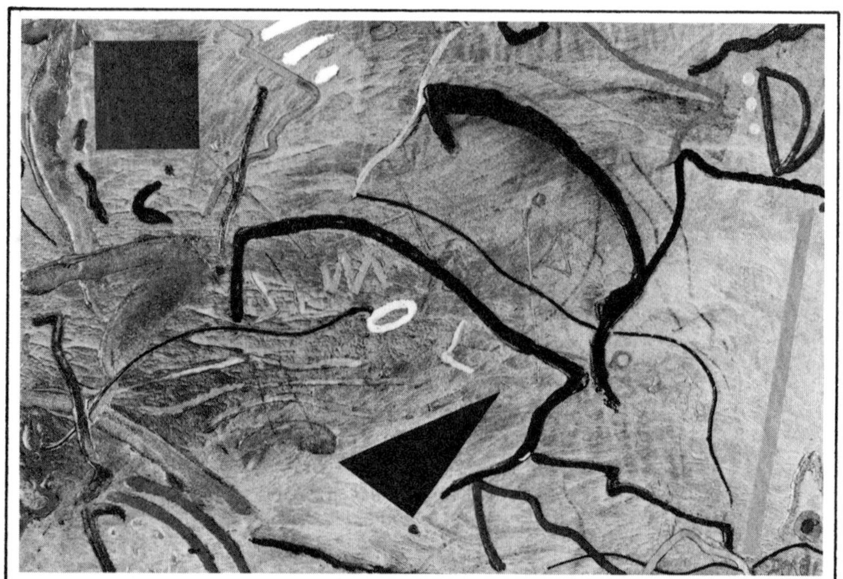

David McCullough, *Alien on
Arabian Desert,* 36½" x 25",
acrylic and sand on linen.
Gallery One.

    An entire room is set aside, however, for the works of naive
painters, mainly French. Among these are Maurice Ghiglion-
Green, a former casino croupier who now paints romantic
landscapes; Raphael Toussaint, another painter of romantic
landscapes who punctuates his scenes with humorous vignettes of
village life; Fernand Boilauges, a onetime sign painter and portrait
photographer whose works depict groups of people posed formally
in front of quaint Paris shops; Jean Axatard, whose landscapes
have a Breughelesque flavor; and Cora Lou Robinson, whose
works recall memories of childhood in and around Minden,
Louisiana.
    Phillips Galleries offers a continuous group show of works by its
regular stable of talents, but once or twice a year there is a special
exhibit focusing on one or two artists. The gallery has a large
selection of prints on hand.

Pruitt Place Galleries   111 N. Houston   Fort Worth 76102
(817) 332-6163   Monday-Saturday: 10-6; and by appointment

Armed with firsthand experience in art sales and marketing,
Donna Pruitt Mattoon opened her Pruitt Place Galleries in April of
1981. The artistic spirit of the West is represented in works by
contemporary Western artists in all media.

The works of A. Kelly Pruitt range from his early works in paint
and bronze to his most recent dimensional "Thunderbow" series.
Lee Herring, a member of the Artists of the West, portrays the
historic West with ultrarealism. The young Jeff Segler's
modern-day cowboys are captured in a style not unlike Norman
Rockwell's, with a slightly graphic influence. Other members of
the Artists of the West are also represented.

Lew Cole's wildlife carvings are far from wooden. Each feather
and lock of hair is carved and painted in startling detail. Renne
Hughe makes small bronzes affordable for everyone.

The gallery carries a full line of limited-edition prints by many of
the Cowboy Artists of America, the Artists of the West, and others.
Framing is also available.

Ps Galleries   2525 Fairmount   Dallas 75201   (214) 741-5576
Tuesday-Saturday: 10-5, or by appointment

Established recently by Michael A. Palmer and Peter E. Spear,
who operate a summer gallery in Ogunquit, Me., and were
looking for a year-round location, Ps occupies a 90-year-old,
two-story frame house near downtown Dallas.

Specialty of the house is contemporary representational work
by U.S. artists. Among those shown regularly are David Shaw,
painter of rural interiors and genre scenes; Stephen Etnier, a
seascape painter; Edward Betts, also a painter of rural scenes;
David Bumbeck, a printmaker whose aquatints of nudes have a
photographic look; and Ralph Hurst, who carves animals and
birds in alabaster.

Exhibits change every month. Once or twice a year the gallery
shows work of special historic significance, lithographs by George
Bellows, for example, or the sun-drenched paintings of Robert
Vickrey, or works from the estate of Rudolph Dirks, who invented
the comic strip Katzenjammer Kids but also produced
vividly colored paintings.

Reminisce Gallery   3322 Camp Bowie   Fort Worth 76107
(817) 335-4295   Monday-Friday: 9:30-5:30; weekends by
appointment   Closed during the Christmas-New Year holiday

Specializing in the art of the West and Southwest, Directors
Barbara Bowden and Ken Johnson carry oil paintings, watercolors,
bronzes, Indian pottery, and hand-woven wall tapestries.

Melvin C. Warren, a member of the Cowboy Artists of America and a participant in the prestigious Western Heritage Sale, paints mood paintings of the American West as it is today and as it was in years past. Other leading members of the Cowboy Artists of America are also represented such as Gordon Snidow, George Marks, Fritz White, James Boren and Gary Niblett.

Patricia Warren, daughter of Melvin C. Warren, uses women of the Southwest as subjects for her sculpture. Walt Gonske leans toward the impressionistic interpretation of Southwest landscape. Recent exhibits have also featured the works of Ramon Froman, Roy Lee Ward, Tony Eubanks, and Donald Teague.

In 1980 a special exhibition of antique and contemporary Navajo rugs drew a wide audience. The 1981 exhibit of N.C. Wyeth and members of his family was a highlight of the year.

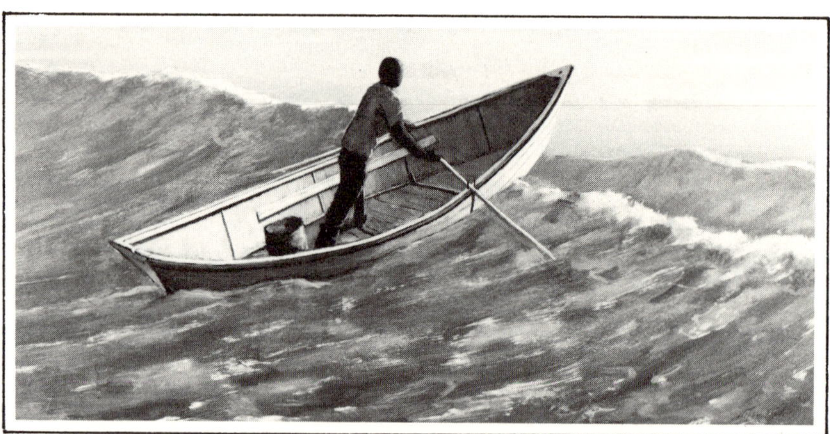

Stephen Etnier, *Inward Bound,* 16" x 36", oil. PS Galleries.

Shango Galleries   2606 Fairmount   Dallas 75201   (214) 744-4891   Tuesday-Saturday: 12-6

Shango

Shango, which occupies the second floor of a turn-of-the-century house in a neighborhood of art galleries, is one of only two galleries in the Dallas area specializing in primitive and tribal art. Founder and owner John A. Buxton constantly roams the world in search of new objects, and he exhibits his latest finds regularly in constantly changing gallery shows.

Buxton describes his tastes as "eclectic in the area of primitive art." Recent exhibits have featured African, American Indian and Pre-Columbian objects, and works from each of these cultures are almost always on display. Within these areas, the gallery tends to specialize in works from Colima, Nayarit, and Jalisco in Western Mexico, and in masks and sculpture from west and central Africa. American Indian art or display comes mainly from Southwest and Northwest Coast tribes.

Shango has also offered some especially fine exhibits of Navajo rugs recently. Sometimes as many as 150 at a time are on display here, some from as early as the 1830s, some as recent as the 1980s.

The gallery's clientele includes both museums and serious private collectors.

SL Art Gallery

SL Art Gallery   2133 Cedar Springs   Dallas 75201   (214) 761-9912   Monday-Friday: 10-5; Saturday by appointment

The sign in front informs the visitor that this is the SL Art Gallery of Dallas and Paris. The Paris connection is longtime French art dealer Francois Lucet. The other half of this transatlantic partnership is Sharon Simons, who met Lucet at Maxim's in Paris during a party thrown by a wealthy Texas oilman.

Lucet says he doesn't want the gallery to have a "look", and since it opened in early 1980, SL has exhibited works by a wide variety of European, American, and, increasingly, local artists. Works have ranged from paintings by British artist Fleur Cowles, and from Carol Greer's mixed-media works suggesting kimonos and dresses, to Robert Einbeck's geometric meditations, to a collection of primitive New Guinea masks, animal figures and ceremonial pieces. The gallery had tremendous success at the annual FIAC exposition in Paris with the paintings of Richard Childers, a local artist who drips and splatters pigment on large canvases.

Other artists whose works have been seen at SL include sculptors Ramon G. Orlina, Eduardo Castrillo, and Michel Beck and painters Don Hathorn, Lary van Haren, and Jean Allemand.

Lucet recently purchased a onetime Dallas Power & Light station in the Knox Street area and is in the process of remodeling it. When finished it will provide some 40,000 square feet of exhibit area. But they are in no hurry, the lease on the present location, which offers 17,000 square feet, doesn't run out until 1984.

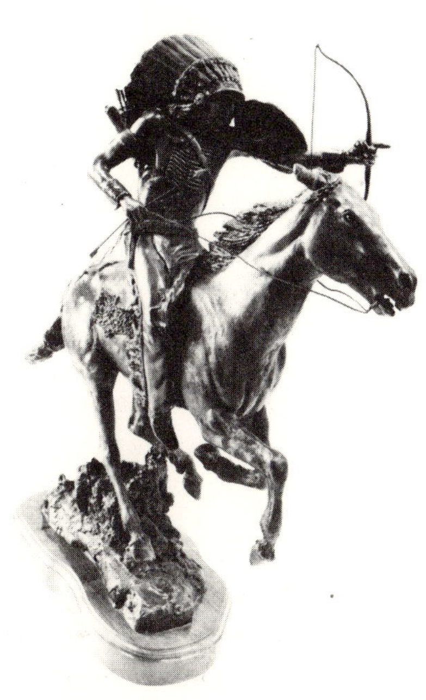

Jack Bryant, *Sacred Stride,* 18" high Bronze. Southwest Art Center.

Southwest Art Center

Southwest Art Center   1428 Preston Forest Square, Preston Rd. at Forest   Dallas 75230   (214) 233-2702   Tuesday-Saturday: 9-6

Southwest Art Center, at its North Dallas location for eleven years, houses 22,000 square feet of art supplies, ready-made and photograph frames, custom framing, prints, graphics, original paintings and sculpture. Most of the many, many works shown deal in contemporary realism from landscapes to still lifes.

The art shown in the gallery has a traditional feeling, with many of the works by Southwestern landscape artists such as W.A. Slaughter, Jerry Ruthven, and Jack Bryant. A wide selection of paintings is available by contemporary European artists such as Antoine Blanchard and Louis Peyrat, who paint Paris street scenes, and Ludwig Muninger and Janez Kenzer, who specialize in "Old World" Bavarian landscapes.

Also shown throughout the gallery are nineteenth-century European paintings and American and European antique furniture. High-quality English "restrike" engravings are prominent in the graphics area. The gallery's sculpture collection consists of Western bronzes by Jack Bryant, Metz Castleberry and Jim Deutsch. Michael Garman's full line of "character" sculpture is also on display. Mixed throughout are some older European sculptures.

Southwest Art Center's large selection appeals to many art tastes especially those in the market for framing. A leasing program is available for commercial accounts. Artist exhibitions are held several times a year in the gallery.

Southwest II Gallery   2710 Boll St.   Dallas 75204   (214) 827-7730   Tuesday, Wednesday, Saturday: 10-6; Thursday-Friday: 10-9

Southwest II Gallery

Southwest II Gallery opened its doors in October of 1978. Under the same ownership as Southwest Art Center, a long-established full-service gallery in North Dallas, Southwest II was established with the intention of specializing in contemporary original graphics, a medium not offered extensively by the parent gallery.

The gallery specializes in contemporary original graphics. Most of the artists exhibited enjoy a national and/or international reputation. In its three years of existence, Southwest II has mounted major exhibits (50 works or more) by artists such as Miro, Dali, Rufino Tamayo, Henry Moore, Erte, R.C. Gorman, Karel Appel, Lowell Nesbitt, and Will Barnet. Where possible, the artists attend the opening receptions of their exhibits—as in the case of Tamayo, Gorman, Nesbitt, and Barnet. Southwest II Gallery is also building a stable of newer, less-established printmaking artists who are also exhibited—Tony Bass, etcher, and Roger Bartlett, woodblock artist, are two of the young artists in this group.

Another medium that the gallery exhibits is contemporary sculpture. Larry Young uses the lost-wax process of bronze casting to create works ranging from 10" to 6'. Sharon Gainsburg works primarily in stone. Tere Metta, from Mexico, works in a variety of materials. David Anderson's work is is of fiberglass.

The gallery occupies a 5,000 square-foot, 2-story refurbished house across the street from the Quadrangle, a cluster of galleries and shops for those seeking the unusual and unique in fine arts and crafts. The gallery opens a new exhibit approximately every two months. However, because of its diverse space, Southwest II is able to exhibit a selection of works by all the gallery artists, in addition to the current one-man show. Where possible, Southwest II also offers posters and books about the artists they feature.

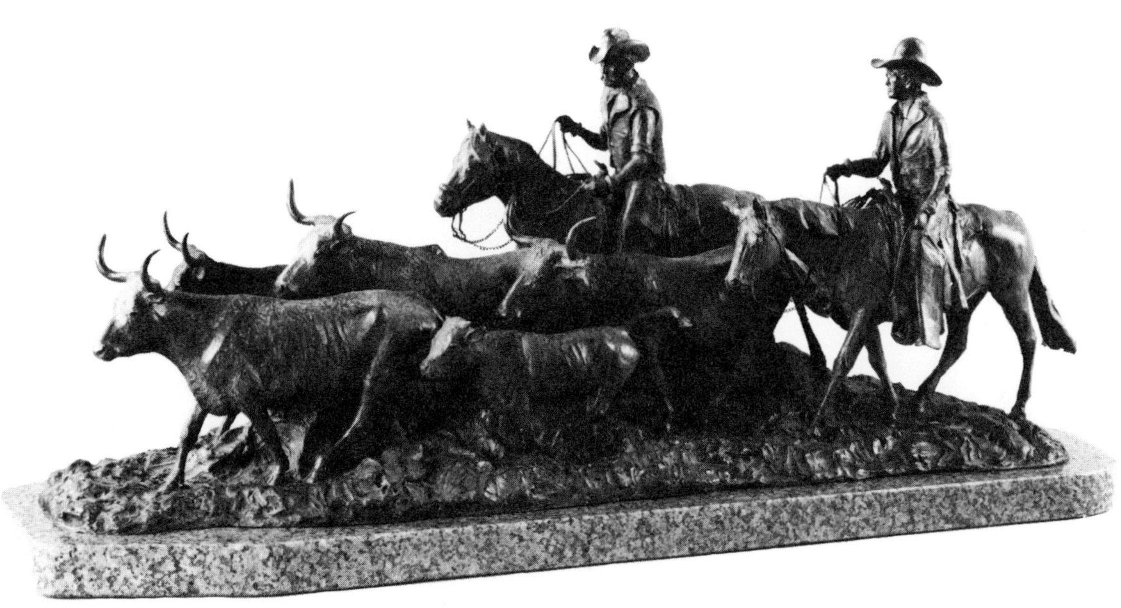

Melvin C. Warren, *Head 'em Up,* Bronze. Reminisce Gallery.

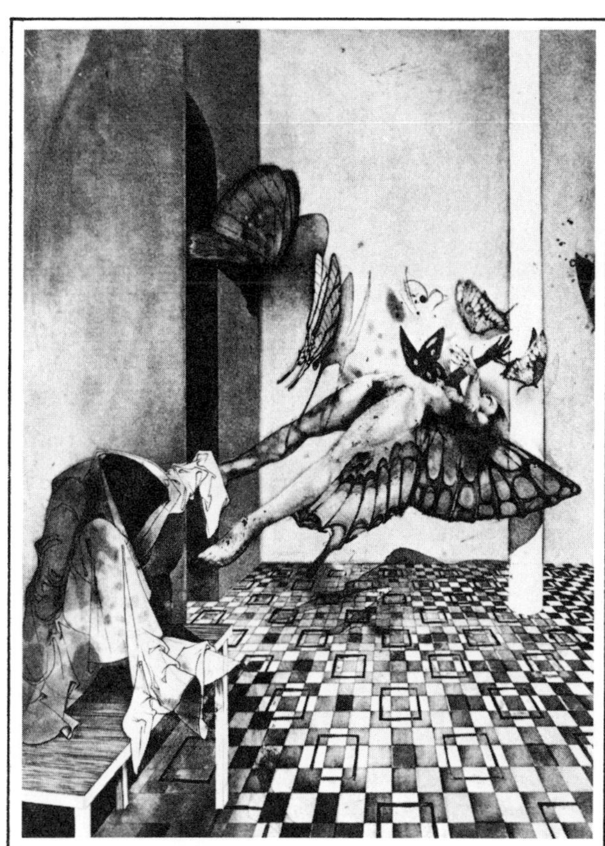

Tony Bass, *Chrysalis,* 24'' x 18'' etching. Southwest II Gallery.

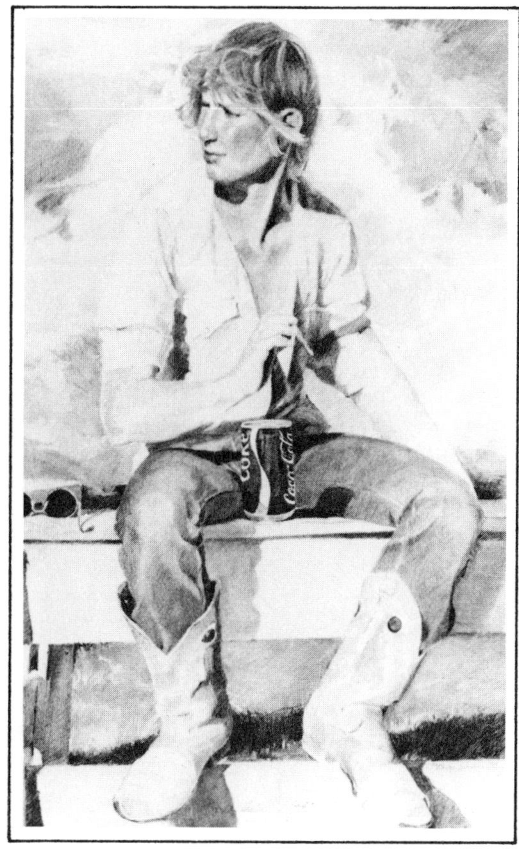

Patricia Warren, *Coca-Cola Cowboy,* watercolor, Reminisce Gallery.

Ann Cushing Gantz opened Cushing Galleries, Inc., in 1961
along with three partners. It operated until 1979 as an important
commercial gallery, representing internationally known
printmakers, painters, and sculptors. In May 1979 the gallery was
closed and Cushing Studio was opened, in order for Mrs. Gantz to
focus on her own painting and teaching, and on showcasing local
artists.

Cushing Studio exhibits one-man and group shows, but does not
represent artists and keeps no work on hand other than what is part
of the current show. The primary function is that of education and
instruction, with exhibitions acting as "special occasions," though
they are presented monthly.

Works by painters Mike Hulme, Audrey Anastasi, Eleanor
Randle, and Pat Magruder have been featured in one-man shows
in recent months, as well as sculpture by Gita Packer and
drawings by Ann Cushing Gantz. The annual exhibition of
paintings, prints, and drawings by students of Ann Cushing Gantz
is presented every September.

Atelier II presents an annual show every February of the work of
a group of artists who have exhibited together for eight years.

Special workshops in serigraphy, woodcut, and mixed media
are conducted three times a year, as are critique programs. Juried
shows are presented twice a year and then travel to university
galleries and such public spaces as KERA-TV's Gallery 13.

Fiske, *gold leaf trotter weathervane,* (nineteenth century). Sundance Gallery.

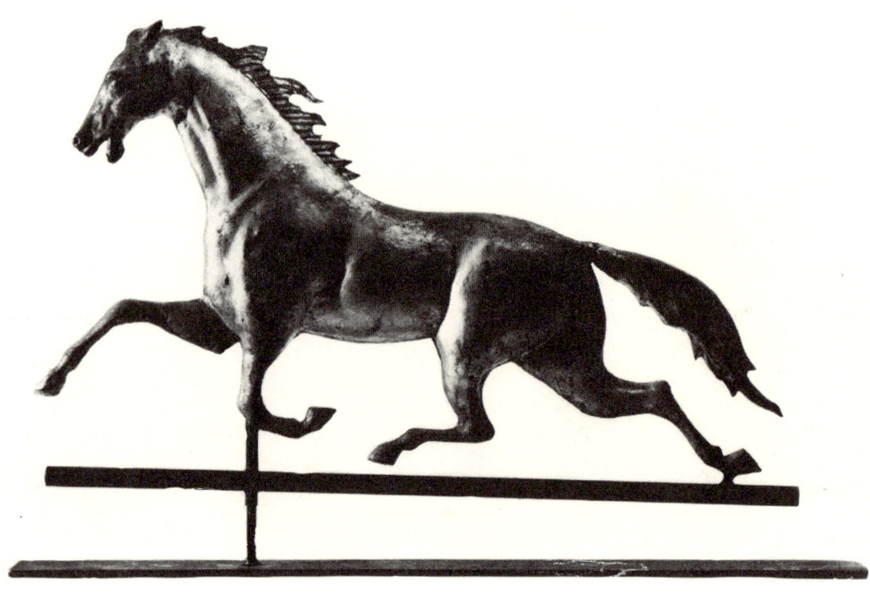

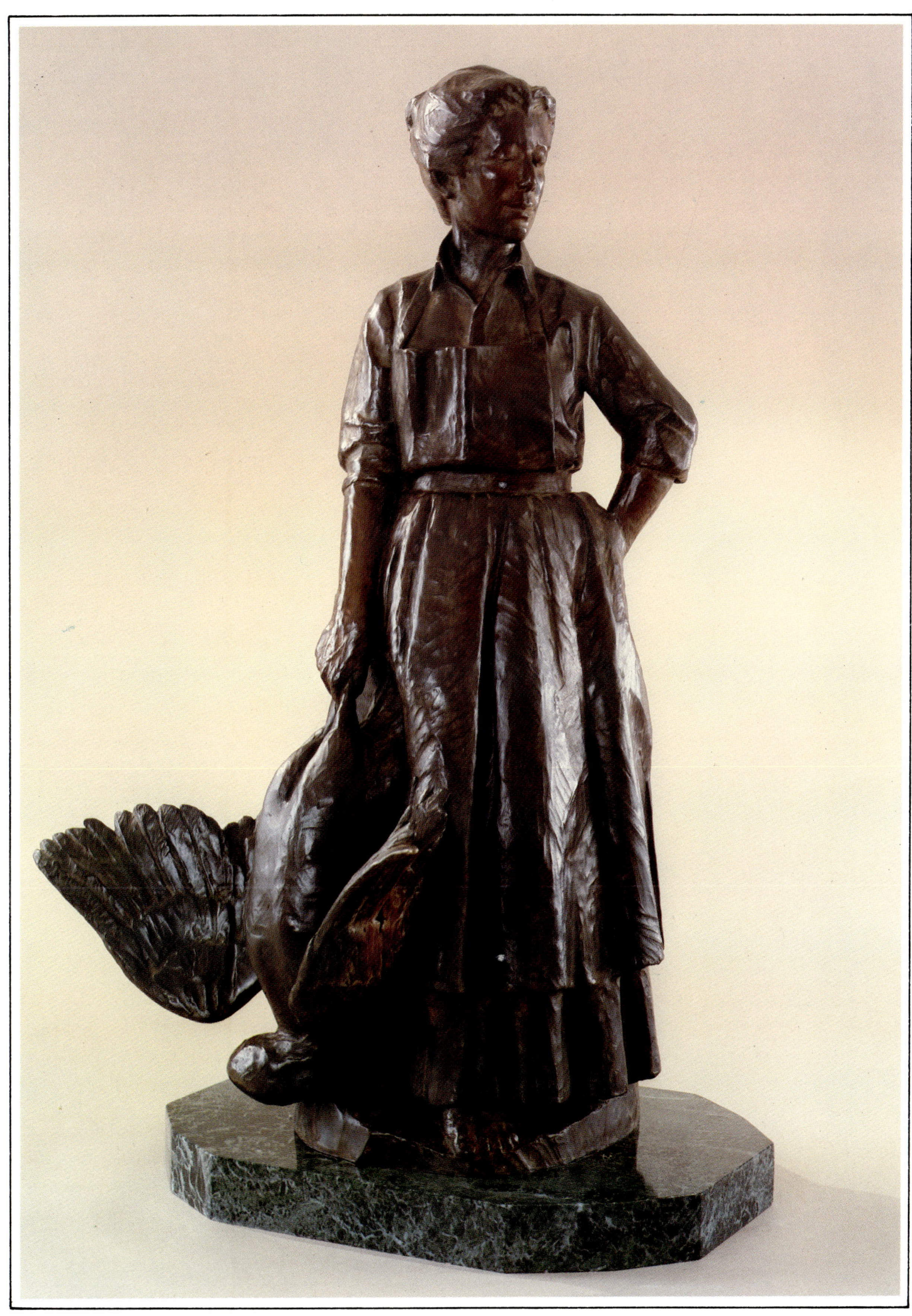

Patricia Warren, *Sunday Dinner,* 35″ high, bronze. Reminisce Gallery.

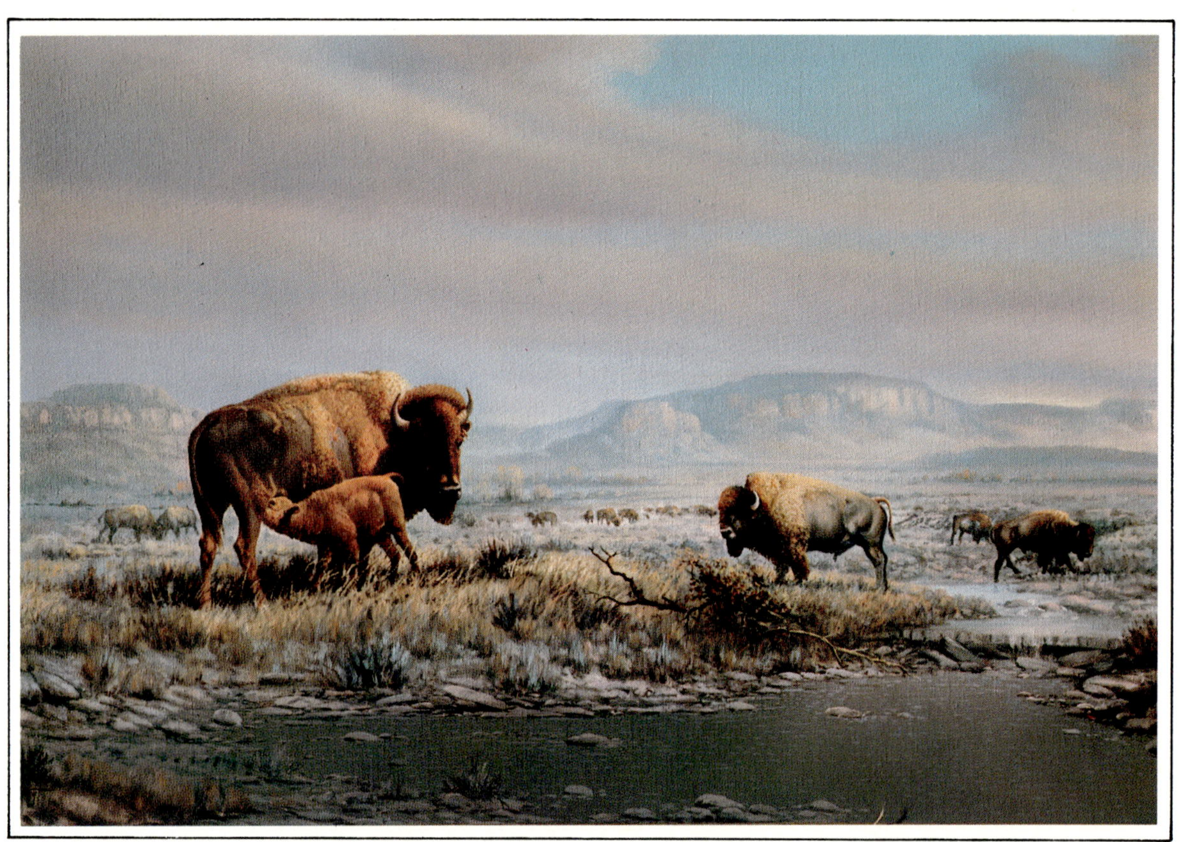

Jack Bryant, *Once the Thundering Herd,* 24″ x 36″, oil on canvas. Southwest Art Center.

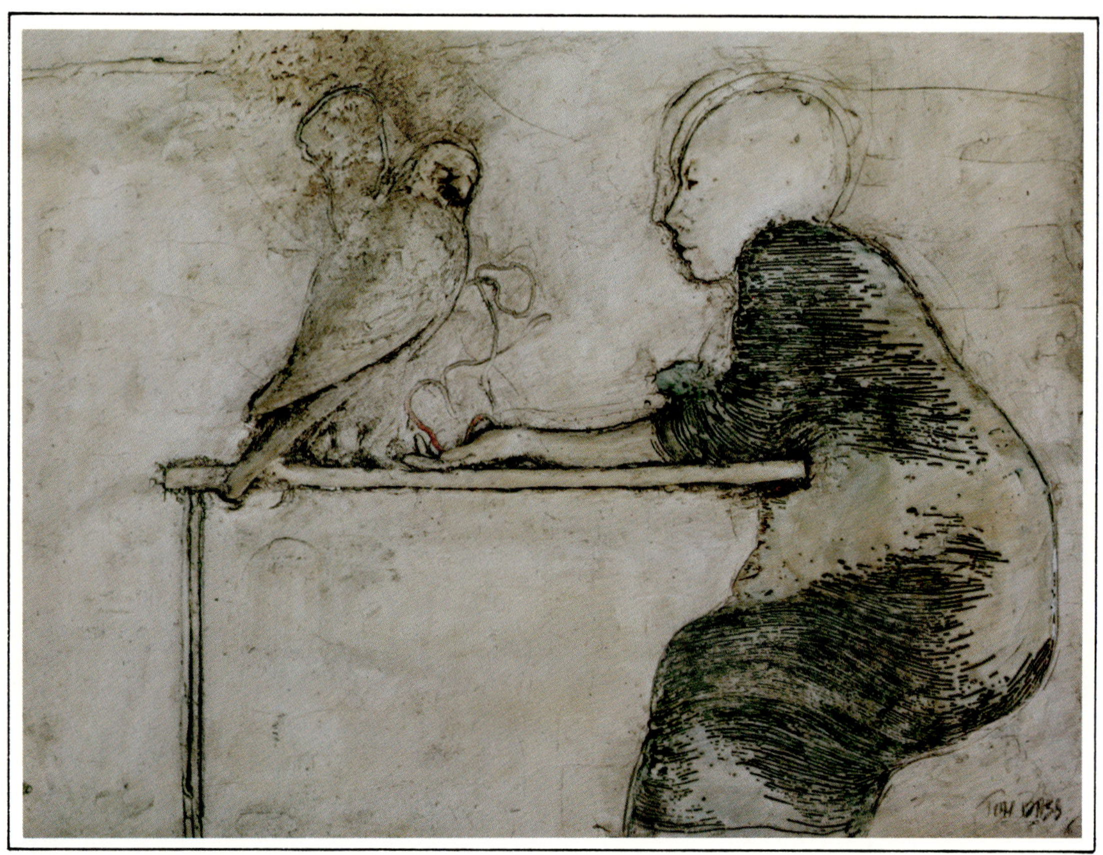

Tony Bass, *Entanglement,* 18″ x 24¼″, mixed-media relief multiple. Southwest Gallery II.

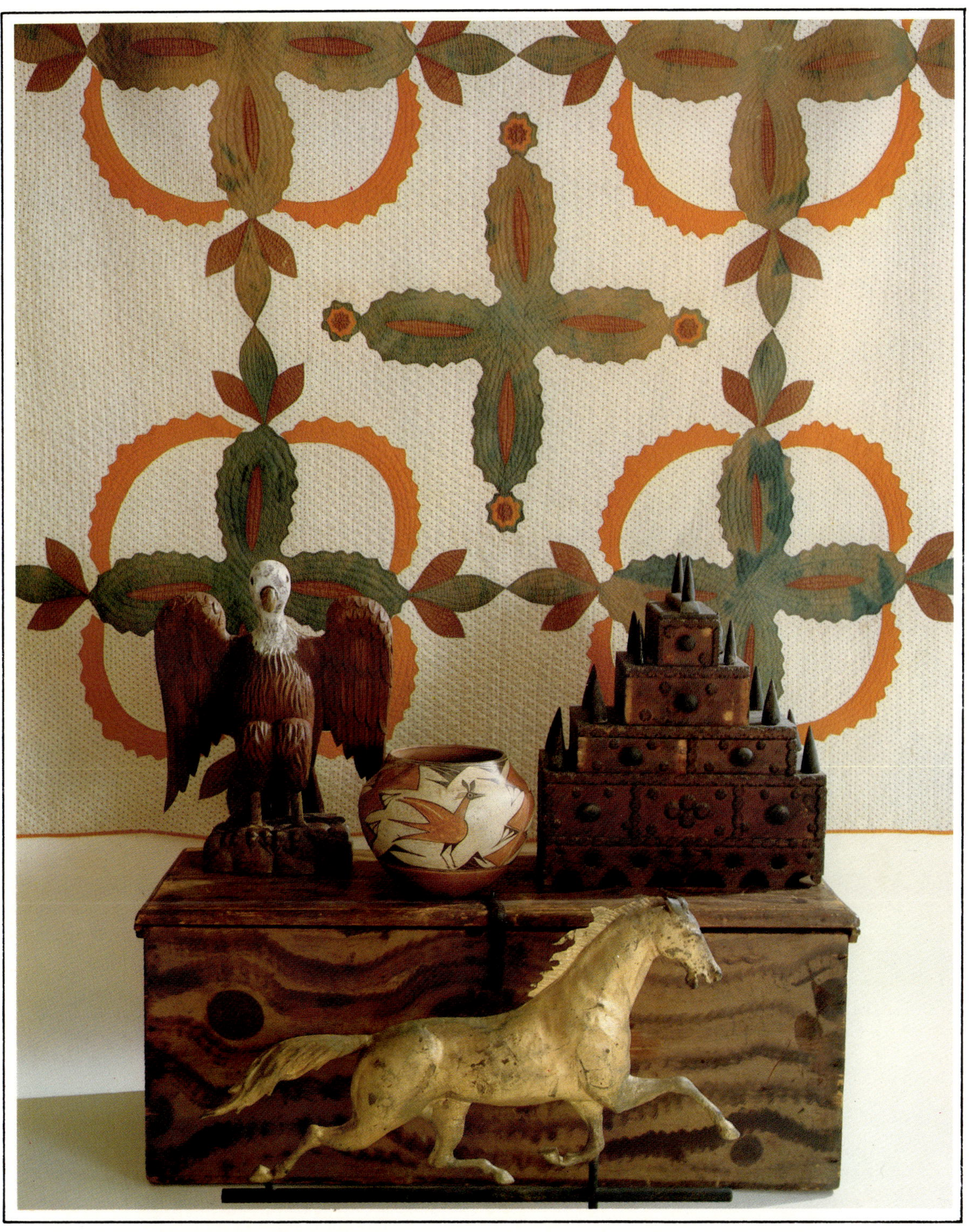

Nineteenth Century Cactus Quilt (background). *Tramp Art Chest,* From right to left (atop chest): *Wood-Carved Eagle Lecturn, Zia Pot, New England Blanket Box. Gold-Leaf Trotter* (foreground). Sundance Gallery.

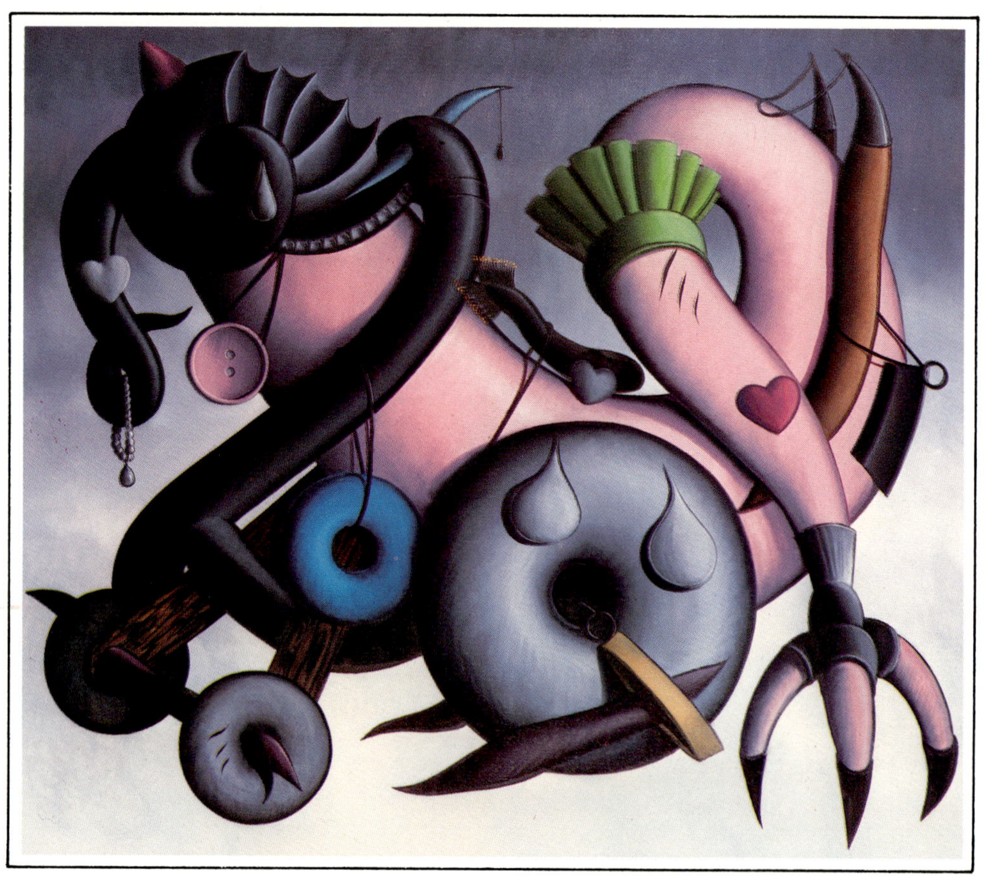

Valton Tyler, *Tap Too's on a Horse,* 74" x 84", oil on canvas. Valley House Gallery.

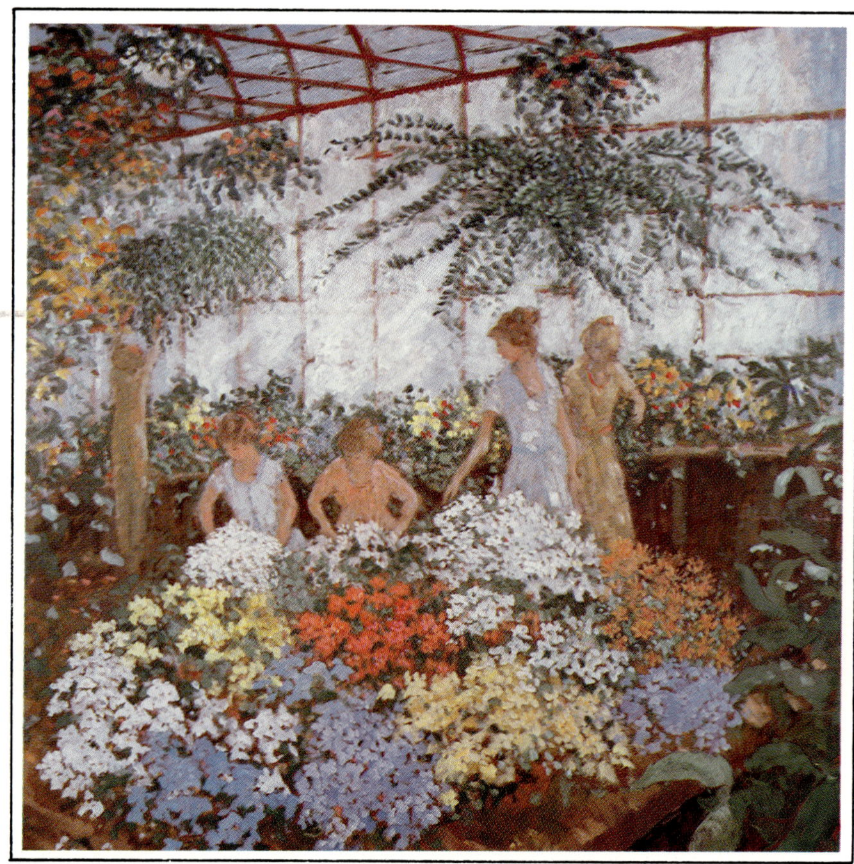

Donald Vogel, *Greenhouse Spring,* 1981, 48" x 48", oil on panel.
Valley House Gallery.

Sundance Gallery   310 Main   Fort Worth 76102   (817) 870-1001   Monday-Saturday: 10-5

Sundance Gallery is Dallas-Fort Worth's first folk art gallery. The nineteenth- and early twentieth-century Americana include domestic objects such as quilts and bowls, ornamentation from homes, barns, shops, and boats, objets d'art such as folk sculpture and ceramics.

As in most folk art, many of the artists are unknown, leaving the works to be judged on their creativity, their unique juxtaposition of utility with visual interest, and their rarity of craftsmanship. Sweetie Ladd, current painter of historic Texan scenes, is represented in the gallery, as are folk sculptors David Alvarez and Felipe Archuleta of New Mexico.

Most of the folk art originated in the Northeast or in the Southwest, especially Texas and New Mexico, and reflects regional habits. From the Northeast are whirligigs, chests, carved signs and symbols, and weathervanes; from the Southwest, quilts, pottery, carved animals, belts, jewelry and kitchen items.

Two or three special shows are held each year: special exhibits of folk art include an entire show of contemporary New Mexican lithographs and crafts and a display of historic Indian pottery.

The gallery is located in a historic building in a restoration area of downtown Fort Worth. The exhibition design employes Southwestern antiques, such as pharmacy cases and a nineteenth-century buggy.

Carol Taylor, Art   2503 Cedar Springs   Dallas 75201   (214) 745-1923   Tuesday-Saturday: 10-5

One of Dallas's newest galleries, Carol Taylor, Art, opened with a bang at the beginning of 1981 with an exhibit of the rigorous, systematic drawings of Bruce Nauman, followed by a rambling installation piece in which Lucio Pozzi painted directly on the gallery walls, hung up photographs and pieces of painted plywood. Then, as if to signal that this gallery would be impossible to type-cast, the third exhibit was of nineteenth-century Cheyenne Indian ledger drawings.

The gallery space is small, no larger than a small shop, but owner Carol Taylor's ambitions are large. She shows what she likes, and what she likes is often very important work that has received national attention but has not yet been shown in Dallas.

Exhibitions at the gallery have featured the madcap collages and constructions of Barton Lidice Benes; photographs of such industrial commonplaces as water towers and mine heads by the German husband-and-wife team of Bernd and Hilla Becher; the spindly wooden sculpture of Mel Kendrick; the lyrical drawings/ paintings of Edda Renouf; cubist-inspired ceramic sculpture by

Andrew Lord; space, geometric paintings by Robert Mangold; and thickly textured canvases by Michael Venezia.

Works by local artists exhibited at the gallery include the photographs of acclaimed independent filmmaker Lloyd Birdwell and mysterious multimedia constructions by Doug MacWhitney. The gallery also has sponsored one of MacWithey's performance pieces in a local theater.

Texas Art Gallery   1400 Main Street   Dallas 75202   (214) 747-8158   Monday-Saturday: 9-5

Texas Art Gallery

The Texas Art Gallery is as good as its name, purveying rip-roaring, rootin'-tootin' bronzes and paintings made by artists who still work in the tradition established by Remington and Russell.

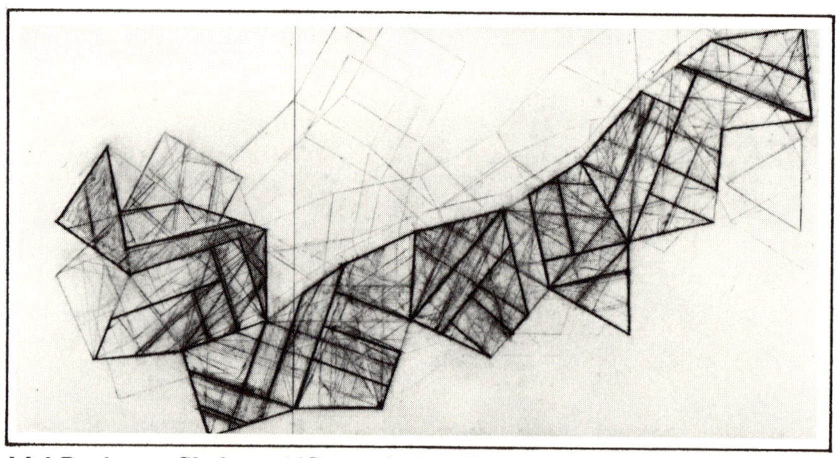

Mel Bochner, *Skeleton *(Syzygy)*, 37½" x 77¼", charcoal on two pieces of paper. Carol Taylor, Art.

As you might expect in a gallery devoted to Western art, landscapes predominate, especially landscapes with a few cows, horses, cowboys or Indians. But some of the gallery's artists are starting to branch out into nostalgic scenes of life in the good old days and pictures of modern cowboys at work and at ease. The gallery's catalog of artists is extensive. Among the better-known are bronze sculptor Joe Beeler; painter James Boren and daughter Nancy Boren, known for her delicately beautiful wildflower paintings; well-known illustrator-turned-artist John Clymer; Penni Anne Cross, who paints pictures of fetching Indian maidens; waterfowl artist Bruce Dines; G. Harvey, painter of the turn-of-the-century small-town West; and such perennial Western favorites as Clark Hulings, Robert Lougheed, Gary Niblett, James Reynolds, Tom Ryan. The gallery also has watercolor drawings by Olaf Wieghorst, "Dean of Western Artists."

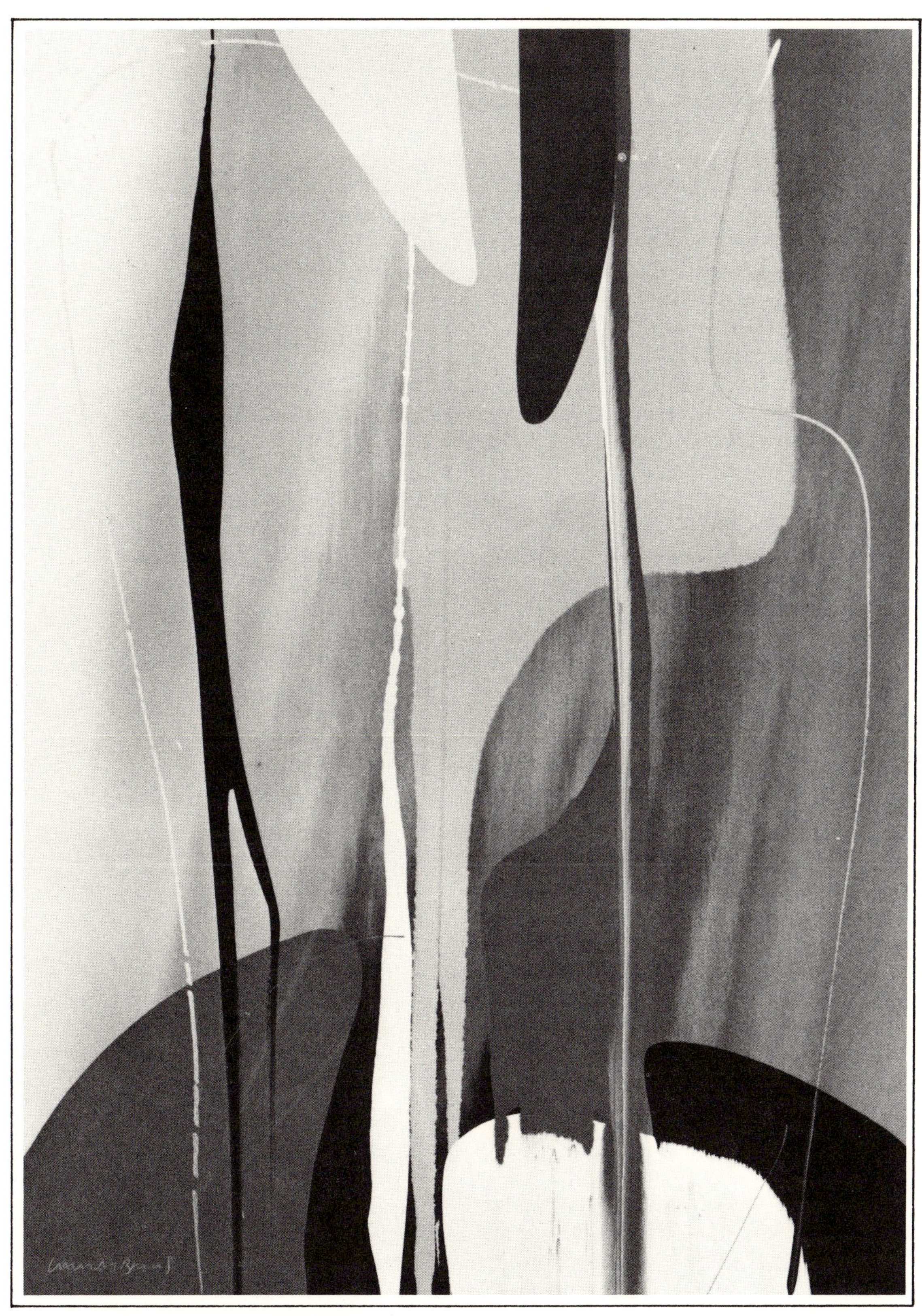

Lamar Briggs, *Ibiza Series #64,* 40″ x 30″ acrylic on paper. Gallery One.

Other gallery artists are Joe Abbrescia, James Asher, Bill
Atkins, Wayne Baize, Tracy Beeler, Michael Coleman, Tim Cox,
Mike Desatnick, Barbara East, Tony Eubanks, Gerald Farm, Bettie
Felder, Martin Grelle, George Hallmark, Gary Kapp, Bob Lee,
Vel Miller, Don McCauley, Lad Odell, Robert Pummill, Donald
"Putt" Putman, Bill Shaddix, Donald Teague, and Robert
Wagoner.

Texas Art Gallery sponsors an annual preview auction at which
millions of dollars' worth of traditional and Western art are sold.
Included are works by its own stable of artists as well as works by
such past masters as Henry Farny, W.H.D. Koerner, Charles
Schreyvogel, Olaf Seltzer, Grandma Moses, Norman Rockwell,
and, of course, Remington and Russell.

The gallery also maintains a small selection of books about the
West and Western artists and, under the name Texas Art Press,
published limited-edition prints by gallery artists.

Gallery 13

Gallery 13   3000 Harry Hines Blvd.   Dallas 75201   (214)
744-1300   Monday-Friday: 8-5

A unique operation, Gallery 13 takes its name from Channel 13,
KERA-TV. The local PBS station provides exhibit space in its
corridors and board room as a service to the community and as an
extension of its involvement in the cultural and artistic life of North
Texas.

Gallery coordinator Patty Tees, a station employee, selects
artists for exhibits. Invitations are mailed out by the station, and
20-second on-the-air announcements are broadcast daily during
the run of each show.

All media and all styles are represented. Among works recently
exhibited at Gallery 13 are Rebecca Best's collages, infrared
photography and photo silk-screened ceramics by Roy Cirigliana
and Mary Hatz-Cirigliana, Xerox collages of jazz greats by Vicki
Meek, and cutout cow sculptures and folded paintings by Wayne
Amerine.

Upstairs Gallery

The Upstairs Gallery   1039 W. Abram   Arlington 76013
(817) 277-6961   Monday-Saturday: 10-5

In 1967, when Eleanor Martin started The Upstairs Gallery, there
were no other galleries in Arlington. Since then, Arlington—
located between Dallas and Fort Worth—has grown to 150,000
people, and more than a few galleries have sprung up. Upstairs
shows an unusual variety of painting, drawing, sculpture, jewelry,
pottery, and prints. Several of the artists shown here have gained
national status and have won awards in national competitions.

The artists who are represented at The Upstairs Gallery show the
richness of the work being done in the area. From Arlington itself:

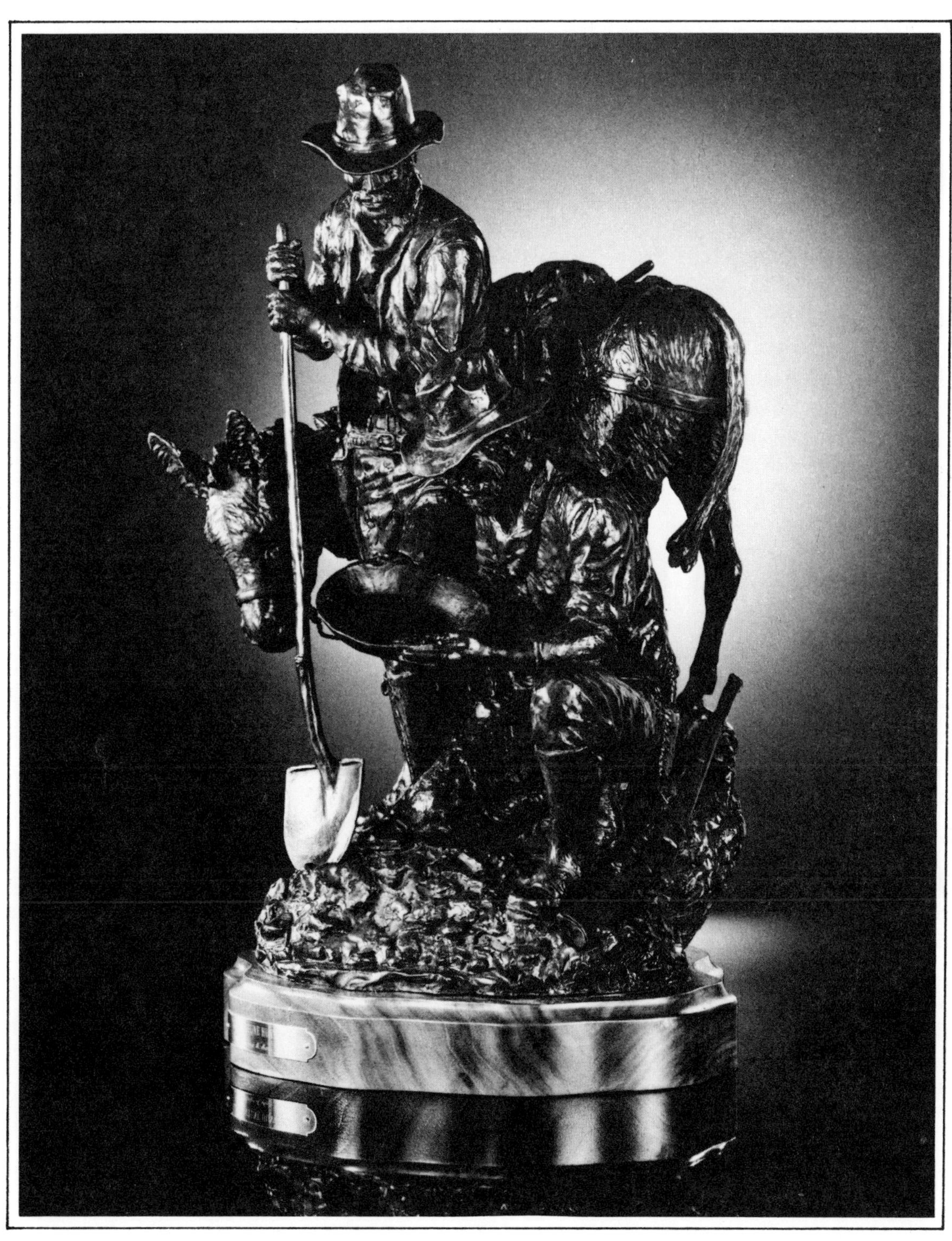

George Marks, *The Fortune Hunters,* Bronze. Reminisce Gallery.

Al Brouillette, who has been with the gallery since 1967, executes
his works in acrylic on paper, canvas, or panel; Jo Ann Bushart,
jewelry in gold, silver, minerals, and precious stones; Jane Jacobs,
hand-built sculpture; Mary Lee Drysdale, commissioned
watercolor portraits; Sherry Dunaway, photographs; Eleanor
Martin, watercolor and collage; Mildred Taylor, graphics;
Stephen Rascoe, impressionistic oil paintings; May White Dyer,
fibers and works on paper; Betsy Collier, oil and watercolor. From
Fort Worth: Alvis Ballew, oils on canvas and drawings with an
emphasis on nature. From Houston: Virginia Cobb, watercolor
and mixed media on paper.

The gallery owns an old, two-story house in the rear where Jane
Jacobs and Jo Ann Bushart have studios. Art classes are conducted
weekly at the gallery; workshops by outstanding artist-teachers are
held four times a year for one or two weeks. Several one-man
shows are held each year, and there is a traditional Christmas
show.

Valley House Gallery, Inc.   6616 Spring Valley Rd.   Dallas
75240   (214) 239-2441   Monday-Friday: 10-5; Saturday: 10-3

Valley House

Valley House was founded by Donald and Margaret Vogel in 1953
and has been a member of the Art Dealers Association of America
since 1964. The gallery is nestled in a 5-acre garden in a
residential area in north Dallas. Valley House was one of the first
galleries to exhibit contemporary art in this region and now
specializes in nineteenth- and early-twentieth-century European
and American paintings, drawings, and prints.

The estates of Hugh Breckenridge and Morgan Russell have
been represented at the gallery with an important catalog
published on Breckenridge. The contemporary artists represented
are working in many media and styles, including abstraction,
figurative, surrealistic. James Twitty and Gottfried Honegger work
in abstraction. Donald Vogel, Loren Mozley, and Fred Nagler
work in figurative manner, both impressionistic, cubistic. Hub
Miller and Valton Tyler work in a surrealistic figurative manner.

A unique aspect of the gallery is the garden which is ideally
suited to sculpture exhibitions including Henry Moore, Sorel
Etrog, Peter Chinni and Charles Umlauf, and Mike Cunningham.

There has been a recent emphasis on master printmakers due to
Kevin Vogel's personal interest in prints and drawings. The gallery
periodically arranges exhibitions of Whistler prints or shows of
several artists with a theme.

The viewing room of the gallery houses the library which is
being compiled for appraisal and research needs.

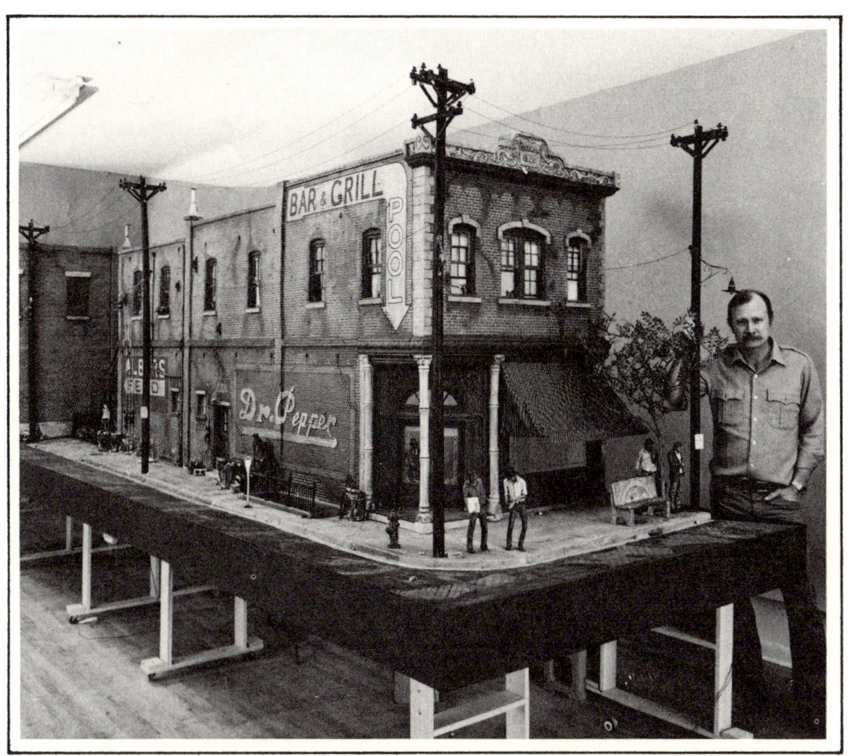

Michael Garman, *Darby Street,* 6' x 17' cityscape, mixed media.
Southwest Art Center.

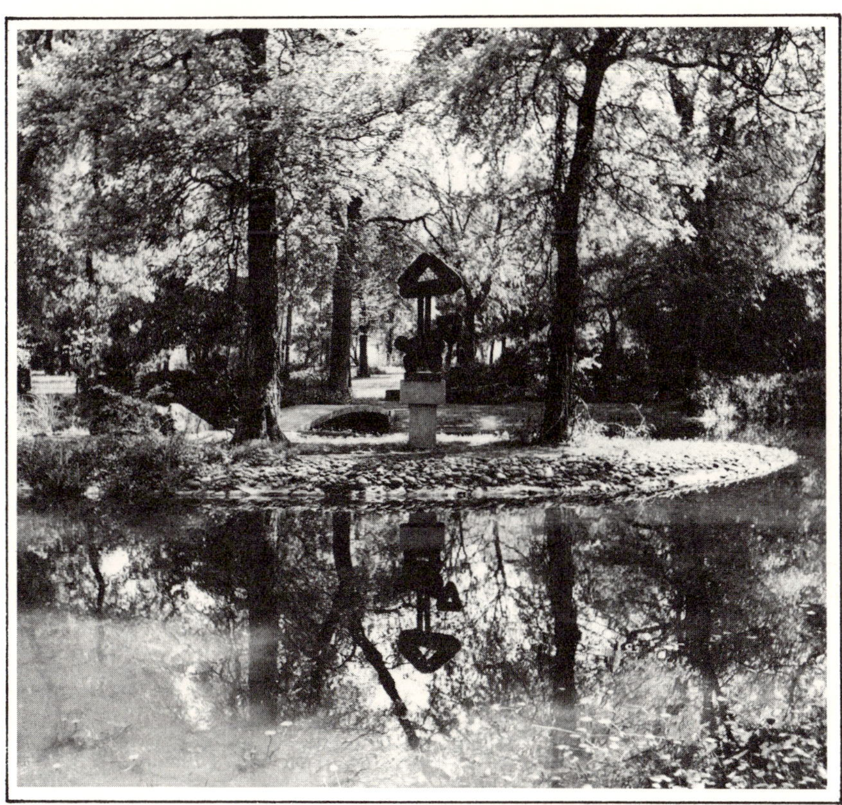

Sorel Etrog, *Two Acrobats and Crusader* (Valley House Gardens),
Valley House Gallery.

Houston & Southeast Texas

Museums and Public Exhibition Spaces

The Art League of Houston   1953 Montrose   Houston 77006
(713) 523-9530   Tuesday-Friday: 10-4; Saturday: 12-4

The Art League of Houston is a fellowship of Houston-area artists
and patrons, founded in 1948 to promote interest in the
achievement of its members by providing a showcase for artists'
work and studio-workshops for learning.

   The nonprofit League, a community-oriented, educational
organization consisting of over 700 members, has become a vital
force in the development of Houston artists. It is the only institution
in the city providing continuous juried exhibitions with the
opportunity of workshops and studio participation. The Art League
of Houston offers a flexible program, designed to meet the needs of
the membership.

The Bayou Bend Collection of the Museum of Fine Arts, Houston
1 Westcott Street   Post Office Box 13157   Houston 77019   (713)
529-8773   Tuesday-Saturday: 10-11:15; Tuesday-Friday:
1:15-2:30. Closed on New Year's, July 4, Christmas, Labor Day,
Thanksgiving and the entire month of August. During the hours of
operation, visitors are escorted by docents in groups of four every
fifteen minutes. Admission is by reservation only. Minimum age is
16, except on Family Tour days (first floor only) each second
Sunday, except March and August, 1-5. No reservations needed
for family tours.

Bayou Bend is the name of the twenty-eight room house built by
Ima Hogg and her two brothers Will and Mike in 1928. Designed
by John F. Staub, an architect who made a career of designing
large homes for the commercial elite of Houston, the house is a
pink-painted stucco structure combining Greek Revival and
Palladian elements in its design. It is surrounded by several acres
of landscaped gardens and is bordered on its north side by Buffalo

Art League of Houston

Bayou Bend Collection

Bayou, the major waterway of the Houston area. Inside is an extremely large and good quality collection of American furnishings arranged in rooms by periods. The William and Mary style Murphy Room showcases furniture and objects from the period 1650 to 1725. The central hall is dubbed the Philadelphia Hall and displays objects made between 1760 and 1790, including the Chippendale furniture made in that city. The Federal Period Music Room presents examples of American taste from 1790 to 1815, and includes a Duncan Phyfe piano made in New York City. The most modern room is the Belter Parlor, an Early Victorian sitting room of the period 1845-1870.

This extraordinary collection requires making reservations well in advance, for a price of $1.00, but is well worth it, especially in Spring when the azaleas and magnolias are in bloom. Although the house was meant to be approached from an entrance on Lazy Lane, out of consideration for other residents of the street the house is now reached by a footbridge over Buffalo Bayou from a parking lot located on Westcott Street, a small appendage off of Memorial Drive. Guests are asked to arrive fifteen minutes before their scheduled tour so that they may be properly registered.

Membership in the Museum of Fine Arts, Houston, qualifies you for listing on a mailing list that keeps you abreast of new events at the Museum and the pleasant previews and receptions for new shows. In addition, you get a 10% discount on purchases at the Museum Shop and film series tickets, discounts on tuition at the Alfred C. Glassell, Jr. School of Art, children's programs, and travel programs. The basic membership costs $35 ($12.50 for students). Other memberships, with additional perks, are from $50 to $1,000 per year.

Beaumont Art Museum

Beaumont Art Museum   1111 Ninth St.   Beaumont 77702
(713) 832-3432   Tuesday-Friday: 10-5; Saturday-Sunday: 2-5

The Beaumont Art Museum was founded in 1950. In 1970, the J. Cooke Wilson family donated their Ninth Street residence to the City of Beaumont, and it is now the location of the museum. A significant work of art in itself, the building was designed by noted Houston architect John F. Staub in his "Latin Colonial" style.

The museum brings to its galleries traveling exhibitions from around the world, ranging from paintings and drawings to photography and crafts. A selection from the permanent collection, consisting mainly of twentieth-century art, is displayed on the second floor.

The museum's commitment to the cultural enrichment of the area is enhanced through its broad range of educational activities: scholarly lectures and seminars; a film and music series; an art library; and a variety of tours, in addition to school programs on the elementary- through high-school levels.

One weekend each May the museum's grounds are filled with
the annual arts and crafts festival, Kaleidoscope. Designed to
emphasize skilled artists and craftsmen from across the country,
there are also children's activities, food booths, and live
entertainment. The museum's wooded grounds are used again
each spring and fall for theatrical, musical, and dance productions
in the Celebration of the Arts series.

When approaching the museum from the east, take the I-10 to
the 11th St. exit, go under the freeway and turn right on 9th St.
The museum is 5 blocks south. Coming from the west, take the 7th
St. exit, and turn right on 9th.

Blaffer Gallery

Sarah Campbell Blaffer Gallery   University of Houston, Central
Campus   Houston 77004   (713) 749-1320   Tuesday-Saturday:
10-6; Sunday: 1-6

The Blaffer Gallery, Houston's only public university museum, is
located on the central campus of the state's second largest
institution for higher education, the University of Houston. It was
named to honor the late Sarah Campbell Blaffer, who during her
lifetime made available to the university what ultimately became a
sizable and highly prized collection of major art works dating
from the fifteenth century to the present day.

In addition to the painting collection, the Blaffer Gallery has a
pre-Columbian collection, contemporary prints, and Mexican
graphics.

The exhibition program is planned for a diverse audience and
has included such acclaimed exhibitions as Three Centuries of the
American Nude (1975); Picasso, Braque, Leger, and Edvard
Munch (1976); Willem de Kooning, and German Expressionism
(1977); Harry Callahan, Ancient Roots/New Visions, and Freda
Kahlo (1978); The Way West, Vienna Moderne: 1898-1918, and
Texas Crafts (1979); Beyond the Box: Architecture of Philip
Johnson and John Burgee, American Fiber Art, and City Segments
(1980); and Artist and Printer and Directions 1981 (1981).

To reach the Blaffer Gallery, use entrance 5 off Cullen Blvd.   *transportation*

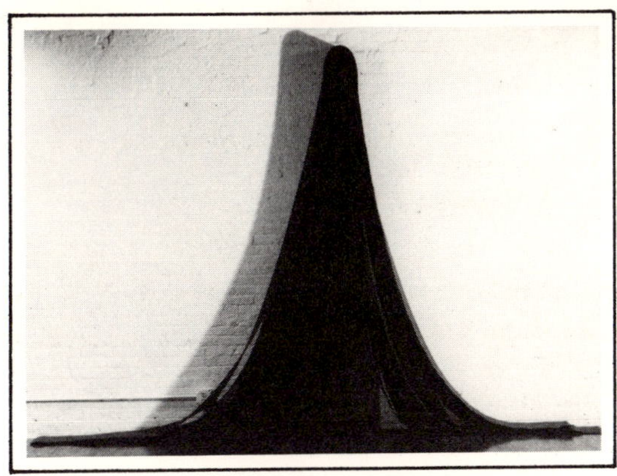

Robert Morris, *Untitled,* 102" x 146" x 8"
variable, felt strips.

Contemporary Arts Museum   5216 Montrose Boulevard
Houston 77006   (713) 526-3129   Tuesday-Saturday: 10-5;
Sundays: 12-6

The Contemporary Arts Museum, one of perhaps a half-dozen
such institutions in the entire United States, is strictly an exhibiting
museum and possesses no permanent collection. It is housed in a
corrugated stainless steel-covered trapezoid shaped building on
the corner of Montrose Boulevard and Bissonet, across the
intersection from the Museum of Fine Arts and in the middle of a
neighborhood that contains a number of good commercial
galleries. Inside the windowless building are two major galleries, a
gift shop, a room sized gallery that is actually the live-in
headquarters of a "gallery without walls" that sponsors theatre
events, lectures, symposia and films, and the Museum offices,
some 12,000 square feet in all.

Normally, the top floor is devoted to one artist currently
producing art in the United States, although retrospectives of
recently deceased modernists and foreign artists make their
appearance from time to time. Recent shows have showcased the
works of Robert Gordy, John Baldessari, Anthony Berlant, Ansel
Adams, and Ed Paschke. The lower gallery, a smaller space,
frequently shows the works of artists local to Houston.

The gift shop sells catalogs of CAM shows, naive art by Texans,
narrative art books, CAM t-shirts designed by punk art queen
Zandra Rhodes, and anything else deemed suitable to the avant-
garde Houston lifestyle.

Basic membership which will keep you abreast of upcoming   *membership*
openings, films, classes and lectures costs $30 per year for
individuals and families, $15 for students. Other categories of
membership begin at $50 and go up to $1,000.

The Museum was established in 1948 as the Contemporary Arts
Association and had the avowed purpose of bringing to Houston
the sort of art that would "interpret the modern world." The
Association did not have a building at first, but as soon as one was
located, near Sam Houston Park, exhibitions of the works of Pablo
Picasso and Alexander Calder were arranged. For many
Houstonians, it was their first experience with the world of
Modernism. In 1954, the building was moved to the grounds of the
Prudential Building, which itself had caused quite a stir in Houston
when a severe Art Deco pair of nudes were unveiled in the
fountain in front of the building in the early post-War years.
Edward Steichen's *Family of Man* and some works of Mark Rothko
were shown there. In 1972, the present building was opened to the
public. Despite the fact that the Houston heat caused the metal
sheathing of the outside to buckle and fall off, necessitating new,
corrugated sheathing, and a typical Houston rainstorm flooded the
lower floor in 1976, destroying the offices and archives along with

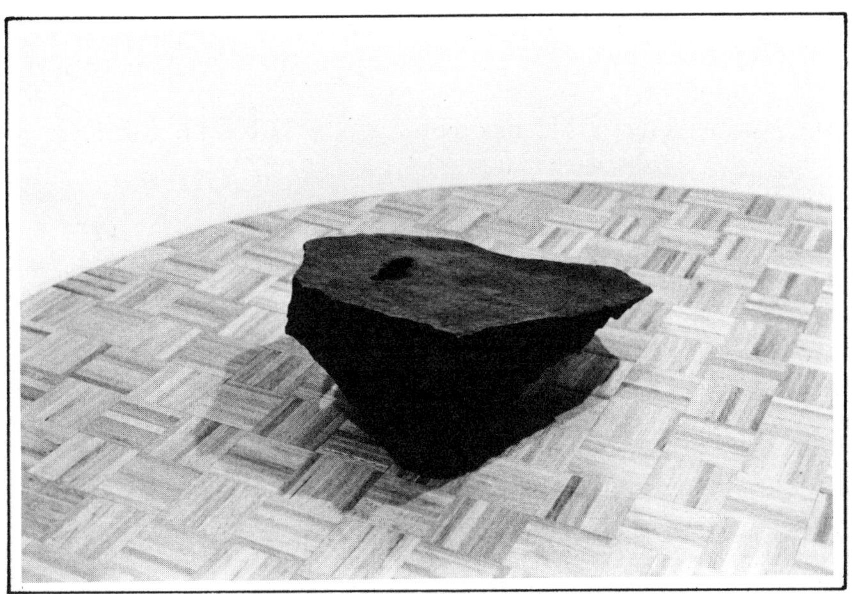

Brian Hunt, *Monolith Quarry,* 36″ x 29½″ x 14″, bronze. Contemporary
Arts Museum.

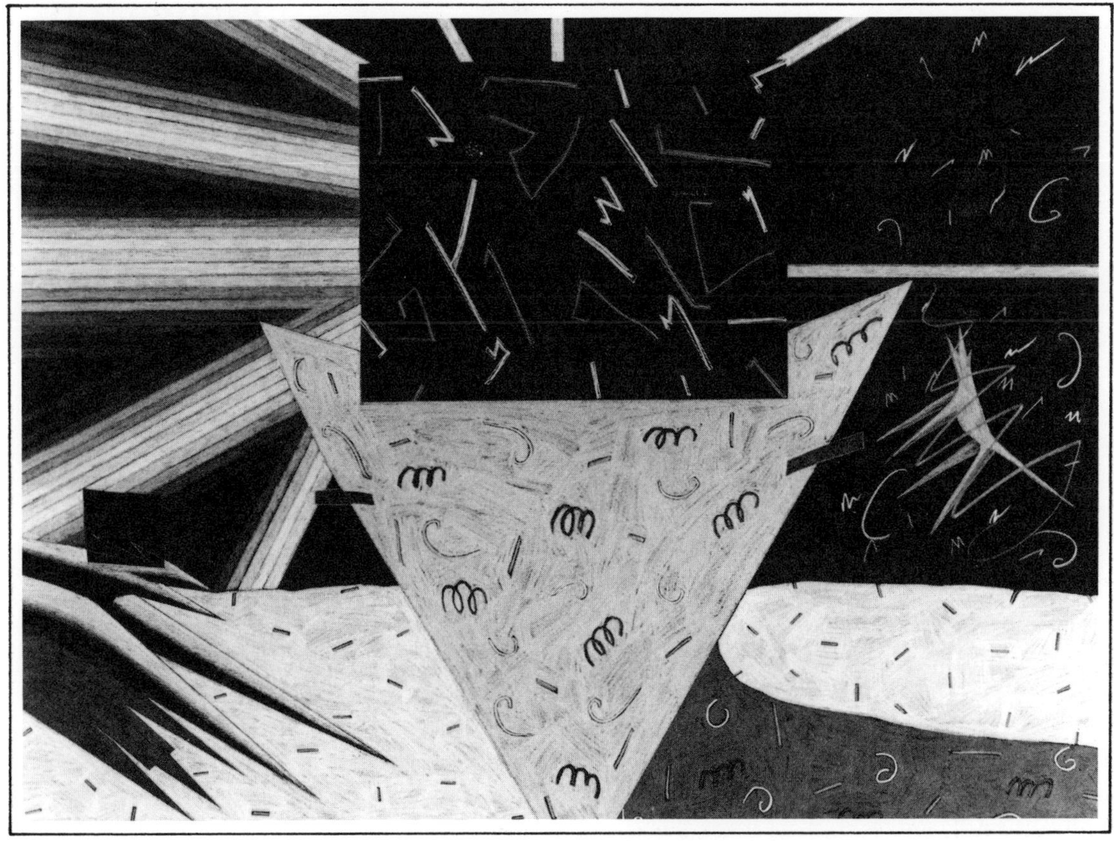

Jean Dibble, *I am Lost,* 22″ x 30″, colored pencil on paper. Contemporary Arts
Museum.

artworks, the CAM as it is known has continued to grow in public acceptance and stature.

<table><tr><td>

Fort Bend County Museum Association   500 Houston St. Richmond 77469   (713) 342-6478   Tuesday-Friday: 10-4; Saturday-Sunday: 1-5; Historic House: Sunday: 1-5; and by special appointment   Admission free; Historic House, $2

</td><td>

Fort Bend County Museum

</td></tr></table>

The museum depicts the history of Ford Bend County from 1822 to 1922, and includes artifacts of Austin's "Old 300 Colonists," and material relating to Jane Long, President Mirabeau B. Lamar, Carry Nation, and others. There is a collection of early photographs, documents, and Texas Revolution artifacts. Rotating exhibits and slide programs feature material relating to nineteenth-century Texas history.

The Doll House exhibits in November and the Candlelight Tours in December are annual events.

The Confederate Museum, which is located at 602 Preston St., is the sheriff's apartment of the 1896 jail. Displays include weapons and swords, pictures of battles, artifacts, and tape-recorded histories.

Galveston Arts Center Gallery   2127 Strand   Galveston 77550 (713) 763-2403   Monday-Friday: 10-6; Saturday-Sunday: 11-5

Galveston Arts Center

When the Galveston Arts Center opened in 1973 as a school for photography, drawing, painting, and ceramics, the gallery was also established as a space for local exhibitions. Through the years the gallery has grown both in size and range of exhibitions. Exhibits of community interest as well as national competitive and invitational shows fill the calendar.

The works presented at the Galveston Arts Center Gallery are varied in subject matter, ranging from strong representational to abstract works. There are twelve exhibits per year: four to six one-person shows, two competitive shows, a special children's show, a college show, and two community shows.

The most outstanding exhibit in recent months was the 30 Americans Invitational, which included artists such as Wendell Castle, Thelma Coles, David Davidon, John Glick, Wayne Higby, Marvin Lipofsky, Sam Maloof, and Toshiko Takaezu. The exhibit was sponsored in part by the National Endowment for the Arts, the Moody Foundation, and the Kemper Fund. The works ranged from blown glass, silver, jewelry, pottery, and furniture, to fabrics.

Other exhibits at the gallery include watercolors, children's drawings, photographs, steel environmental sculpture, large environmental paintings, ceramics, both functional and nonfunctional, and etchings, litho, serigraphs, and three-dimensional prints. Some of the artists who have mounted one-person shows during the 1981-1982 season are: Nick Nicosia

exhibitions

and Stephen Dennie, photographs; James Drake, environmental
steel sculptures; Charles James, large drawings and performance
pieces; Vicki Teague Cooper, large paintings.

<h1>Harris County Heritage Society</h1>

Harris County Heritage Society Restoration   Sam Houston Park
1100 Bagby   Houston 77002   (713) 223-8367   Monday-Friday:
10-3; Saturday: 11-2; Sunday: 2-4

The park, in the reflection of Houston's downtown, is a restoration
of the city's oldest structures, restored and furnished in
nineteenth-century fashion and open for guided tours every day.

The Kellum-Noble House, built in 1847, may be the oldest brick
house in Houston. It is joined by the Nichols-Rice-Cherry House, a
Greek Revival House built about 1850 by a native of Cooperstown,
New York; San Felipe Cottage, a simple six-room house built on
the western edge of Houston but restored in this location as a
typical Texas cottage of the 1870s; Pilot House, a mid-Victorian
structure believed to have the first indoor kitchen in Houston; The
Old Place, a cabin moved from the west bank of Clear Creek, the
oldest structure in Harris County, and built about 1824. St. John
Church still has its original altar-pulpit and cypress plank pews.
The Long Row is Houston's first business building, originally
constructed in 1837. The Bandstand is a copy of the original
turn-of-the-century Houston City Park Bandstand, and a focal
point for a varity of special events held in Sam Houston Park.

The Heritage Society owns several portraits, some with subjects
and painters identified, some not. The portraits date from the
beginning of the nineteenth century. A partial list includes an oil
portrait of Sam Houston (c. 1850); an oil painting of William Marsh
Rice (c. 1850) (Mr. Rice was the driving force behind Rice
University); and oil portraits of the mother-in-law and brother-
in-law of Sam Houston (c. 1850) by George R. Allen. Miniatures
and watercolors by artists such as Adam Buck, Gabriel Max, and
Mrs. E. Richardson Cherry are also in the collection.

A shop and tearoom are popular Houston attractions.

<h1>Museum of American Architecture and Decorative Arts</h1>

Museum of American Architecture and Decorative Arts   Houston
Baptist University   7502 Fondren Rd.   Houston 77074   (713)
774-7661, Ext. 311   Tuesday-Thursday: 10-4; and by appointment

The Museum of American Architecture and Decorative Arts has
evolved into a warm, intimate, and friendly setting for its
collections of early Americana.

The early American room has an early Texas bed with a
sensuous, hand-rubbed finish covered by a hand-loomed Jacquard
spread dated 1846, worked into the design of the Capitol at
Washington, D.C. An armoire complete with antique rat hole, an
early jam cupboard, and a washstand with bowl and pitcher
complete the room.

A collection of eighteenth- and nineteenth-century retablos hangs on the walls, examples of a flourishing folk art. Folk retablos served as household shrines for a people who centuries before had shifted their worship from pagan images to Roman Catholic saints.

More retablos, ex-votos, and early American silhouettes are on the walls of the adjoining Colonial Texas Room. They tell the lively history of Texas. Wonderful cast-iron pots and a collection of antique dolls complete the scene.

Nineteenth-century dolls from the Theo Redwood Blank collection number over 1,000 examples. The pieces of doll-sized furniture on display were often salesmen's samples. A case houses a number of dolls from the collection of Lafitte Desirate whose dolls were used by mantua makers (or dressmakers) to exhibit ladies' fashions.

A Victorian bedroom of the 1880s is complete with four-poster bed and bedding, a New Orleans Cheval mirror, and a needlepoint chair. Framed prints from Godey's Lady's Book adorn the wall.

Paintings by Indian artists of Oklahoma, collected by Woody Crombo, are woven through the collection. In the adjoining Victorian dining room is a collection of paintings by Emma Richardson Cherry, who founded the Art League of Houston which eventually evolved into the Museum of Fine Arts.

The massive oak table (c. 1875) was a gift to the Bringhurst family from Zaviah Noble, who founded the first school in Houston.

A wonderful early Houston bookcase and drop-front desk (c. 1868) by Usener, whose memorabilia of Houston fill it now, occupy one corner. Another desk is a campaign desk brought to Texas by George Bringhurst in 1835. Important documents, including a Cherokee treaty, were said to have been signed on it.

The Museum of Fine Arts

The Museum of Fine Arts, Houston   1001 Bissonnet   Houston 77005   (713) 526-1361   Tuesday-Saturday: 10-5; Sundays: 12-6

The Museum of Fine Arts, Houston, began most modestly on April 13, 1900 as the Houston Public School Art League. The five women who comprised the membership of the League had gotten together with the idea of acquiring reproductions of famous paintings and monuments so that the sons and daughters of wildcatters, rough-necks and cowpunchers could be exposed to the morally uplifting sight of La Giaconda and the Petit Trianon. The effort enjoyed a *succes d'estime* and in 1913 the organization was chartered as the Houston Art League, with a small collection hung in the Mayor's office and City Council chambers. By 1924, a site and building funds had been acquired and a small, Spanish Colonial-and Neo-Classical structure was erected to house a collection consisting of twenty-five paintings, an engraving, five bronzes, and a few carved Medieval ivories and fragments of

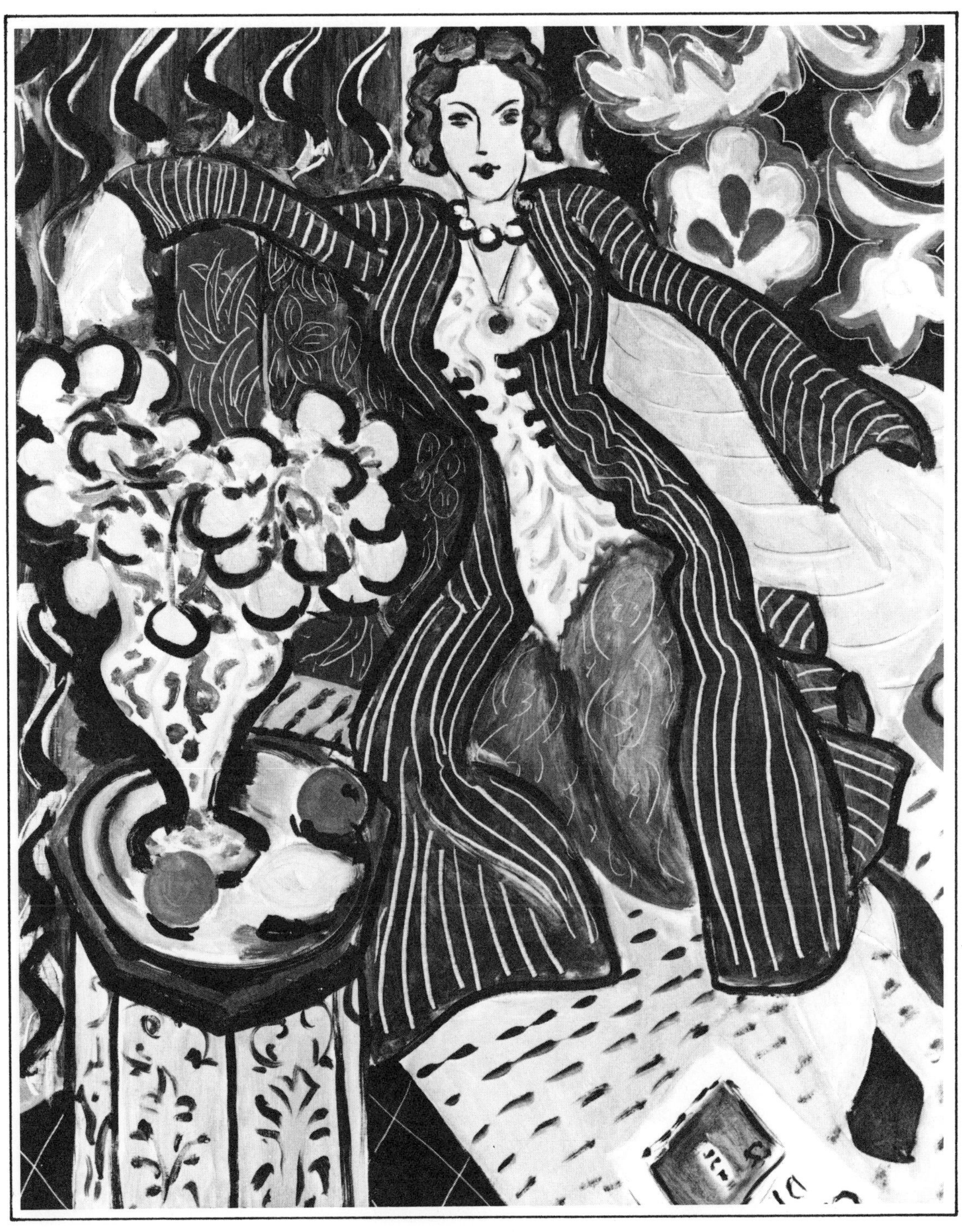

Henri Matisse, *Woman in a Purple Coat,* 1937, 32″ x 25¾″, oil on canvas. The Museum of Fine Arts, Houston.

stained glass cathedral windows.

In 1926, per the architects' plans, two wings were added to house five galleries in one wing and the Museum School in the other wing. With the exception of a small gift of antique lace and Classical Greek, Roman and Egyptian items and one hundred works on paper by leading contemporary and recently deceased artists in 1939, the Museum continued to drowse in the torpor-inducing subtropical heat through the 1930's and early '40's. In 1943, Miss Ima Hogg, daughter of the celebrated 1890's reform Democrat Governor of Texas, Jimm Hogg, donated a collection of Frederick Remington paintings and a bronze. In 1944, a gift of North American Indian art from the Hogg estate and eighty-three works from the Italian and Northern Renaissances and eighteenth century France comprising the Straus collection broadened the Museum's erratic scope.

Continuing to grow in the fitful, capricious way that so much of Houston has grown in, the museum added a small square wing in 1953, the Robert Lee Blaffer Memorial Wing designed by Kenneth Franzheim. In 1958, Cullinan Hall, a large gallery space in the glass-and-steel international style was grafted onto the Classical-Spanish Colonial facade of the original building. This unnatural mating was legitimized by the fact that the architect was none other than Ludwig Mies van der Rohe, who had invented the whole glass-and-steel International style was grafted onto the Classical-following World War I. In 1974, five years after van der Rohe's death, the second phase of his design was completed, the Brown Pavilion. The Pavilion extended the Museum out to Bissonnet Boulevard, doubled the gallery space to an impressive 75,331 square feet, and added an auditorium, a cafeteria, a museum shop and a library to the Museum's facilities. This is the building visitors to the Museum now see.

In addition to the Bissonnet complex, the Museum operates the Bayou Bend Collection, a twenty-eight room house filled with American decorative arts and furnishings created during the two centuries prior to the early Victorian era. The house is located five miles from the Museum site on the banks of Buffalo Bayou, the main waterway leading from Houston to the Gulf of Mexico. The house and property were donated to the Museum by Ima Hogg over a nine-year period from 1957 to 1966, when it was opened to the public.

The Museum has always had a school attached to it since it acquired a permanent building in 1924. The school is now housed in a new glass brick building across the proposed Lillie and Hugh Roy Cullen Sculpture Garden from the Museum and is now known as the Alfred C. Glassell, Jr. School of Art.

Since 1969, several large endowments and collections have broadened and deepened the Museum of Fine Arts' collections.

Blaffer Wing

Glassell School

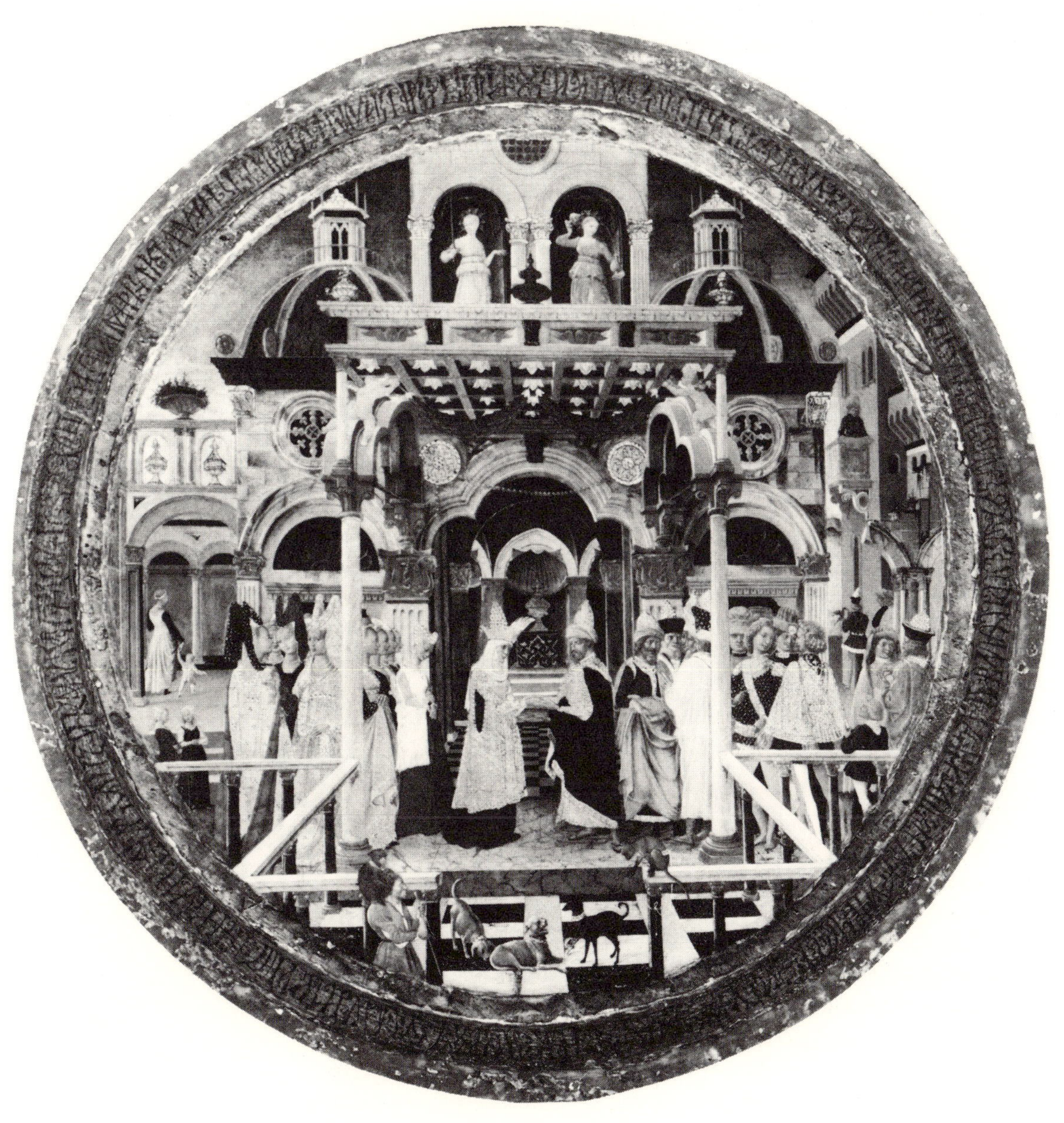

Unknown Italian (Ferrarese), *The Meeting of Solomon and the Queen of Sheba* (late 15th Century) 26″ diameter, tempera on wood. The Museum of Fine Arts, Houston.

The material represents a survey of art history from around 2000 B.C., with an Early Cycladic Period female idol being the oldest piece, through samples of Egyptian, Assyrian, Hellenic and Roman art to the Middle Ages, the Renaissance and up to the present. In addition there are samples of painting, sculpture and applied arts from China, Tibet, India, the great pre-Columbian civilizations of Mesoamerica, and tribal art from West Africa, Oceania and New Guinea.

While no one area of the Museum's collecting activity outside of the Bayou Bend edifice possesses great depth, breadth or celebrity, there are a number of pieces of singular individual merit. The oldest of these is a Third Century Roman bronze remnant known as the "Portrait of a Ruler." It is generally considered to be a copy of Lysippo's lost *Alexander with the Lance,* but as the head is missing, the provenance unsure (It is thought to have been recovered in an area of modern Turkey), and the subject indefinite, it is best admired for its Classical harmony and idealized anatomy.

Other pieces of interest include but are not limited to a *Reliquary Monstrance from the Guelph Treasure* made in the 15th century in Lower Saxony, a Hans Memling *Portrait of an Old Woman,* a Veronese entitled *The Dead Christ with Angel and a Monk,* a Frans Hals *Portrait of a Woman,* and some Impressionist pieces such as a Renoir *Still Life with Bouquet,* van Gogh's *The Rocks,* the seminal Fauvist canvas by Andre Derain entitled *The Turning Road,* an early Braque cubist painting of *Fishing Boats,* and some works by leading American artists. Chief among those are Georgia O'Keeffe's *Grey Line with Black, Blue and Yellow* of 1923, Jackson Pollock's *Number 6* of 1949 and Kenneth Noland's *Half* of 1959.

The collection of various types of primitive art includes a good selection of Southwestern Indian bowls from prehistoric to recent times, Mayan pottery, and some pre-Columbian carvings from Mexico and Guatemala. Among the objects from various Pacific peoples, there is a carved crocodile totem from the Karawari people of New Guinea notable for its size, nearly 23' long. The carving was used for holding the severed heads of tribal head hunting victims among other uses.

The Museum of Fine Arts, under a grant program from Target Stores and other sources, employs a curator of photography and is acquiring a good collection of contemporary American photography.

The Museum of Fine Arts, through an ongoing relationship with the Museum of Modern Art in New York and other institutions, regularly brings major shows to the Houston area. A sampling of recent efforts, which are usually displayed in the immense (300') Upper Brown Gallery include the record-breaking MOMA

Cezanne show, an exhibition of Leonardo da Vinci prints from the collection at Windsor Castle, a look at Joan Miro and his influence on American artists, a collection of the watercolors of the British master J.M.W. Turner from the British Museum, and a look at the Costakis collection of Soviet-era Russian abstract art that included films and a performance of an early Constructivist play on a set designed by an artist of the period and reproduced in the Cullinan Hall. A number of the smaller side galleries regularly show exhibits devoted to anything from etchings based on Rubens's paintings to rare bookbindings to photography from its invention to state-of-the-art experiments with new films and emulsions.

In addition to art objects, the Museum's Brown Auditorium is the scene of various film series such as a retrospective look at the works of American director Vincente Minnelli, Japanese director Kenzo Mizoguchi's treatment of women in Japanese society, or the current Dutch cinema, to name some recent topics. The Brown Auditorium is also the place where guest lecturers deliver talks about various shows at the Museum, contemporary writers and poets read their works, and, usually on Sunday afternoons, documentaries on art and artists on exhibit are screened. There is a charge for the feature films ($1.50 for members, $2.00 for non-members) but all the other events, like the Museum itself, are open to the public free of charge.

The Museum's Department of Art History and Education offers visitors free Gallery Lectures on Wednesday and Sunday afternoons at 1:00 and 2:00 p.m. At 1:00 p.m., the Museum Instructors give an introductory talk entitled *The Collection: An Introduction to the Museum of Fine Arts.* The 2:00 p.m. topics change regularly. Individual group tours are available by calling the Museum's Department of Art History and Education (526-1361.)

The Alfred C. Glassell, Jr. School of Art   5101 Montrose Boulevard   (713) 529-7659

The Museum of Fine Arts, Houston operates an art school across the planned Cullen Sculpture Garden (designed by Isamu Noguchi) from the Museum. Housed in an attractive glass block and concrete building designed by Eugene Aubrey of S.I. Morris Associates, the 41,000 square foot structure houses studios and classrooms where students from age 4 on can take lessons in art history and technique. Drawing, printmaking, ceramics, photography, jewelry-making and sculpture are all taught here by recognized artists. A new artist-in-residence type of program will bring nationally recognized artists to work at the school for short and long periods. While college degrees are not offered here, adults can earn a Certificate of Achievement for a two-year course of study. The current tuition schedule is $50 per course for children aged 4 through 12, $65 for high school age children, and

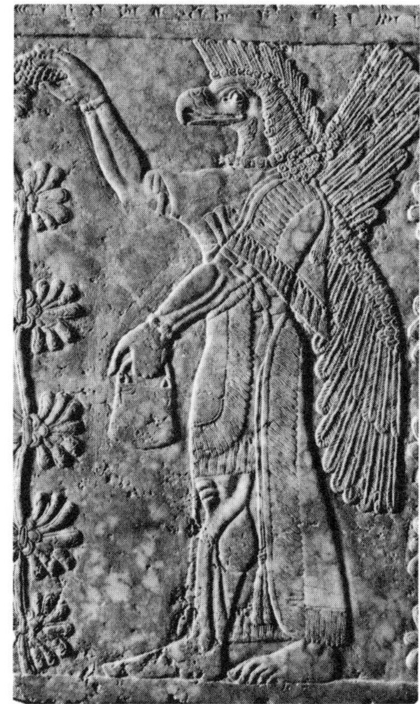

Assyrian, bas relief (c. 883-859 B.C.), *Eagle Headed Deity*, 42¾" x 26¼", Gypsum. The Museum of Fine Arts, Houston.

Glassell School

between $115 and $135 for adults, plus lab fees. New students must present examples of work before enrolling if they wish to take art courses, but there is no requirement for Art History classes.

O'Kane Gallery   1 Main St.   Houston 77002   (713) 479-1950
Monday-Friday: 10-5   Closed July & August

O'Kane
Gallery

The Harry W. O'Kane Gallery, established in 1970, was made possible by gifts from Harry W. O'Kane, South Texas Junior College Athletic Director and Dean of Students; Mary W. Bingman, an instructor with STJC; and the Humphreys Foundation.

During the past decade the gallery has strived to become a showplace for up-and-coming local artists. Gallery exhibits have been coordinated to present a rich and varied fare of mixed-media works by Houston area artists specifically and Texas artists in general.

For students at the University of Houston Downtown College, the gallery offers an enriching and broadening educational experience. For the community, the gallery forms the nucleus of a cultural center for downtown Houston and local communities.

The 1981-82 season has featured a number of outstanding shows: Cynthia Morgan Batmanis, mixed media and drawings, semi-abstract in tones of white, black, and grey; Tommy McAfee, whose painting of the Star of Hope Mission is reminiscent of Hopper; David Wood, photographer; Dean Woodruff, jewelry; Pat Till, acrylics; Judy Blossman and Jean Wetta; Frank Gerriettte, sculpture and acrylics; and Clarence Talley, acrylics.

Since the eleven-year history of the O'Kane Gallery has so dramatically paralleled the growth of Houston from a thriving Southwestern town to a major, dynamic metropolis, the show "Impressions of Houston," which ran during the month of November, 1981, was particularly appropriate.

Rice Museum   Institute for the Arts, Rice University/Houston, Texas   Entrance 7 (University Boulevard at Stockton Street) (713) May-August.

Rice
Museum

This small, excellent exhibition space is the gift of Dominique de Menil to Rice University, via the de Menil Foundation Museum which will be built at another site in the near future. Mrs. de Menil is the Museum's Director as well as its chief patron. Begun in 1968, the Museum mounts three exhibitions a year, often with works from the vast de Menil collection, and issues catalogs for the exhibitions that are reknowned for the excellence of their scholarship and printing. While Mrs. de Menil favors Surrealism (some credit her with "rediscovering" Max Ernst), the Museum puts on a variety of exhibitions ranging over many continents and eras.

Recent exhibits include such topics as: "Form and Freedom:
a gathering of Northwest Coast Indian Art," "Art Nouveau from
Belgium and France," "Ten Centuries that Shaped the West:
Greek and Roman Art in Texas Collections," "Jim Love Up to Now"
(a retrospective of Houston sculptor Love), "Max Ernst: Inside the
Sight," "Secret Affinities: Words and Images by Rene Magritte,"
and shows of material by Yves Klein, Joseph Cornell, Roman
Opalka, de Menil collection prints and Byzantine locks, keys,
weights and seals. There is no charge for admission.

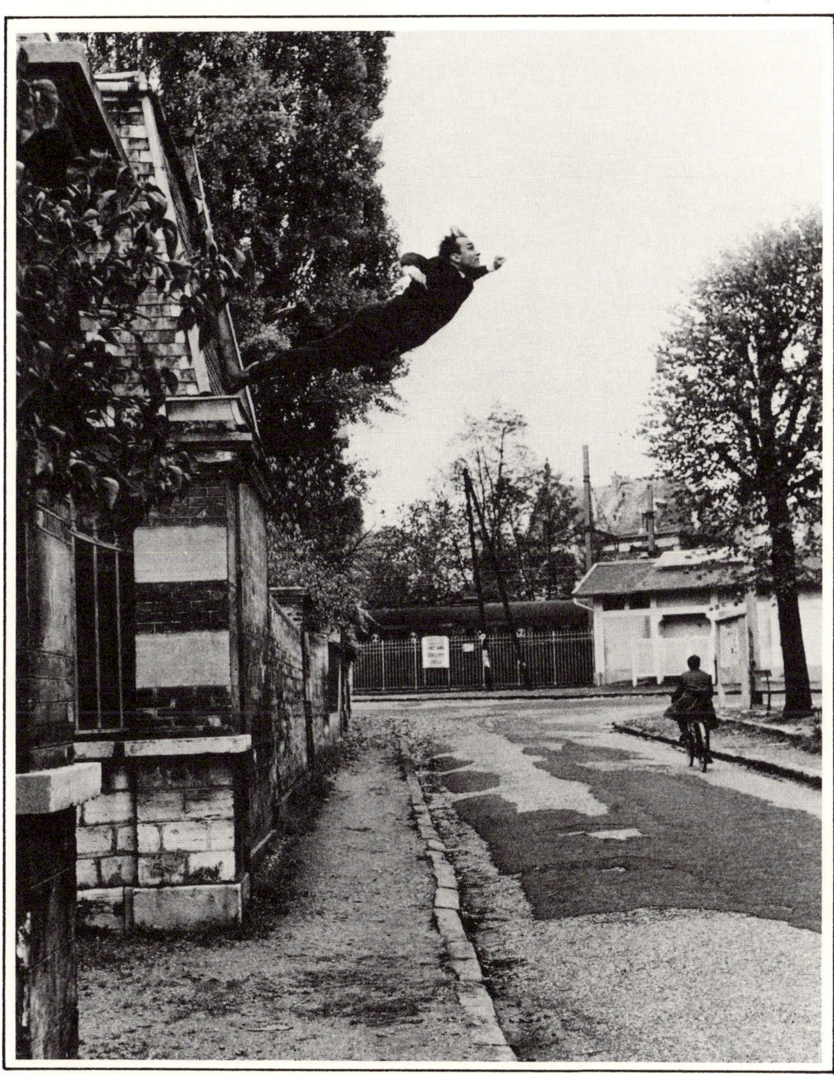

Yves Klein, *The Leap,* 1960, Photograph. Institute for the Arts, Rice
University.

Rosenberg Library   2310 Sealy Avenue   Galveston 77550
(713) 763-8854   Monday-Thursday: 9-9; Friday-Saturday: 9-6

The Rosenberg Library was given to the citizens of Galveston by
Henry Rosenberg (1824-1893), whose will left an endowment for a
free public library for the use of the people of the city. The brick,
stone, and terracotta late Italian Renaissance-style building
opened its doors in 1904. In 1971 a new wing was added.

There is exhibit space throughout the building. The Harris
Gallery is for paintings, the Hutchings Gallery features material
on the history of Galveston and Texas, and the Lykes Maritime
Gallery features exhibits relating to the sea.

In the permanent collection are paintings by Edgar Paxson,
Thomas Moran, Ernest Moore, and E. Irving Couse; Russian icons
from 1575-1895; a collection of over 150 watercolors done by
Boyer Gonzales (1867-1934); and works by Julius Stockfleth, a
Gulf Coast marine and landscape painter (1857-1935), who
provided a lasting memory of schooners, pilot boats, and sailing
vessels.

Special exhibits are held throughout the year. 1982 will feature
Grace Spaulding John, A Woman Ahead of her Time; and Prints
and Drawings by Eric Avery. In 1983 the paintings of Mary
Frances Judge will be shown.

Rothko Chapel   1401 Sul Ross Street   Houston 77006   (713)
524-9839   open daily

As befits an ecumenical spirit, the Rothko Chapel is a
contemporary building set on property owned by a Catholic
university named after an English archbishop killed by
Protestants, was paid for by a French Catholic industrial heiress
married to an aristocrat, and showcases the last works of a Russian
Jewish expatriate who committed suicide. In addition, the chapel
has been the site of religious observances by Hindus, Buddhists
and Moslems as well as the religions more common to the West,
and has hosted symposia with such personages as the Dalai Lama
and seen performances by Turkish whirling dervishes.

The octagonal chapel, located in the middle of a quiet
residential and university neighborhood, contains a narthex and a
central room. In the middle of the room is a circle of simple
benches and pillows where visitors can sit while contemplating the
encircling space which displays five immense paintings and three
painted tryptichs. Done in the dark colors favored by Rothko in his
last phase and covered with the endless pentimenti common to his
work, the works at first confront the viewer with what is almost a
non-experience of dark rectangles. In a little time however, as the
eyes adjust, the dark colors begin to take on distinct tones of black,
brown, grey green and plum and their many combinations. In a

few more moments, the flat surfaces acquire surprising depths and motion. For those who have never quite felt at ease with Greenbergian esthetics, this chapel is perhaps their best explication. In another way, it is a sort of Taj Mahal of Modernism, a grand edifice that never lets one get off feeling that it is a tomb. The late Mark Rothko, at any rate, never came down to see the installed paintings before his suicide. The chapel was dedicated on February 27, 1971.

In front of the chapel is a reflecting pool containing Barnett Newman's "Broken Obelisk." It is one of an edition of three and one of the very few sculptures created by the New York artist who devoted most of his artistic life to solving the question of how to divide a flat, painted surface with a colored line.

Currently, a number of other modern sculptures adorn the grassy spaces around the chapel and pool. Dominique de Menil, the patron of the Chapel and one of America's foremost living art collectors, is currently overseeing the construction of a new museum in the immediate vicinity which will house her extensive collection.

San Jacinto Monument and Museum

San Jacinto Monument and Museum   San Jacinto 77536 (21 miles east of Houston)   (713) 479-2421   Monday-Saturday: 9:30-5:30; Sunday: 10-6; Labor Day through May: closed Monday

The museum depicts the region's history in a continuous, chronological line from the Indian civilization that Cortes encountered in the New World, to Texas, a state in the Union. The displays include documents, maps, books, broadsides, engravings, paintings, daguerrotypes, photographs, coins, costumes, and other memorabilia.

Emphasis is on the cultural development of Texas and the region under the Spanish-Mexican and Anglo-American civilizations.

The monument, 570 feet high, is built of reinforced concrete faced with Texas fossilized buff limestone. The museum proper, which forms the base of the building, is 125 feet square. On the museum's four bronze doors are flags in relief of the six governments which exercized sovereignty over Texas.

Sewall Art Gallery

Sewall Art Gallery   Cleveland Sewall Hall, Rice University 6100 Main Street   Houston 77005   (713) 527-8101, extension 3502   Monday-Saturday: 12-5; closed from May through August

This small gallery belongs to the art department of Rice University. Since it opened in 1971, it has staged four to six shows every academic year. Like most university galleries, the final exhibition of the year is devoted to the work of students earning their BA and BFA degrees. Unlike most college galleries, the Sewall has a permanent collection under the curatorship of Director Esther B.

de Vecsey and the shows, which are designed to supplement
courses being taught by the Rice art department, are often taken
on tours around the United States to other galleries and museums
subsequent to their appearance at Sewall. Examples of shows that
have traveled from here recently include "American Abstraction
from the CIBA-Gigy Corporate Collection," "Contemporary
Sculptors Drawings," (which contained drawings by such artists as
Robert Morris and Robert Smithson) and "Leonardo's Return to
Vinci." The last included some works on paper by the Renaissance
mega-genius and a panel attributed to him.

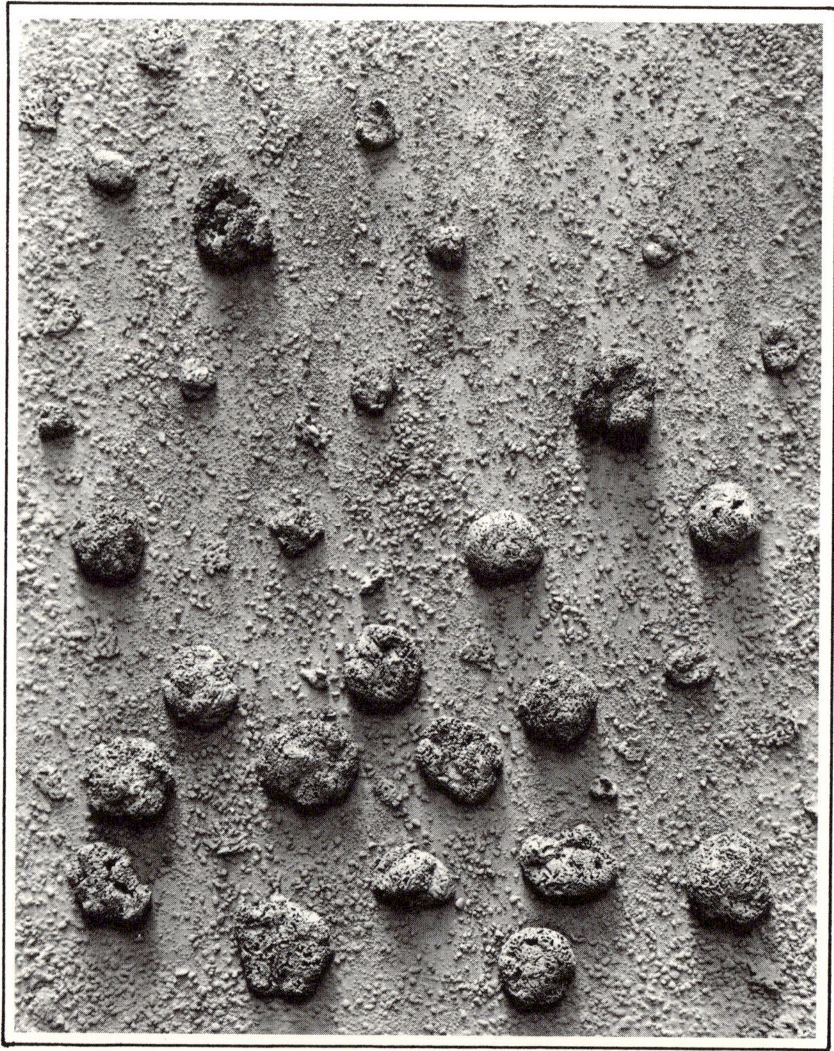

Yves Klein, *Requiem* (*RE20*), 1960, 78" x 64¾", paint, sponge, and
pebbles on board. Institute for the Arts, Rice University.

Stark Museum

The Stark Museum of Art contains exhibits which reflect the Stark family's interest in the land, wildlife, and people of the American West. The museum is housed in a contemporary, two-story building whose focal point is the corner entry where the second-story mass of marble block forms a dramatic contrast to the expanse of open space created by the recessed entrance on the first floor. The building is constructed of Vermont white imperial Danby marble.

The collection of Western American art is one of the finest in the country. It includes prints, paintings, sculpture, rare books, manuscripts, and letters which span the entire history of Western art beginning in the 1820s and continuing to 1980. Of special interest are prints made by Audubon of birds of Louisiana and Texas, sketches made by Paul Kane as he traveled in the 1840s from the Great Lakes to the Pacific Northwest, bronze sculpture by Frederic Remington and Charles M. Russell, and paintings by the twentieth-century artists of Taos, New Mexico.

The American Indian Collection consists primarily of material crafted by the tribes of the Great Plains and the Southwest— clothing, body ornaments, and beadwork. It also includes baskets from major basket-producing cultures in the West; Pueblo pottery, including the work of Maria Martinez of San Ildefonso; kachina dolls of the Zuni and Hopi; and an outstanding collection of Navajo rugs and blankets.

The entire series of Doughty birds is represented in the museum and is permanently on view. The only complete set of the *United States in Crystal* is a series of Steuben bowls engraved with scenes relating to the history of each of the fifty states.

Special exhibitions focusing on particular areas of the museum's collection are held in Gallery 5.

Take Simmons Dr. off I-10 to Green Ave.

Houston
Gallery Specializations

Many of the galleries found below exhibit a wide variety of art styles and mediums. The following list represents concentrations of a particular artistic mode and not necessarily the individual focus of the gallery. Thus, some galleries which exhibit many styles may be found in several listings. Some, but not all, of the galleries which are listed under a specialization are classified on the basis of excellence in that respective area, rather than for the size of their collections.

American:

contemporary: Archway, Arena Art Gallery, Circle, Cronin, Rachel W. Davis, Davis McClain, DuBose, F.A.M.E., Gibson-Riley, Graham, Harris, Hooks-Epstein, James-Atkinson, Jones, Kaufman, Koski-Long, Lee, Long, M.E.'s, Meier, Meinhard, Millioud, Moody, Robinson, Watson/de Nagy, Wurzer

periods: Rachel W. Davis, James-Atkinson, Long, Meinhard, Rice, Sotheby's

European & other continents:

contemporary: Atelier, Duveen, F.A.M.E., Graham, Hooks-Epstein, Kaufman, Meinhard

periods: Duveen, James-Atkinson, Meinhard, Millioud, Rice, Sotheby's

Graphics:

contemporary: Atelier, Circle, DuBose, F.A.M.E., Marjorie Kaufman, Off the Wall Graphics, Post Oak Fine Arts, Wurzer

periods: Millioud, Wurzer

Sculpture: Brush Gallery

Photography: Mancini

Primitive/Ancient: Balene, Collins

Western & Native American: Meinhard, Pritchard, Random Canyon

Houston
The Galleries by Location

The Galleria: Brush, Circle, Marjorie Kaufman Graphics, Pritchard, Wurzer

Montrose/Near Town: Harris, Hooks-Epstein, Jones, Mancini, M.E.'s, Robinson, Watson/de Nagy

Post Oak Road: F.A.M.E., Meinhard, Post Oak Fine Art, Robert Rice

River Oaks: Balene, Cronin, Davis/McClain, DuBose, James-Atkinson, Kaufman, Long, Moody, Sotheby Park Bernet

Southwest: Arena Gallery, Off the Wall Graphics

West Central: Collins, Millioud

West University Vicinity: Archway, Atelier, Davis, Graham, Lee, Meier

Outlying: Duveen (Woodlands), Gibson-Riley, Koski-Long, Random Canyon

Archway Gallery   2517 University Blvd.   Houston 77005   **Archway**
(713) 522-2409   Monday-Saturday: 10-5:30

Archway Gallery is a partnership of regionally and nationally recognized professional artists. The gallery opened in 1976 and moved to its present location in August 1980. A wide variety of original abstract and representational art is available: paintings in oil, watercolor, acrylic, and collage; drawings in ink, charcoal, and pastels; sculptures in bronze, terracotta, and stone; pottery in raku, porcelain, and stoneware; fibers in felted and woven compositions; wood reliefs and Eskimo stone carvings.

Archway painters offer a wide variety of style and media. June Adler does large abstract oils and watercolors; Dae-Duck Cha combines airbrush and fine brush work for an over-all effect of realistic/surrealistic representation in both acrylic and watercolor; Judy Richardson Gard concentrates primarily on impressionistic watercolors and acrylics and figure paintings; Stephanie Nadolski combines watercolors and metallics on a textural rice-paper collage surface to create exciting abstracts and semi-abstracts. She is also well known for her finely detailed oil and watercolor landscapes. Fiber artists include Mary Jean Fowler who specializes in weavings and stitchery reflecting her interpretations of her environment, and Marlean MacDougal who does felt compositions both abstract and semi-abstract in nature.

Sculpture is by Carma Anderson who does innovative latex-concrete pieces as well as abstract and semi-abstract bronzes, terracotta, and stone, and Ann Armstrong who specializes in sculptural portrait commissions in bronze and terracotta. Ron Vellucci does intricately pieced wood reliefs in both rough and polished finishes. Potters include Jo Zider whose primary emphasis is on raku cylinders and wall pieces and Ann Lee who specializes in beautifully colored glazes on stoneware and porcelain.

The gallery is also one of the few sources in Houston for Eskimo stone carvings.

Arena Art Gallery   7322 Southwest Freeway #110   Houston 77074 (713) 271-8818   Monday-Friday: 10-6

Owner-director Lillian Blakesley opened Arena Art Gallery in 1981. The gallery specializes in the exhibition and sale of original works by professional Houston artists in particular and Texas artists in general. Original paintings, drawings, sculpture, and other multimedia works are on display. The gallery also deals in Western art by artists from all over the country.

Styles range from traditional through abstract. Some of the more important artists shown are David Hickman, Bo Newell, Ron Ratliff, Beth Eidelberg, and Ron Arena. Hickman's "Nightgarden" series portrays the colorist's specialties in a realistic style. Bo Newell, a wildlife artist, handles the brush in an incomparable fashion. Ron Ratliff paints with great intensity in a true abstract style. Beth Eidelberg's delicate watercolors blend the past with the present to formulate a strong statement. Ron Arena paints in the traditional style with a Taos-school influence. Of course no gallery can ignore the presently popular Western influence—let alone one in Texas.

The gallery holds two guest artist shows annually. Artists who have been invited include Don C. Smith, George Marks and Bill Moyer of the Cowboy Artists of America, Wayne Baize, and others.

Atelier 1513   2530 Time Blvd.   Houston 77005   (713) 522-7988 Tuesday-Saturday: 11-5 and by appointment to the trade

Atelier 1513 aims to be a working studio as well as a sophisticated print gallery featuring works of contemporary European artists. Two large rooms downstairs are devoted to continuous exhibits of prints in original editions only.

The unique combination of gallery/workshop enables the visitor to learn firsthand about original editions and avoid the heartache of purchasing a print that is nothing more than a fine-quality offset reproduction.

Ceramic sculpture by the owner, Marie Leterme, is also shown, demonstrating better than words the unique relationship of her works in clay to those on paper. Emphasis is placed on texture and relief with very luminous, warm colors.

Four times a year special exhibits are organized to show the work of visiting artists who are not necessarily printmakers themselves, although on that occasion the artists are given the opportunity to produce one or more series of etchings.

Etching classes are held upstairs, and press time is available for lease to artists who do not have the equipment to produce their own editions.

Balene, Inc.   2005 West Gray   Houston 77019   (713) 523-2304   # Balene
Monday-Friday: 12-5

This new addition to the Houston art scene, opened in March of
1981, represents a culmination of sorts for owner Balene
McCormick, who has been collecting primitive art for some twenty
years. The primitive art shown is from West Africa, the Southwest
United States, and Pre-Columbian Mexico and Central America.

A visit to a show organized around the theme "birds and beasts"
revealed marvelously beaded, eerie elephant masks from the
Cameroons; prehistoric pottery of the Southwest produced by
vanished tribes such as the Formile, Mimbers, Hohokam, Soccoro
and Tularosa; human- and animal-shaped pottery jugs from the
Colima people of pre-Columbian west-central-coast Mexico, and a
number of other artifacts.

Additional items found in the gallery include excellent
examples of Southwestern Indian rugs and blankets ranging in
vintage from 1850 to 1930; turn-of-the-century Apache baskets;
silver and turquoise concho belts, bracelets and necklaces from
the 1930s to the present; Acoma and Zia tribe pottery from the
historical past of the Southwest; a superb century-old Tlingit
weaving from the Pacific Northwest coast; a Mayan pottery head;
and some contemporary examples of Southwestern Indian pottery
and basketmaking.

All of the items are of very high quality and beautifully
displayed in a spare, subdued setting. Although the price range is
reflective of the rarity of many of the pieces, a visit here is
worthwhile for the student or afficionado of primitive art as well as
for the serious collector.

Brush Gallery   5015 Westheimer Road, Suite 3197, The Galleria   # Brush
Houston 77056   (713) 961-0033   Monday, Wednesday, Saturday: # Gallery
10-5; Thursday and Friday: 10-9

It should first be said that the Brush Gallery sells very few
paintings. The gallery derives its name from its owners, the
sculptor Arthur Charles "Chuck" Brush and his wife Kathy. The
main thrust is contemporary sculpture, by Mr. Brush, and a group
of Texas and Southwestern artists. A friendly, comfortable place
tucked at the end of a corridor on the third level of the Galleria
mall, Brush Gallery began in 1977 and has expanded
considerably in the last year.

Most of the artists shown are either Texans or New Mexicans
from the Parnassian terrain around Santa Fe. One of the featured
artists is Amado Maurillo Pena, Jr., a Texas artist working in
Austin who is known for his serigraphs and etchings of mestizo
women and traditional family life. Bob Boomer is a California
sculptor who carves his state's native manzanita wood, cedar and
walnut into studies of Indians. Larry Young is a sculptor who

creates smooth, soaring abstract shapes in bronze and marble. Candace Knapp of Houston carves bas-relief screens and three-dimensional pieces depicting Indian faces and mythical animals out of smoothly laminated wood. Richard Erdman creates light, fluid shapes out of marble and more exotic stones such as Pakistan onyx and alabaster. Excellent-quality small bronzes of mythical animals and of marine mammals are available from the Santa Fe artist, Norman Boyles, and the California artist, Rebecca Sylvan, respectively. Carolyn Sale produces abstract slab work pottery forms in raku fired clay with glazed markings. Kay Ritter produces humorous fabric mache caricatures of old women, flappers and other in nearly life-size sculptures, a sort of comic Duane Hanson.

Painters represented by the Brush Gallery in Houston include the work of Chicago-based satirical realist Aaron Bohrod, photo realist portraitist Robert Cox of Texas, and Western historical portraitist Francis Woodahl, who paints meticulous oils of cowpokes and Indian persons. The gallery also displays magnificent mineral specimens from around the world.

The Brush Gallery now incorporates art of the former Frank Wood Gallery.

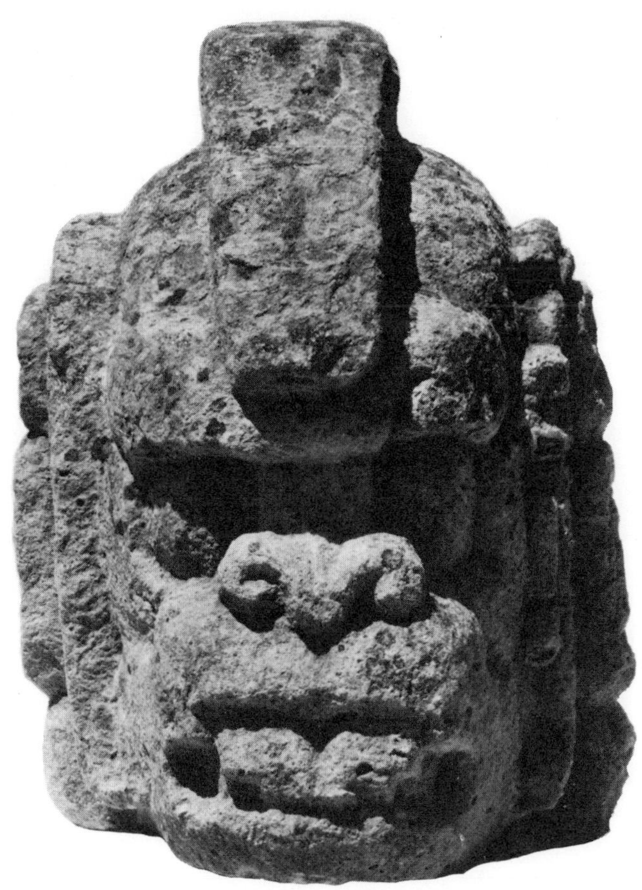

Mayan (from Copan), *Ahau,* 18" x 14", andesite stone. Lowell Collins Gallery.

Circle Gallery, Ltd.   5085 Westheimer Road, Suite 2895, The Galleria   Houston 77056   (713) 961-7241   Monday-Friday: 10-9; Saturday: 10-6

This gallery, formerly known as the Magic Circle Gallery, is a branch office of the largest commercial gallery chain in the world. The Circle Gallery company is headquartered in Chicago and has forty-six branches around the world. This branch is located in a large space on the second level of Houston's reknowned Galleria mall. Dorothy Burris is the gallery director.

This gallery displays the works of artists, photographers and commercial illustrators in little alcoves subdivided out of the total space, an unusual arrangement in the art world but well suited to this establishment's highly commercial style. A visit revealed displays of such varied talents as the octogenarian Russian emigre fashion illustrator Erte, the color photography of Robert Varga (who is known for his photos of wild horses), the illustrations and prints of Norman Rockwell, the psychedelic silkscreens of Peter Max, and the hard-edge abstractions of Israeli printmaker Yaakov Agam. In addition, there are small sculptures and art jewelry on display. For those with an interest in the best commercial art, a visit here is always rewarding. Receptions for individual artists are held about once a month to launch new editions of prints and photographs.

Lowell Collins Gallery   2903 Saint Street   Houston 77027 (713) 622-6962   Tuesday-Saturday: 11-5

Located in a yellow steel building on a leafy side street off of the 3600 block of Westheimer Road, Lowell Collins Gallery is a fascinating place to visit for anyone interested in antique ethnic art and classical antiquities from every corner of the world. Owner Lowell Collins and his son preside over a three-part enterprise that trades in ethnic art, provides appraisals for insurance and various estate purposes, and has an attached art school.

While the gallery is particularly strong in pre-Columbian and Mesoamerican art and artifacts, there are also many fascinating items of South American, Korean, West African, Chinese, Tibetan, Oceanic and Sepik River, New Guinea provenance. In the European area, there are classical items from Greece and Rome, Byzantine icons, and even some early Renaissance items.

Mr. Collins is a Senior Member of the American Society of Appraisers, with a specialty rating in Fine Arts. Both he and his son are members of the International Society of Appraisers. Depending on the client's needs, the gallery provides written and/or oral appraisals on a fee basis, by the item ($125.00 minimum), by the hour, or per diem. Scheduled appraisals for insurance purposes are also supplied.

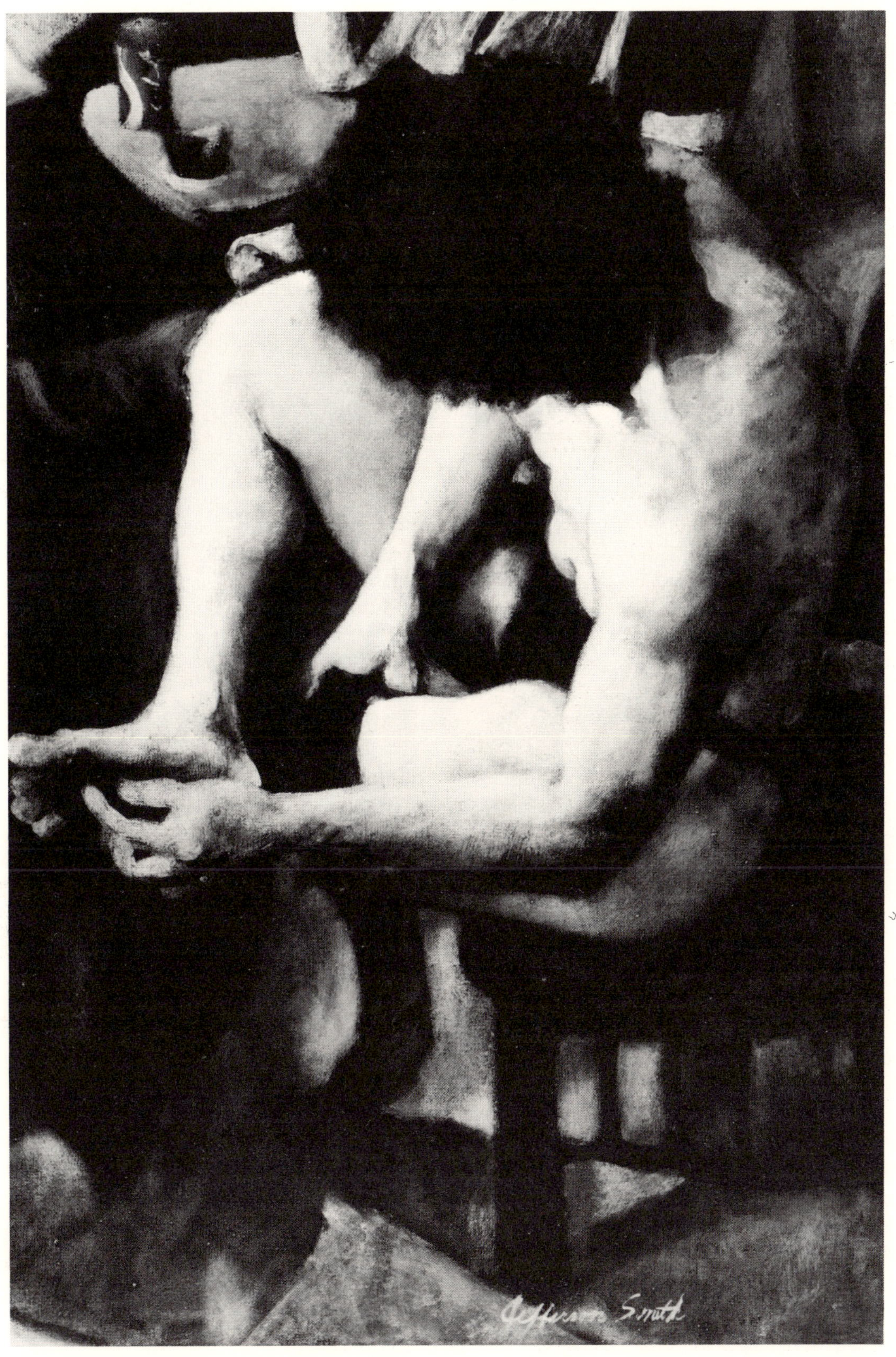

Jefferson Smith, *In the Dressing Room*, 22″ x 30″, oil on canvas. Rachel W. Davis Gallery.

The school offers classes for adults and children in life drawing, painting and design during the days and evenings. In addition, there are Pre-Columbian history lessons taught by Mr. Collins, who has spent much time traveling in Mexico and Central America.

Robin Cronin, Inc.   2008 Peden   Houston 77019   (713) 526-2548   Tuesday-Saturday: 10-5; closed in August

Robin Cronin, Inc. is the latest development in the six-year history of the Cronin Gallery. After specializing for a number of years in twentieth-century American photography, the gallery will now extend its focus to contemporary painting, sculpture, and photography.

The gallery handles the work of contemporary California artists such as Lita Albuquerque, Laddie John Dill, Steve Kahn, and Ron Cooper, who are painters, sculptors, and photographers. Kahn and Cooper's photographic work will be the focus of a special exhibition. Figurative painters Jim Sullivan and Derek Boshier will also be represented by the gallery. Continuing in the tradition of photography the gallery will continue to exhibit the photographs of Gay Block, Sally Gall, and the collaborative team, Manual. Ed Grazda of New York City will continue to be represented by Robin Cronin, Inc.

Following in the new direction of the gallery will be a number of shows featuring artists from California, New York, and Texas whose works deal with similar tasks and problems. Installation pieces and performance works are scheduled for the gallery's 1982 season.

Robin Cronin, Inc. is divided into three exhibition areas. The initial entry into the gallery is an introduction to the two main gallery rooms. Preliminary works, drawings, or studies fill the entry space to the gallery. The two large exhibition spaces with the vast height of the gallery ceiling respond equally well to large paintings or sculpture. Photographs in intimate groupings are equally comfortable in the gallery's exhibition spaces.

Rachel W. Davis Gallery   2402 Addison St.   Houston 77030 (713) 664-4130   Monday-Friday: 10-4, (by appointment)

Rachel W. Davis Gallery specializes in American art of the twentieth century. Focusing on figurative works, the gallery is situated in a unique courtyard building near Rice University.

The gallery has a special interest in the artists of the American Realist School, especially those who worked between World War I and World War II. Artists such as Sloan, Bacon, Lewis, Landeck, and Lozowick are among those available.

Local and national artists who currently work from the same

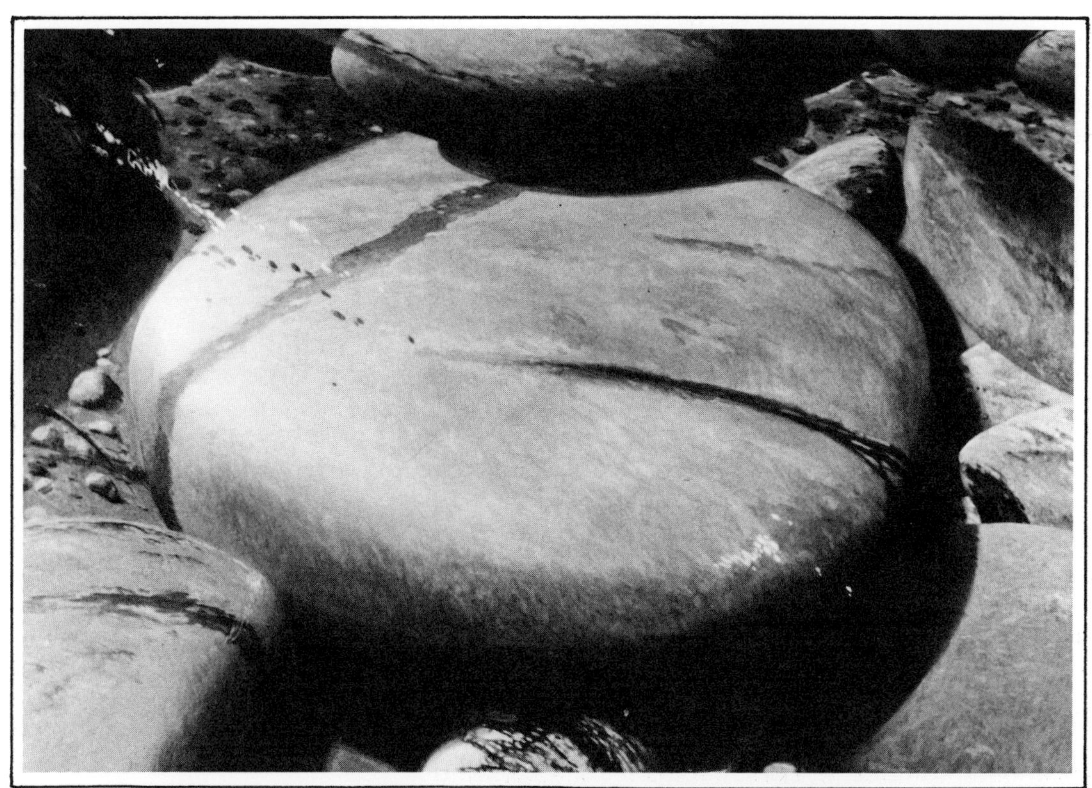

Bill Shepard, *Flat Bi-Lateral Rock,* oil on canvas. Davis McClain Galleries.

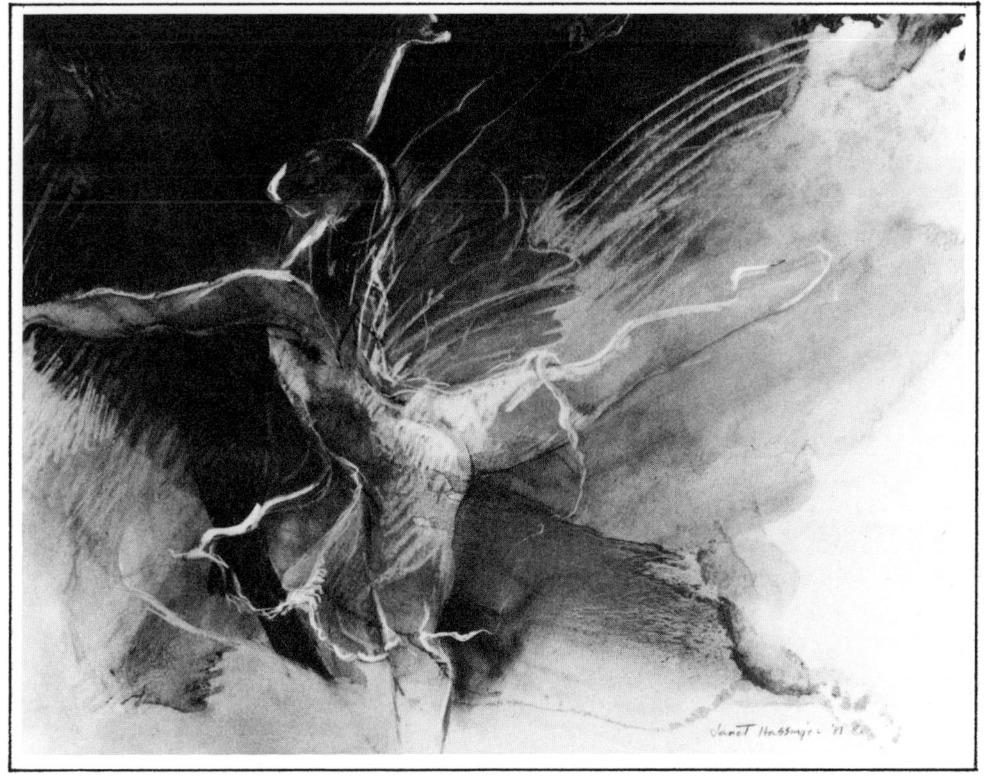

Janet Hassinger, *Titania,* 22″ x 30″, pastel. Rachel W. Davis Gallery.

point of view are also featured in the gallery. Pastels, paintings, and sculpture are the primary mediums shown. Gallery artists include: Houstonians Janet Hassinger and Jefferson Smith, New Yorkers Louis A'Davila and Rick Harrison; Fort Worth artist Daniel Blagg; Minnesota artist Ann Royer, and Bernard Greenwald of New Haven. Steel sculptures by Bill Heise of Vermont are also featured.

The gallery is particularly interested in combining the visual arts with the performing arts. Each spring a special exhibition is held to show the relationship between the two art forms. Examples include performances of dancers with an exhibition of drawings on the subject and an exhibition based on the works played at a piano recital at the gallery. Rachel W. Davis gallery also provides lectures and tours for visiting groups.

Davis/McClain Galleries   2818 Kirby Drive   Houston 77098
(713) 520-9200   Monday-Friday: 10-5:30; Saturday: 11-4

Davis/McClain

Owners Barbara Davis and Bob McClain are committed to introducing a variety of emerging regional and national artists. Though emphasis is on the contemporary work being done in painting, sculpture, photography, and printmaking, they also offer substantial traditional works suitable for collectors and corporations.

An area of concentration is color-field. Foremost examples are Anne Vaccaro and Dean Gillette, who combine color-field and action painting; Larry Flukinger and Clark Harrah, who explore color with neon sculpture.

Sheila Zeve deals with color in a soft lyrical style with large stained canvases. Contemporary realism is strongly represented by P.S. Sheldon who does Southwest landscapes and cowboys with a Fauvist use of bright, strong colors. Nancy Conrad's landscapes combine painterly strokes and airbrush.

Woody Gwyn's superrealist Western landscapes are truncated by sleek, shadowy highways. Bill Shepherd's paintings are realistic closeups of rocks and water that are at once landscapes and abstract representations of light and form. Tom Berg paints landscapes as a backdrop for scenes of pools and poolside settings.

Fine art photography is another area of concentration. Blue-chip photographers such as Brett Weston, as well as promising regional photographers Gary Faye and J. Barry Thomson, deal with abstractions in nature. Bob Brewer's abstractions in nature are printed in color.

Three exhibition spaces allow a variety of works to be shown. A print room features decorative original prints as well as name collectibles. The rear gallery often features fiber and clay works.

DuBose Gallery   2950 Kirby   Houston 77098   (713) 526-4916   # DuBose
Monday-Friday: 9-5:30; Saturday: 11-4:30

DuBose Gallery has been opened for fifteen years and is one of
Houston's oldest and largest galleries. A variety of contemporary
paintings, graphics, and sculptures are shown.

The contemporary work ranges from abstract paintings to more
traditional landscapes. Charles Schorre, Robert Weimerskirch,
Herb Mears, and David Adickes represent the variety of abstract
paintings shown. The more representational approach of Kermit
Oliver, Ellen Soderquist, and Brad Braune is another important
aspect of the gallery.

A recent addition is the newly remodeled print room. The
fantasy imagery of Don Allison's color etchings and the well-
known works of such artists as Appel, Baskin, Friedlander, and
Vasarely are outstanding examples.

A selection of stone, wood, and brass sculptures are also shown.
James Groff works with stone to create his freely flowing abstract
sculptures. David Anderson and Bob Holsch also work with
abstract shapes. Anderson works with metals and acrylics and
Holsch with wood.

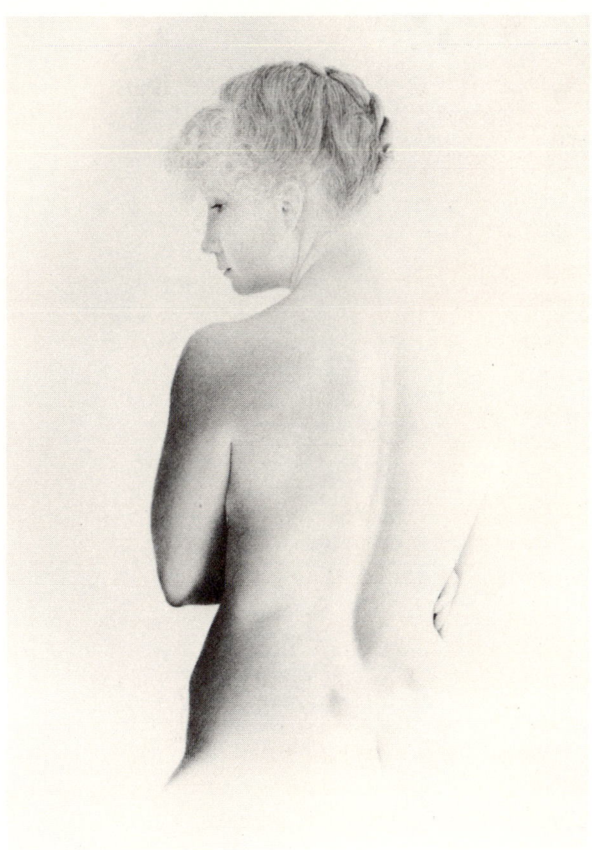

Ellen Soderquist, *Lucia II,* graphite on paper.
DuBose Gallery.

Duveen Inc.   The Wharf Shopping Mall P.O. Box 7463   The
Woodlands   (713) 367-3659   Monday: 1-5; Tuesday-Friday:
10-5; Saturday: 10-3

Director-owner Peggy R. Duveen opened the gallery in December
1978. Works shown are both European and American, although
European nineteenth- and twentieth-century works are the
gallery's main interest. Peggy Duveen was born and raised in
Amsterdam and studied five years in Brussels. Her main interests
are art restoration and history.

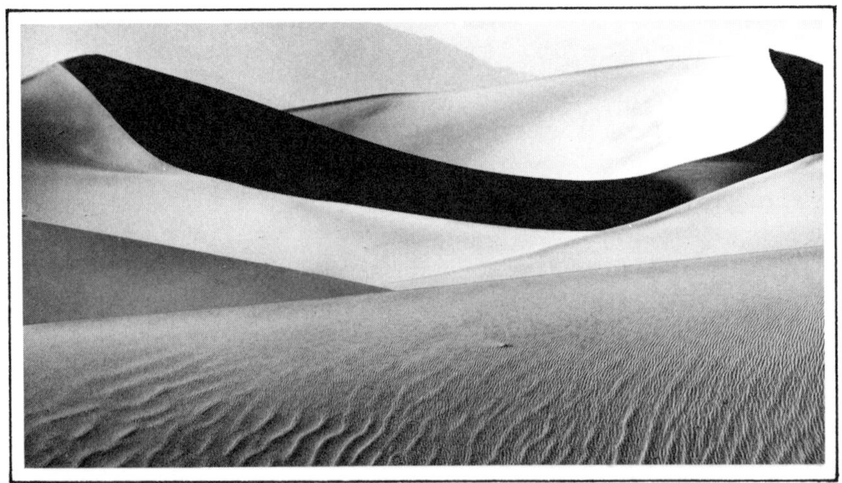

Gary Faye, *Sand Dune, Death Valley,* 10¼" x 19¾" Photograph. Davis
McClain Gallery.

Most of the works are representational, with an emphasis on
figurative paintings. Among them are oil pastels on canvas by
Flemish artists Renee Monnoye and Nicholas. Also shown is Paris's
famous Saidi, who executed murals and oils on canvas of an
elegance seldom seen. Masterpieces by Dutch Dirk Kruizinga
(1894-1972) are still-life oils on canvas (collection Rijksmuseum,
Amsterdam).

Beautiful abstracts by the famous Belgian artist Jean Rigaux, the
Western realism of Gerald Collins, and French Impressionist-
style paintings by Pierre Doyen are secondary areas of
concentration.

Young artist David Headrick works in mixed media and
watercolors, mostly with sports subjects, but with a unique style
and technique.

A small part of the gallery is reserved for top-quality Delft-blue
china and Gouda Plateel.

Peggy Duveen also works in the gallery on restorations of old
paintings and brokers investment-quality art from private
collections.

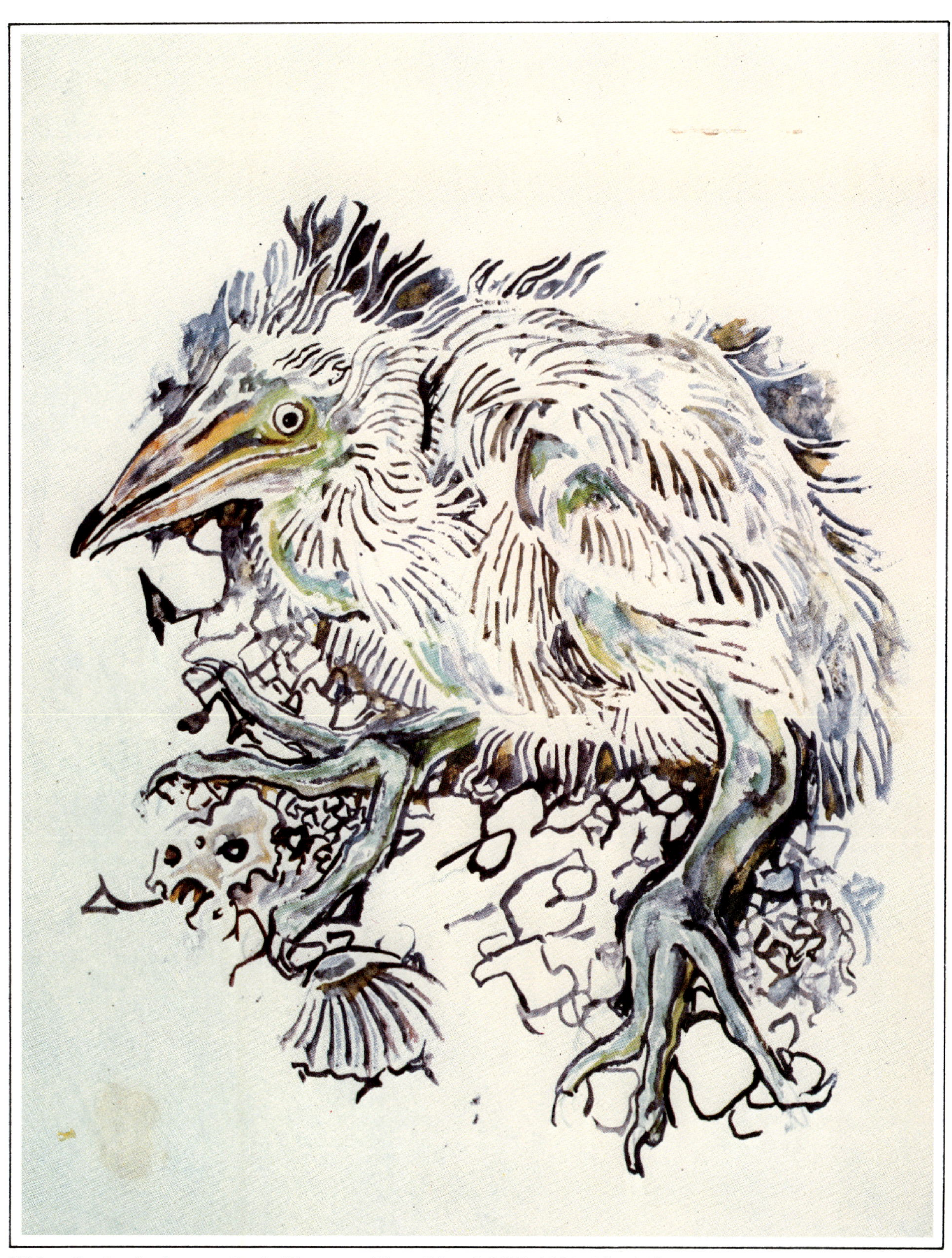

Walter Inglis Anderson, *Little Heron on Horn Island,* 1950-1960, 8'' x 11'', watercolor. Rachel W. Davis Gallery.

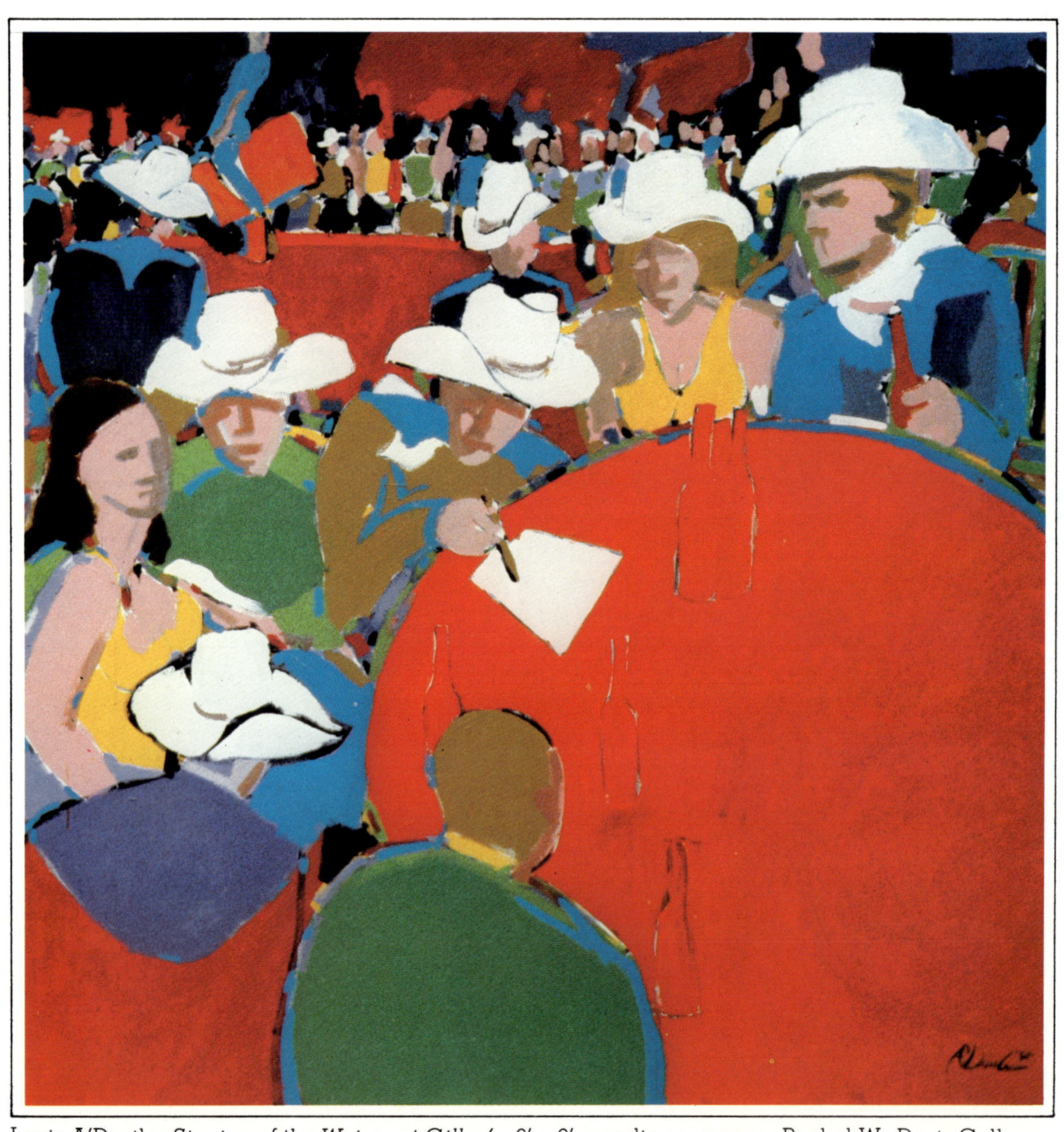

Louis A'Davila, *Signing of the Waiver at Gilley's*, 6' x 6', acrylic on canvas. Rachel W. Davis Gallery.

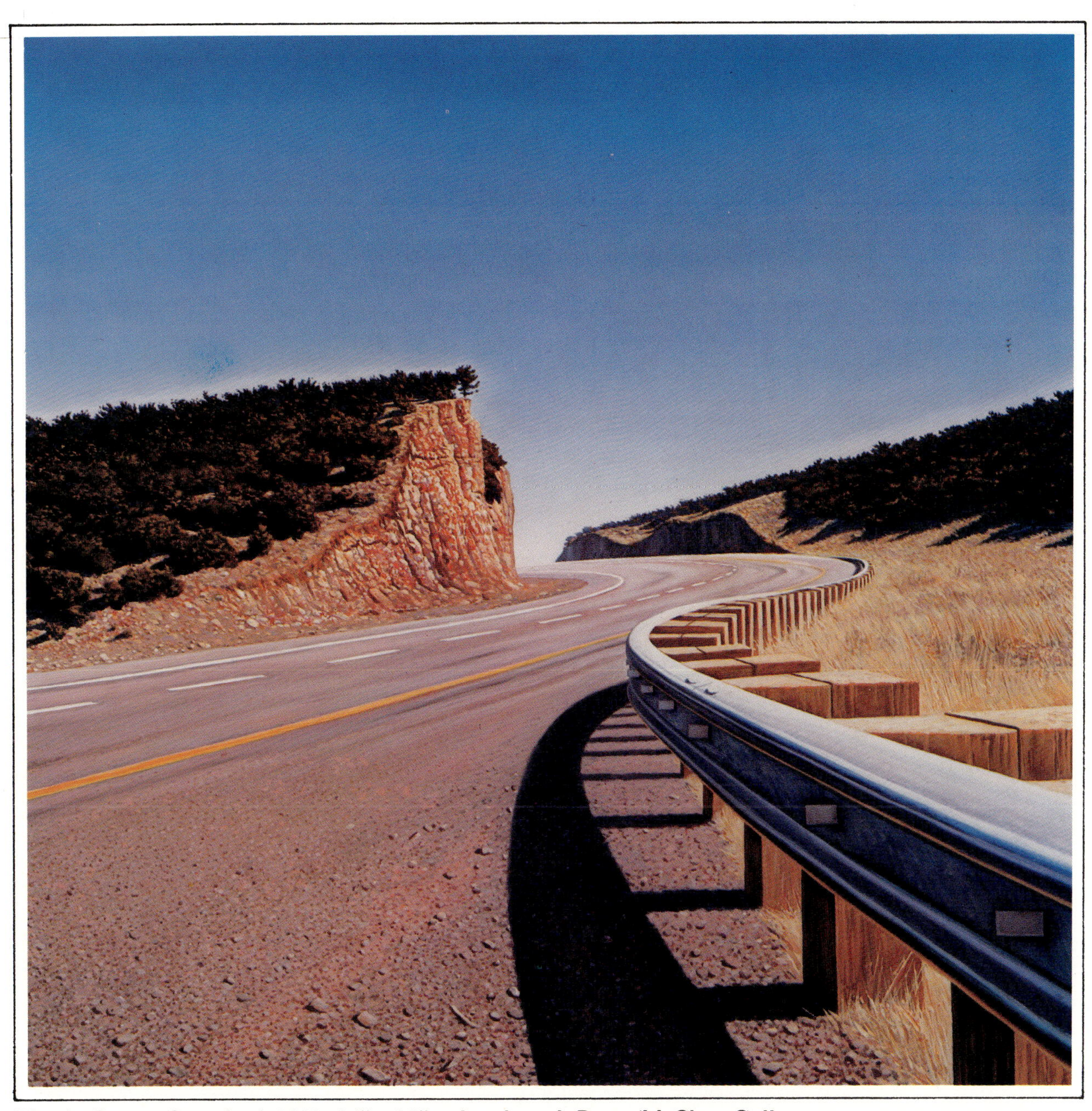

Woody Gwyn, *Guardrail,* 1981, 24″ x 24″, oil on board. Davis/McClain Gallery.

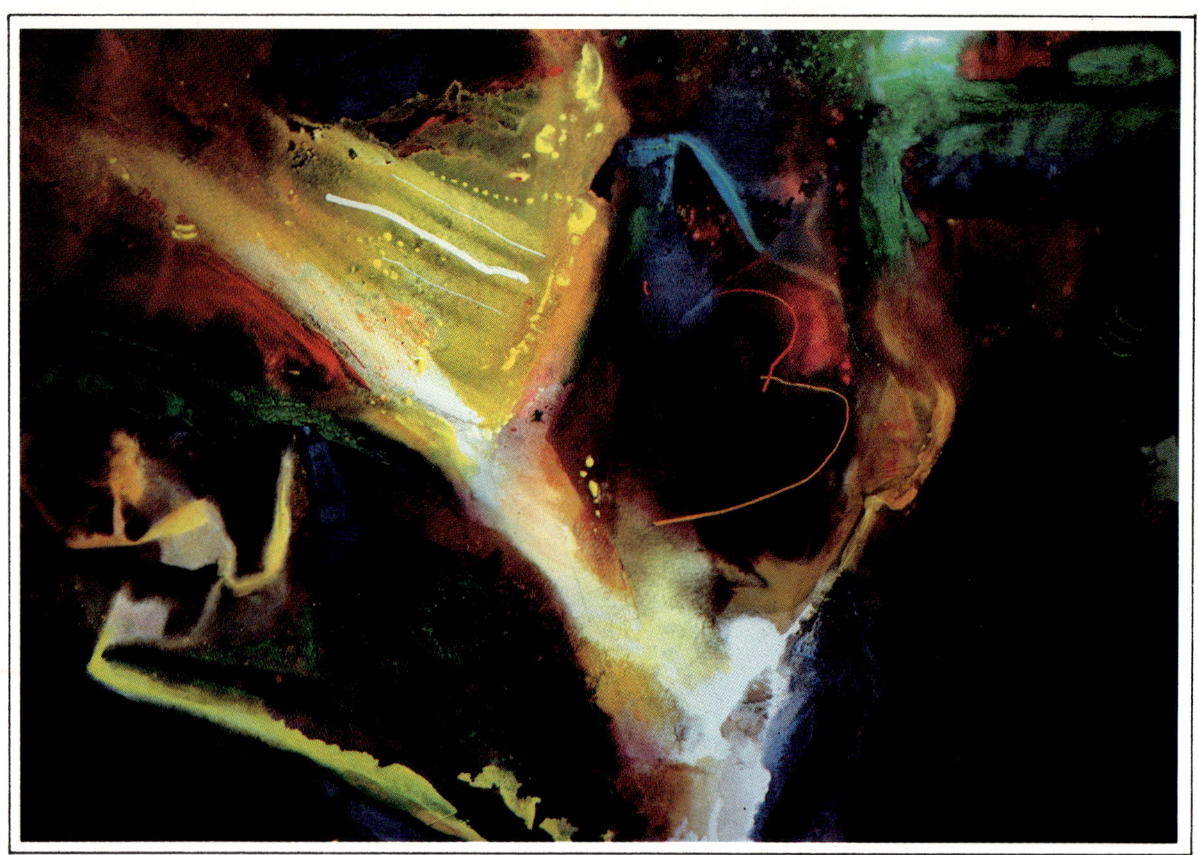

Charles Shorre, *LAZ 3,* 58″ x 90″, oil and acrylic on canvas. DuBose Galleries.

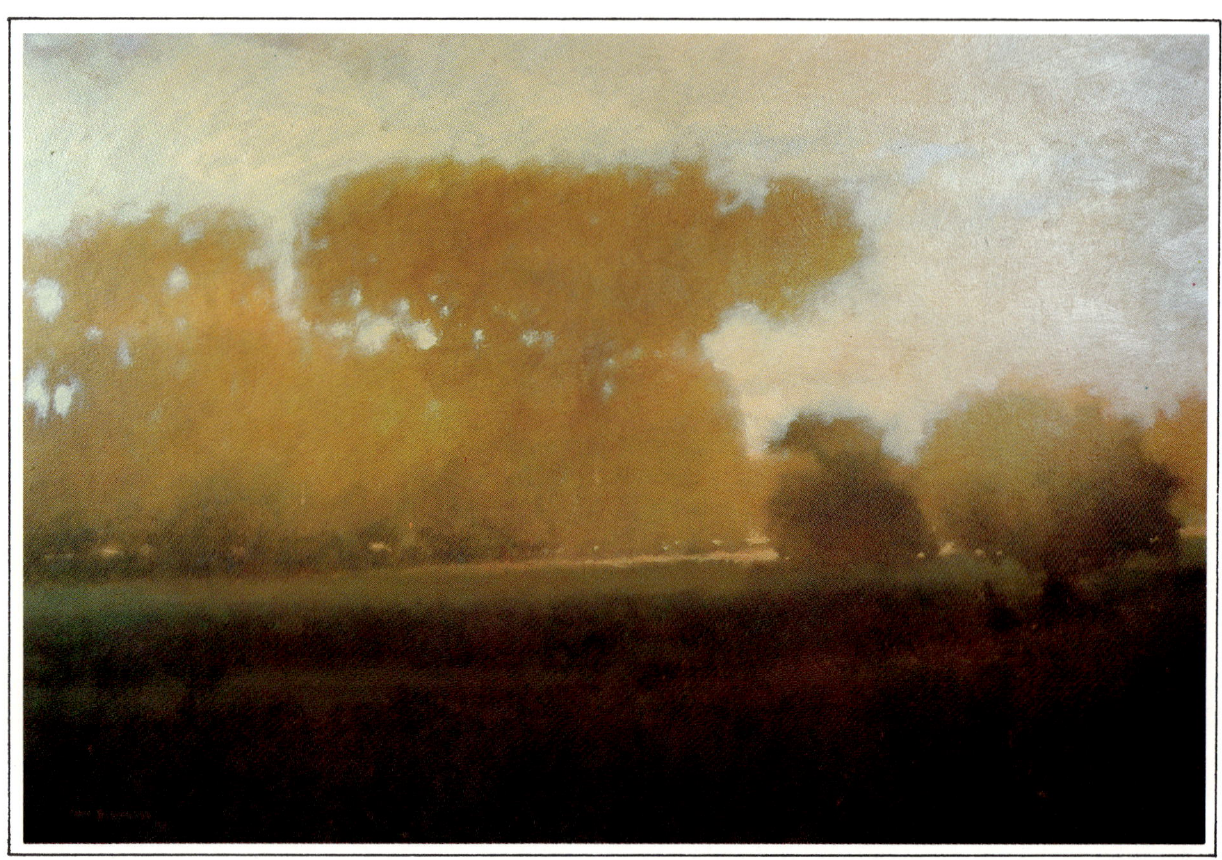

Chris Burkholder, *October Light,* 24″ x 36″, acrylic on canvas. Harris Gallery.

F.A.M.E. Gallery   1980 Post Oak Blvd.   Houston 77056
(713) 627-7024   Monday-Friday: 10-5; (other times by appointment)

As publishers/distributors of limited-edition prints, F.A.M.E. has issued more than 70 separate editions by leading contemporary artists of America and Europe. Its showroom has been open to the public since 1980 as a marketplace for paintings and prints. Special exhibits of jewelry and sculpture are also featured.

Prints by Picasso, Miro, Chagall, Dubuffet, Matisse, Lichtenstein, and others are offered for sale. Among the contemporary prints are Romare Bearden's scenes from the rural south; cityscapes by photorealists John Baeder, Tom Blackwell, Fran Bull, Ron Kleeman, Richard McLean, and C.J. Yao; abstract works by Larry Zox and Conrad Marca-Relli; and Western subjects by Conrad Schwiering and Frank Wootton.

New this year is a six-print mural of Manhattan by Mori Shizume —a dramatic 360-degree view from the Waldorf-Astoria. Michel de Saint-Alban's lovely oils and serigraphs offer Impressionist scenes of the French countryside.

Selected nineteenth-century oils and watercolors by leading Victorian artists include such names as Benjamin Williams Leader and John Ritchie, whose landscapes and architectural scenes are admired for their outstanding draftsmanship.

Finally, lighted-glass display cases feature changing exhibits of gold and silver sculpture and jewelry, art glass, and art greeting cards. A color catalog of contemporary prints is available by contacting the gallery.

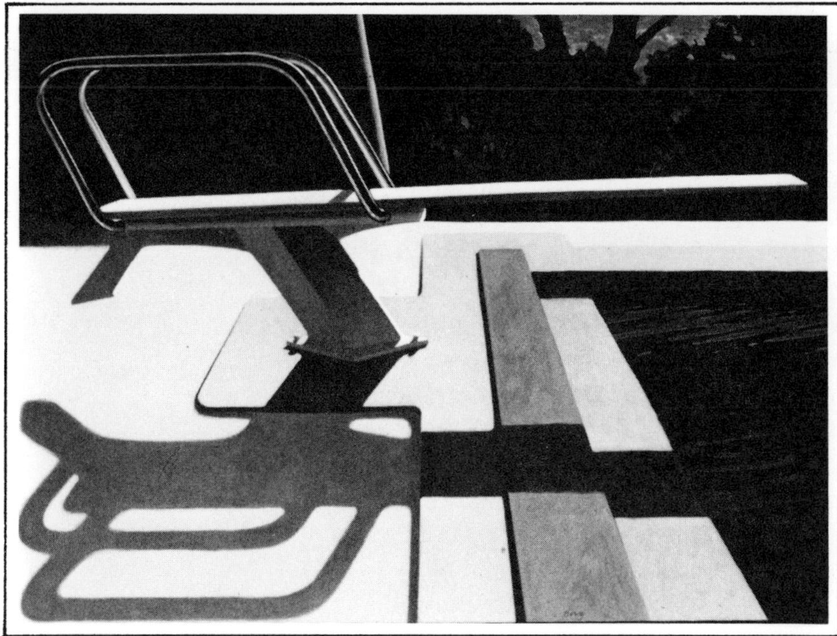

Tom Berg, *Landscape with Diving Board,* 56" x 76" oil on canvas. Davis McClain Gallery.

Gibson-Riley Gallery   1027 Bay Area Blvd.   Houston 77058
(713) 486-0828   Monday-Friday: 10-6; Saturday: 10-4

Gibson-
Riley

Gibson-Riley Gallery opened in October 1977 in the NASA-Clear Lake area of Houston. The gallery offers a wide selection of paintings and graphics. Included are original works by Paul Maxwell, Guillaume Azoulay, Paula Crane, Charles Bragg, Marcus Uzilevsky, and Arthur Secunda. Gallery artists featured include watercolorist Shirley Sterling, traditional impressionist Dearon Bailey, and sports artist Don Boyer.

Well-known Texas artists Robert Summers, G. Harvey, Larry Dyke, and Dalkart Windberg are represented in limited-edition prints, as are many nationally known artists, both contemporary and traditional.

Gallery shows are held approximately three times each year.

Professional craftsmanship in conservation framing and unique design are specialties here.

Graham Gallery   2411 Bartlett   Houston 77098   (713) 528-4957
Tuesday-Saturday: 10-6

Graham

In 1969 William Graham assumed the direction of a gallery in New York City and for one year worked with art and artists living and working in the New York area and in Paris. In 1970 Graham moved to Paris and opened his own gallery in which he exhibited contemporary Europeans, primarily Frenchmen and Paris-based painters and sculptors, and American artists from the New York area. The Graham Gallery is one of Houston's newest.

Although the gallery exhibits contemporary painting from both America and Europe, it concentrates on Southwestern and Texas artists, both figurative and abstract. Abstract and "new figuration" painters such as Brian Mains, Ron Hoover, and Perry House; assemblagist-sculptors such as Charles Rutynowski, Gertrude Barnstone, and Vicy Barnett; and photographers Alain Clement, and Peter McClennan are featured. Pat Musick, who paints abstract oils and watercolors, lyrical watercolorist Simone Bateman, abstract painter Sansy Heppenheimer, figurative watercolorist Hitch Lyman, video and graphic artist Andy Mann, and narrative painter Lee Brevard are also represented by the gallery. Modern European masters such as Man Ray (an American who lived and painted in Paris most of his life), Charles Lapicque, Aleco Fassianos, Rene Laubies, and other younger Europeans have been introduced to Houston through the Graham Gallery.

Original limited lithographs and engravings and drawings are also available, with concentration on modern European masters.

The gallery mounts regular exhibitions at approximately four-week intervals and is particularly interested in young American painters and photographers.

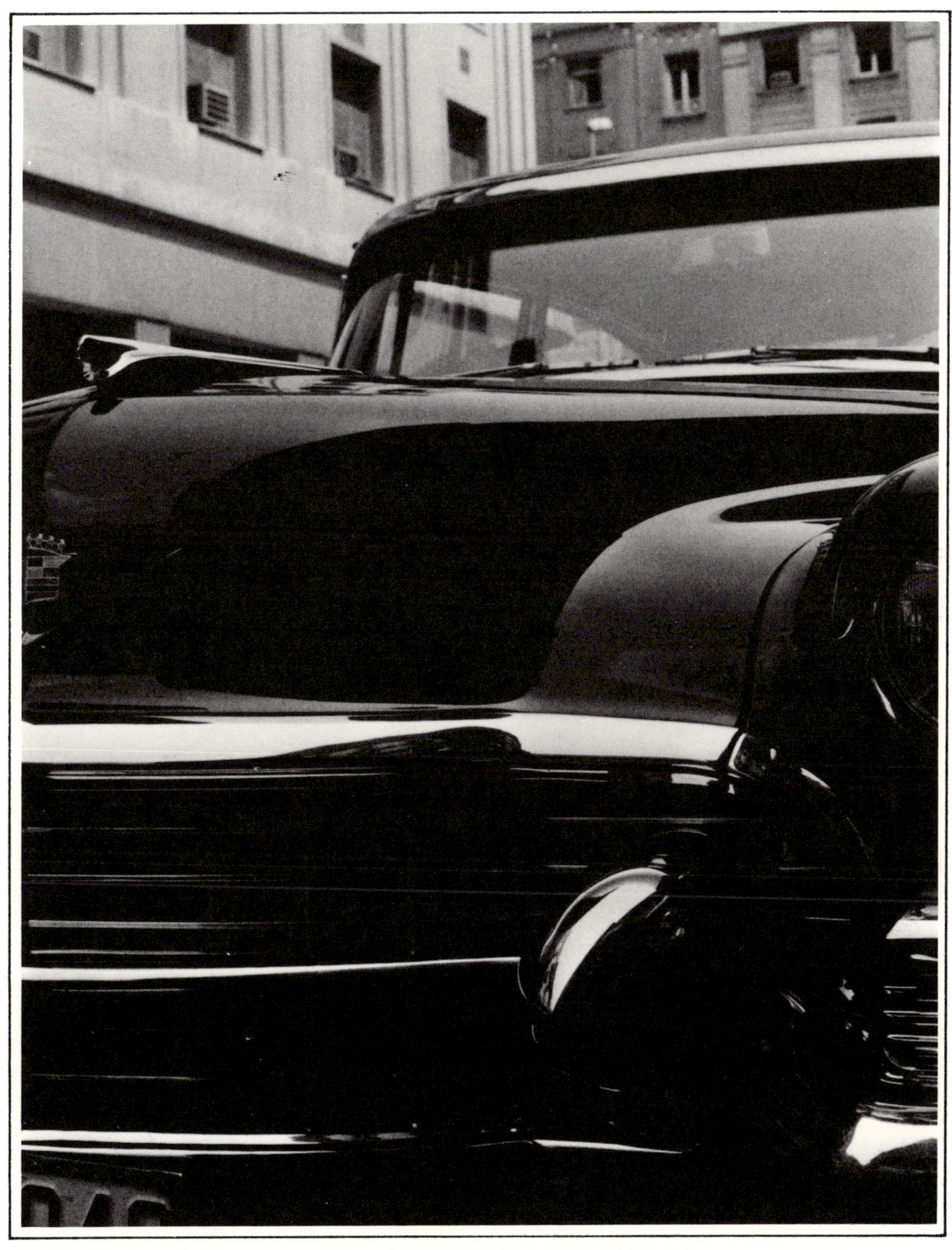

Alain Clement, *Cadillac*, 30″ x 24″, Silver Photograph. Graham Gallery.

Harris Gallery was established four years ago and recently relocated to a 4,000-square-foot house adjacent to the Contemporary Arts Museum.

Harris Gallery is more interested in a consistent high level of quality than in maintaining a "look" or attitude. In the past, the gallery has exhibited master prints by Rembrandt, Whistler, drawings and prints by Gene Davis, American Contemporary prints by Motherwell, Stella, Frankenthaler, Rauschenberg, Lichtenstein, etc., besides working with regional artists.

Texas artists include Pauline Howard, Linda Obermoeller, Chris Burkholder, Susan Smith, Mark Lavatelli, and Linda Graetz. Pauline Howard uses the figure as a basis for study of light and compositions. Her pastels and watercolors deal with ballet dancers, beach scenes, polo matches, and other situations that involve complex compositions of the human figure. Linda Obermoeller also works with watercolor, but her subjects tend to be focused in more of a portraiture attitude. The landscape of East Texas fascinates Chris Burkholder as he explores the light and atmosphere of the countryside peculiar to that area.

Employing the contemporary subject matter of high-fashion mannequins in store windows, Susan Smith paints dramatic tableaux that seem to comment on the quality of commercial attitudes in modern society. Linda Graetz and Mark Lavatelli work in the most abstract direction of the artists in the gallery. Graetz concentrates on space and landscape in her rich gouache paper paintings, whereas Lavatelli abstracts constructions of buildings and streets in his strong acrylic and collage compositions.

During the last year, Harris Gallery has been compiling a major inventory of contemporary landscape. Artists from all over the nation were included in a landscape exhibition, July 1981. Although each artist approached the landscape with a contemporary attitude, the work was diverse in every way possible. Ed Mell paints Southwestern canyons and valleys. He reduces the rock formations to geometric abstractions that vibrate with the hot/cool reds, oranges, blues, and purples of the desert. Using the sky as a panorama, Willard Dixon also paints the desert of Death Valley as it interplays with the clouds and space. The golden rolling hills of Central California are the subject matter of Don Irwin. Like the titles of his paper-painted works, he slices the ground into fragments only interrupted by spherical trees.

Off of the main gallery space is an area where rotating exclusive six-state-area basis (Arizona, Arkansas, Louisiana, New Mexico, Oklahoma, and, of course, Texas). They include the painter Hib Sabin and sculptors Jay Lefkowitz and Helen O. Gross. The gallery additionally shows such unusual mediums as rugs made after artists' designs by the Modern Masters Tapestries.

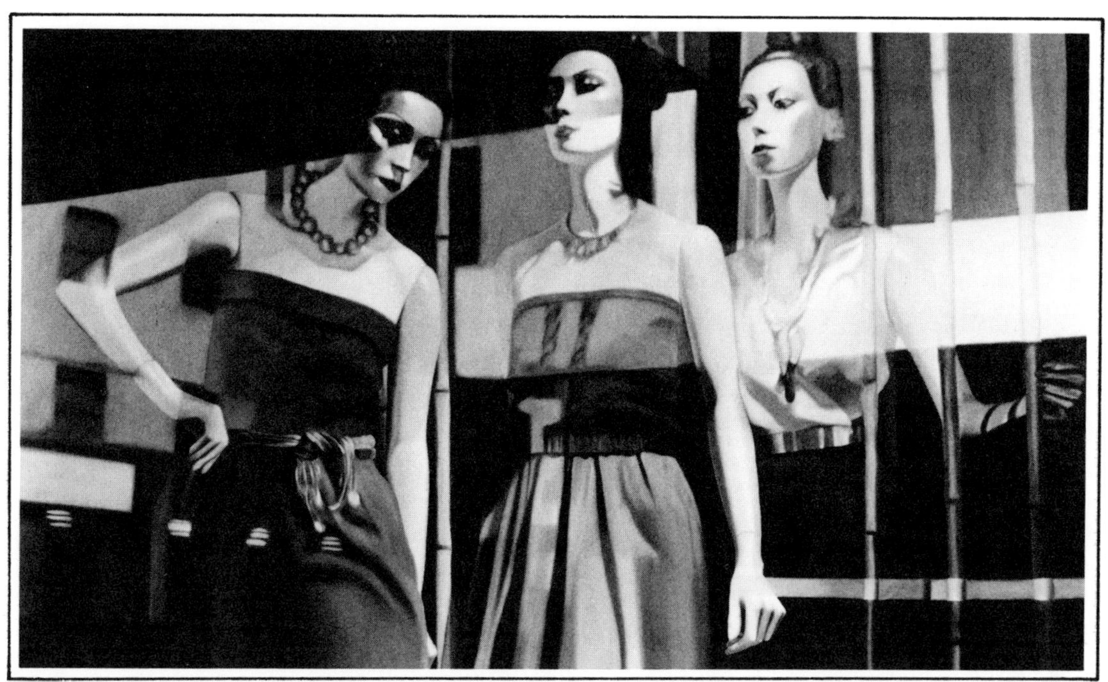

Susan Smith, *Caged,* 41″ x 72″, oil on canvas. Harris Gallery.

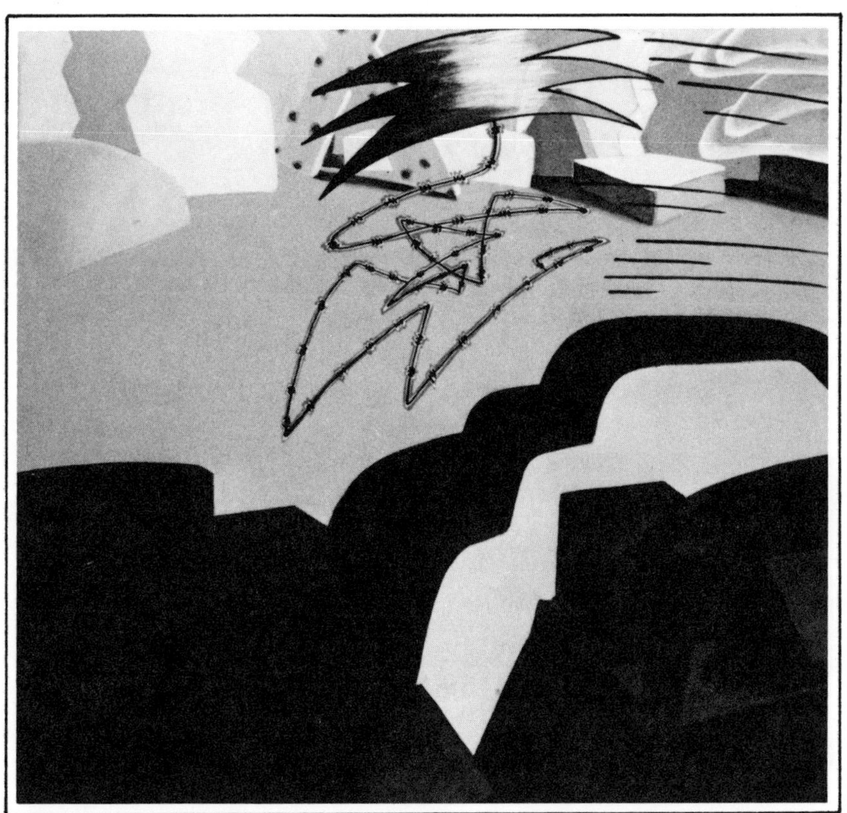

Perry House, *Untitled,* 42″ x 41″, acrylic on canvas. Graham
Gallery.

Hooks-Epstein Galleries, Inc.   1200 Bissonnet   Houston 77005
(713) 522-0718   Monday-Saturday: 11-5 (closed during the month
of August)

Hooks-Epstein

This gallery, located in a spacious old house two blocks down the
street from Houston's two art museums, was started in 1970 with the
idea of selling established artworks to established collectors in
Houston. Presided over by its owners, Charles and Geri Hooks,
the gallery today exhibits works on paper and sculpture primarily.
The emphasis is on late nineteenth- and twentieth-century
European artists with name recognition, such as Picasso, Miro,
Dubuffet and Baskin.

A group of some twelve to fifteen contemporary artists are also
represented by the gallery. The most important is the
Philadelphia-based painter and printmaker Peter Paone, who is
represented in the United States exclusively by Hooks-
Epstein. He is known for his wry, satirical figurative imagery, often
with a certain erotic flavor. Other artists are represented on an
exclusive six-state area basis (Arizona, Arkansas, Louisiana, New
Mexico, Oklahoma and, of course, Texas). They include the
painter Hib Sabin and the sculptors Jay Lefkowitz and Helen O.
Gross. The gallery additionally shows such unusual mediums as
rugs made after artists designs by the Modern Masters Tapestries
firm, Paone's tiny watercolors on ivory, and the jewelry of Anthony
Piazza. A new sideline is the representation of the estates of
deceased artists, such as the estate of the painter Kenneth Frazier
(1897-1949).

Hooks-Epstein has an exhibition policy of a new one- or
two-person show every six weeks, with a minimum of six shows a
year. Occasionally, a print show featuring a dozen artists or more
is presented. The gallery founded the Houston Art Dealers
Association, which now numbers twenty members, and
participates in their July "Introductions" show series which
presents new talent to the Houston market.

James-Atkinson Gallery   2015 W. Gray   Houston 77019
(713) 527-8061   Tuesday-Saturday: 10:30-4:30

James-Atkinson

Though small and unassuming, the gallery carries important works
from American and European schools of Impressionism. The
two-tiered gallery which looks much like a French salon was
founded by Paul Atkinson and his late wife Nancy James, both
private dealers in Lake Forest, Illinois, a suburb of Chicago.

Almost all the works are representational dealing with
American, British and French painters from the turn-of-the-
century. Some contemporary art is also shown including the works
of Robert Vickery and Gage Taylor. The gallery is mounting a
show of the paintings of Megan Bowman whose art is strongly

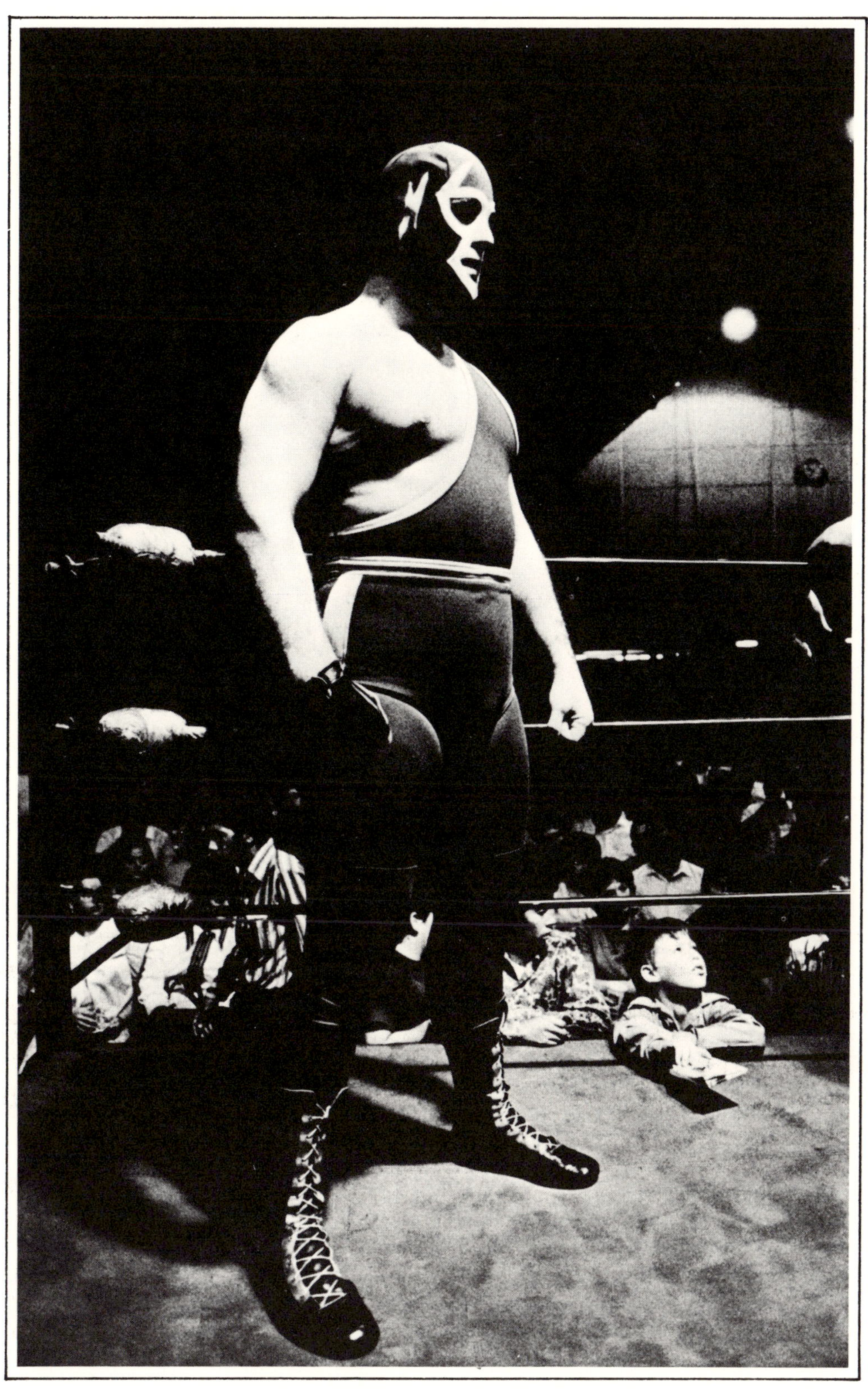

Geoff Winningham, *The Spoiler,* 20″ x 24″, photograph. Harris Gallery.

influenced by her husband, New York painter Frederick J. Brown.
Works of Margaret Fisher, daughter of renowned American
Impressionist, Mark Fisher, may also be found.

A strong theme of the gallery is British Impressionism from the
Victorian period. Works from important painters of The New
English Art Club, a maverick group which broke from the Royal
Academy, tend to predominate. Post Impressionists John D.
Ferguson and Ethel Walker are represented with their nudes and
florals. A lesser, though important parcel of French Impressionism
is shown, highlighted by an extensive collection of painter Charles
Agard's works. Works of Henri Martin, Achilles Lauge and Paul
Signak are also found.

American Impressionists by no means take a back seat, and in
fact some of the best art in the gallery is represented in this facet.
"The Eight" and "The Ten" of the Ash Can School are some of
Atkinson's best finds. Thomas Dewing, Ernest Lawson, Robert
Henri and Theodore Robinson are part of the extensive collection.

Toni Jones   1200 Bissonnet   Houston 77005   (713) 528-7998
Monday-Saturday: 9-6

Toni Jones

A somewhat eclectic contemporary arts gallery located upstairs
from the Robinson Gallery in a building two blocks away from the
city's two museums. Owner and Director Toni Jones began the
gallery a few years back in order to give emerging artists from the
U.S. and Europe a Houston outlet.

Some of the main artists exhibited include Reinhart Wolf, who is
known for his photographs of New York City; the German-born
"space artist" Andreas Nottebohm, who has done pieces for the
Smithsonian's National Air and Space Museum and for NASA; Ted
Echt, a New York artist who does humorous narrative
constructions; Pam Nelson, an artist who creates small figures with
painted canvas over frames and large "icons;" Mark Todd, a
South West Texas State College professor who paints in a variety of
styles, as does his wife, Susan; Tom Allen, a furniture maker whose
wooden chairs and other objects have a sinuous, Art Nouveau
flavor; and the Yugoslav icon maker Adolf Arzensek, who goes
by the *nom-de-stylus* Adi and scratches his Byzantine-inspired
images directly onto engraver's plates, which are then plated or
colored and displayed as finished art.

The Houston area artists handled by Toni Jones form a large
group and include Stevè Adams, Kersti Anderson, Carol Badner,
Fernando Casas, Sheri Constantine, Barbara Gerry, Norene
Hering, Ann Pace, Rick Roederer and Marc Rosenthal.

The 2,200 square feet of gallery space here also contains a
framing shop. New shows are put up every six weeks or so and are
devoted either to one or two artists or to themes. For instance,
during the annual Houston Livestock Show and Rodeo, the gallery

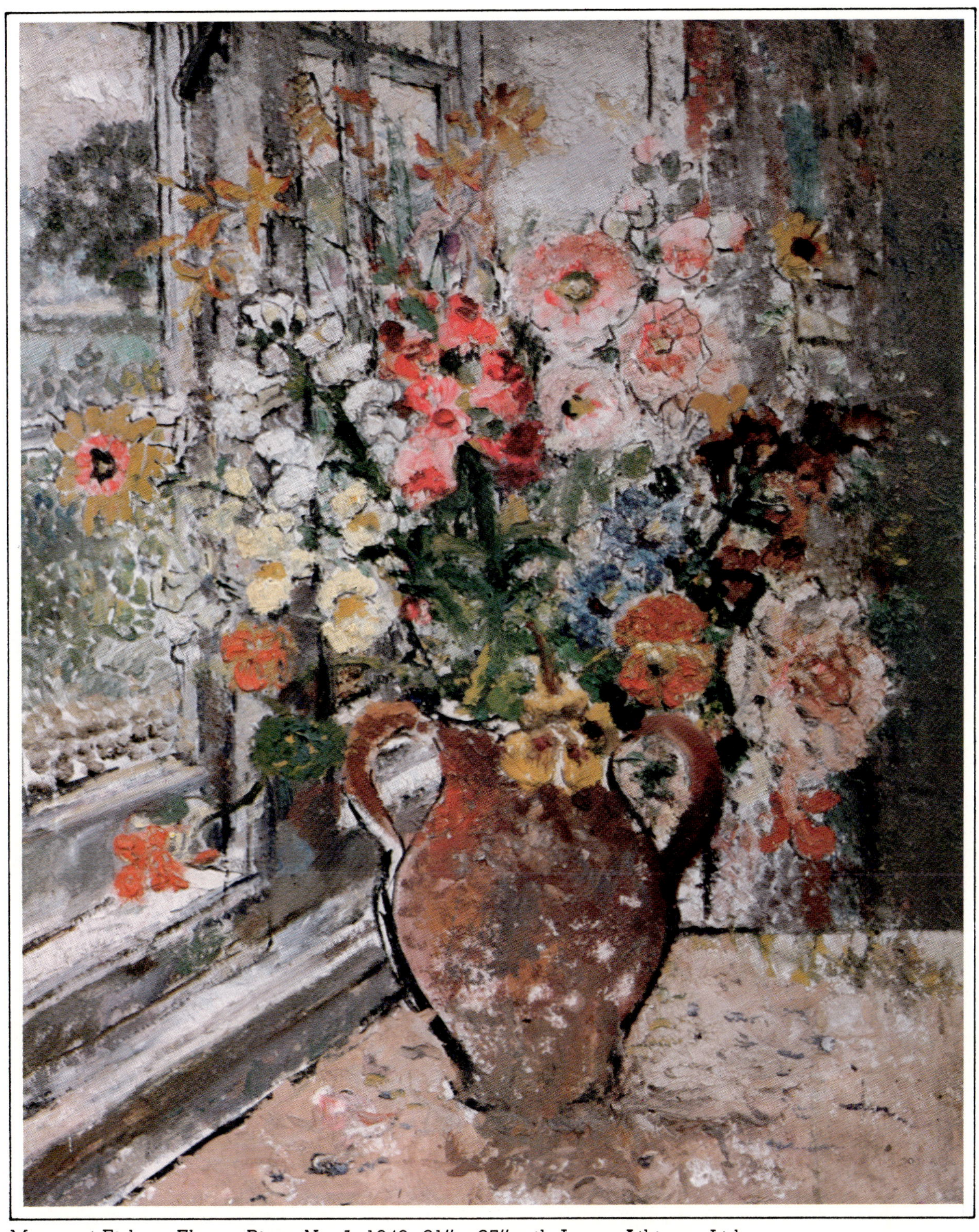

Margaret Fisher, *Flower Piece No. 1,* 1949, 31″ x 25″, oil. James-Atkinson Ltd.

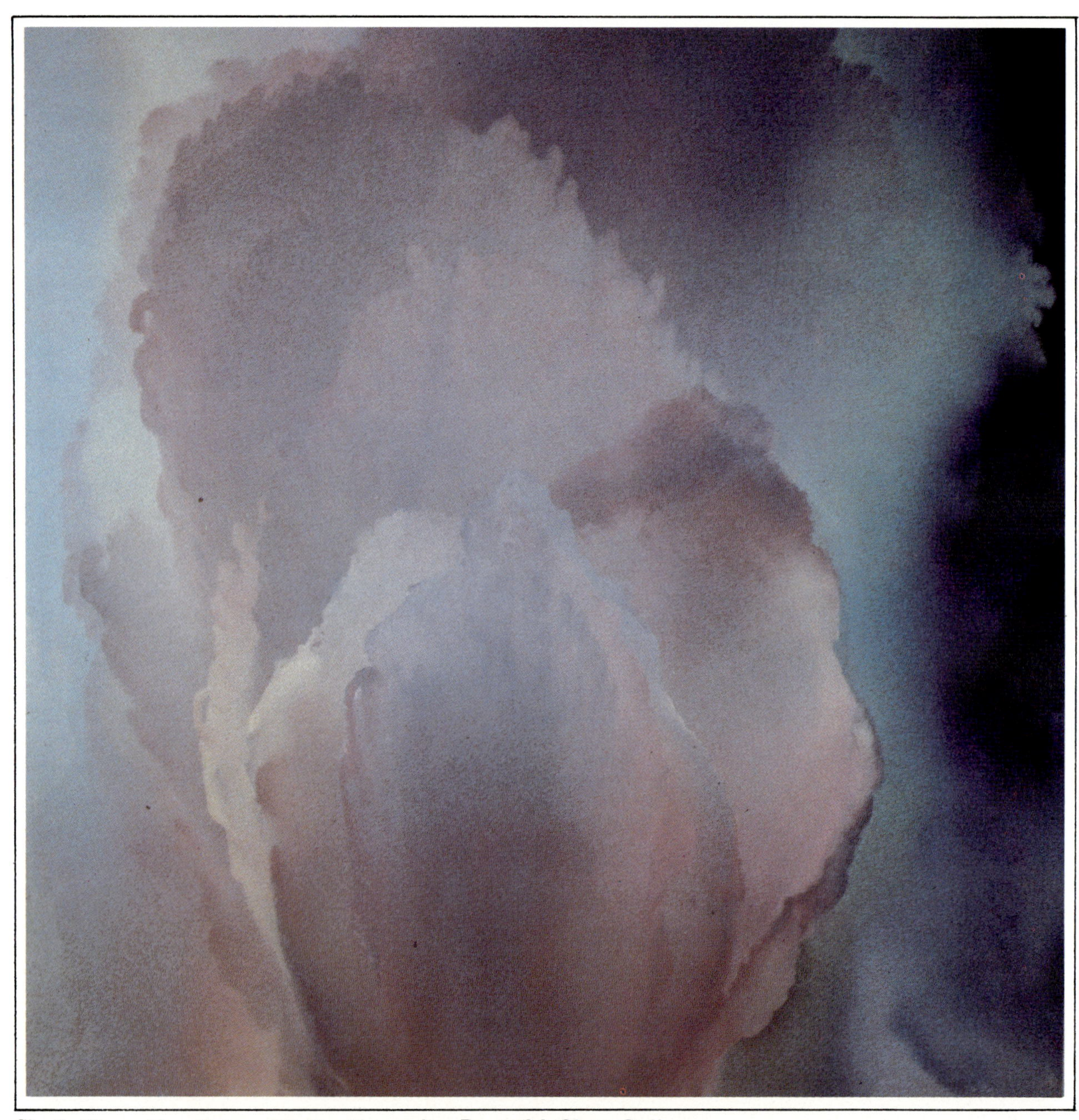

Sheila Zeve, *New Nature III*, 5' x 5', acrylic. Davis/McClain Gallery.

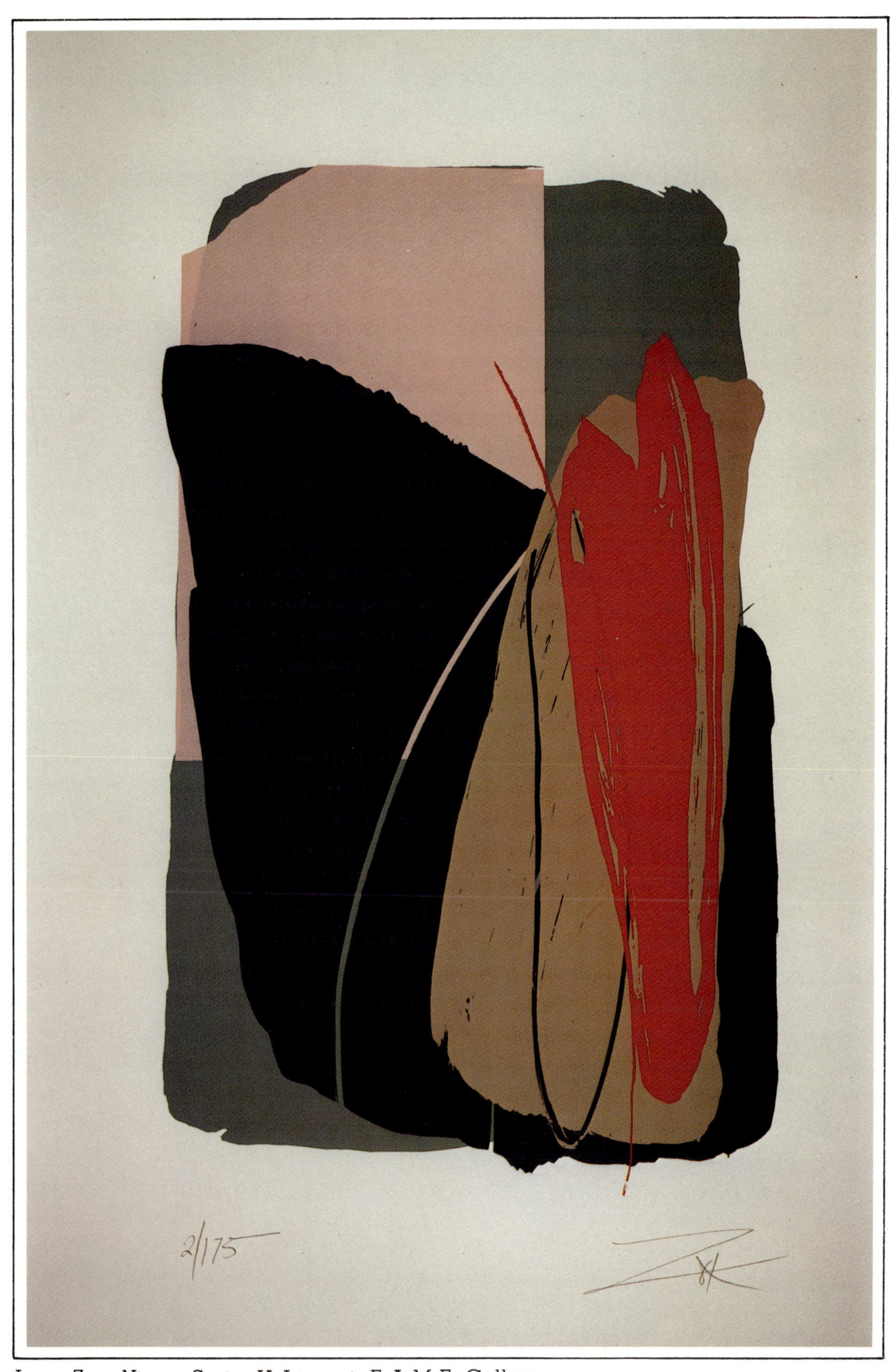

Larry Zox, *Niagra Series V*, Linocut. F.A.M.E. Gallery.

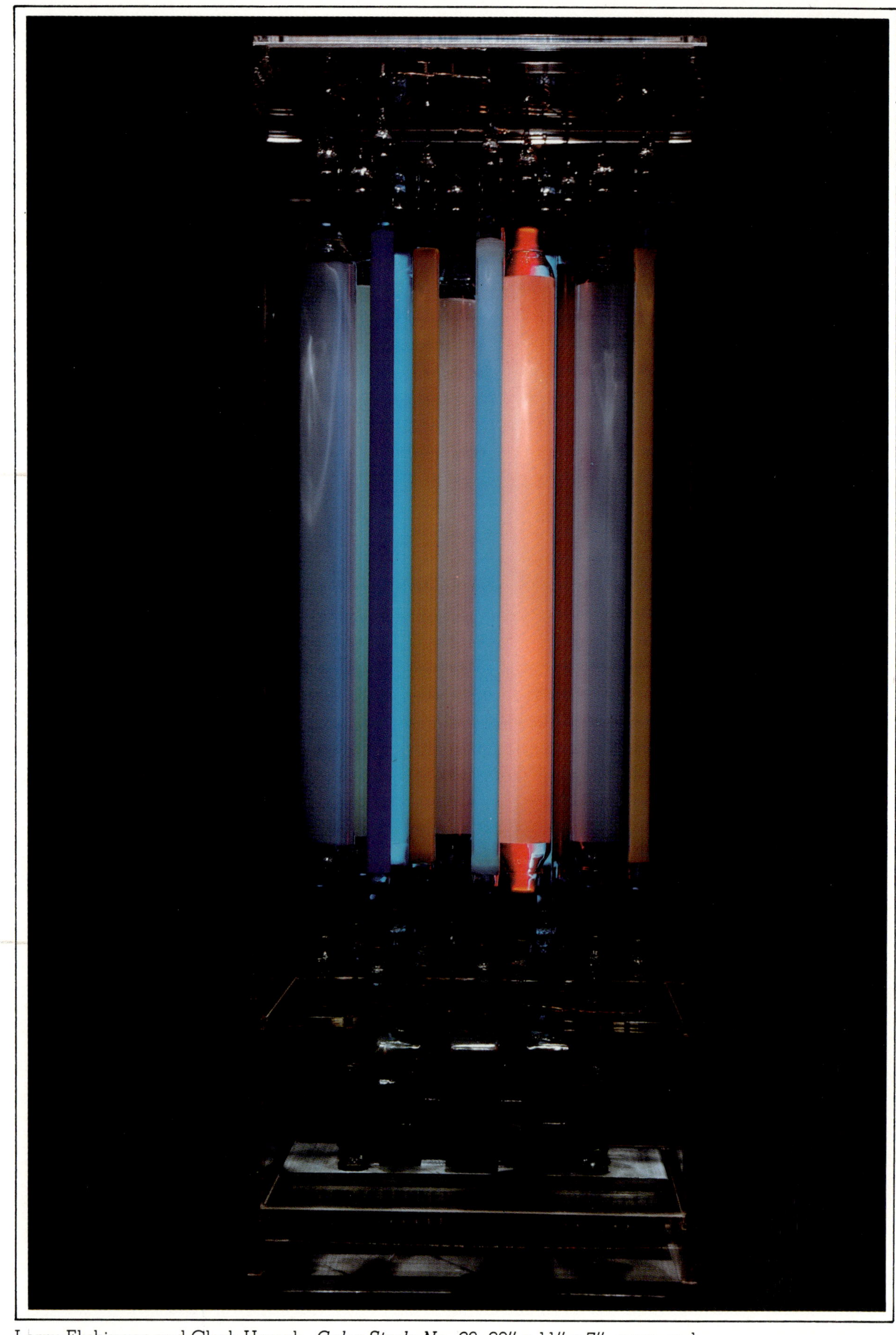

Larry Flukinger and Clark Harrah, *Color Study No. 29,* 29″ x 11″ x 7″, neon and plexiglass. Davis/McClain Gallery.

had a Western art exhibit and in March there was a show of photographs of Ireland in conjunction with St. Patrick's Day.

Kauffman Galleries 2702 W. Alabama Houston 77098
(713) 528-4229 Monday-Saturday: 10-6

Marjorie Kauffman of the gallery at the Galleria which bears her name, founded this gallery in 1980. Kauffman emphasizes works on paper in all media by over 100 living artists, from well known to unknown, from the United States and many foreign countries. Paintings, sculpture, and fiber works are also important in the gallery's inventory.

The following artists are featured: Louise Nevelson, prints and handmade paper works; Jim Dine, recent etchings and aquatints; Carol Summers, woodblock prints; Alexander Calder, lithographs; Fritz Scholder, lithographs; R.C. Gorman, lithographs and ceramics.

A strong showing is also made by the following artists: Wayne Toepp, who works in acrylic on canvas, and produces deep, emotional, colorist paintings involving elements of geometry and Abstract Expressionism; Nick de Vries, a sculptor who executes strong architectural ceramic forms, salt-fired, with subtle colors and surface textures; Piero Fenci, who fashions elegant raku ceramic vessels and nonfunctional objects; and Nance O'Banion, who makes handmade paper and bamboo constructions.

Contemporary Japanese printmakers are a strong sub-specialization. Saito, Hoshi, Tanaka, Mori, and others make up the extensive collection.

Contemporary fiber works include woven, braided, and hand-constructed works by Karen Chapnick, Barbara Nelson, and Alexandra Hart.

Exhibitions are scheduled every five to six weeks. The gallery's efforts are devoted to offering top-quality work to both private and corporate collectors.

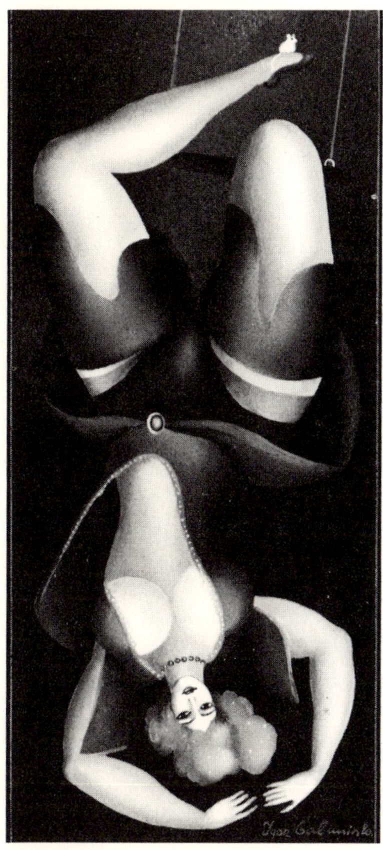

Igor Galavin, *Girl on Trapeze*, 11¼" x 5¼", acrylic on board. Kauffman Galleries.

Marjorie Kauffman Graphics

Marjorie Kauffman Graphics 5011 Westheimer Road, Suite 3220, The Galleria Houston 77056 (713) 622-6001 Monday-Friday: 10-9; Saturday: 10-6

A small, brightly lit space located on the third level of the Galleria mall, Marjorie Kauffman Graphics is a branch office of the Kauffman Fine Arts gallery located at 2702 West Alabama Street. Director Ilene Haney presides over an extensive collection of original prints by a variety of contemporary artists and quality posters and reproductions of work by everybody from Houston poster artist Jack Boynton to Impressionist master Toulouse-Lautrec. A framing service is available on the premises.

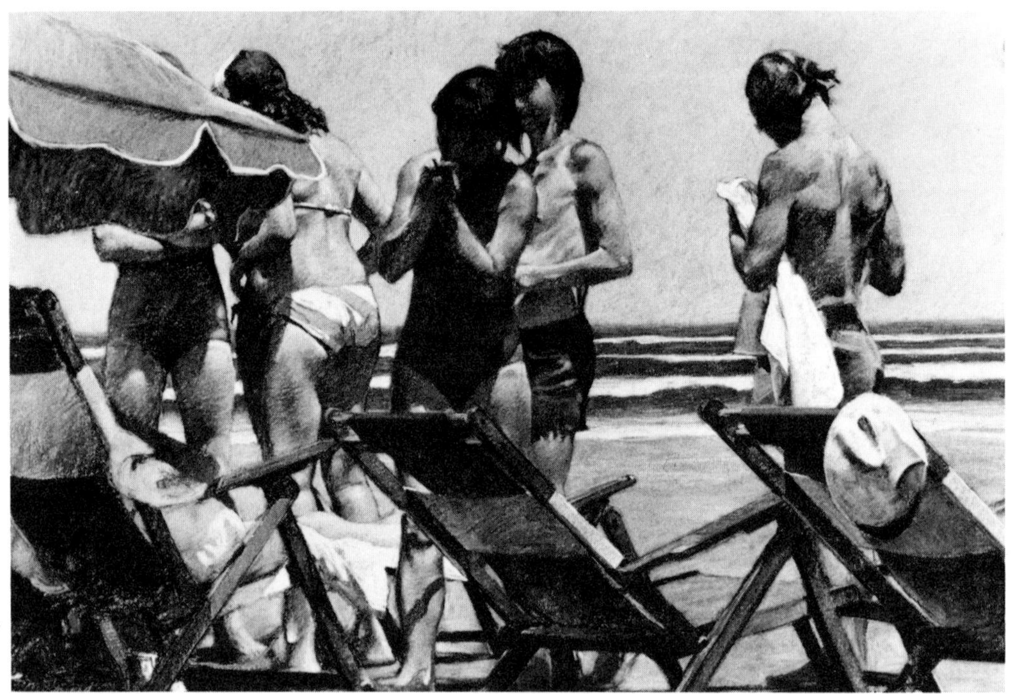

Pauline Howard, *Five Figures,* 28″ x 40″, pastel on paper. Harris Gallery.

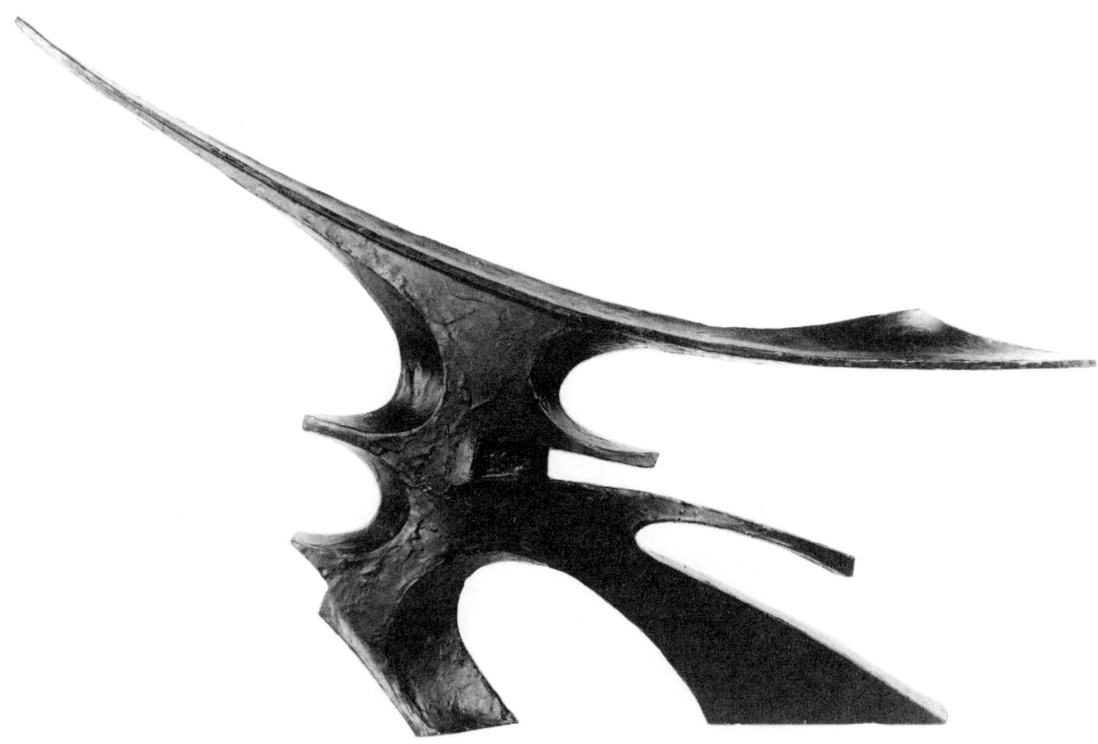

Hannah Stewart, *Galileo,* 26″ x 45″, cast bronze. DuBose Gallery.

Koski-Long Galleries   2405 S. Gessner   Houston 77063
(713) 783-0015   Monday-Saturday: 10-6

Koski-Long

Koski-Long Galleries is one of the newest faces in Houston.
Opened two years ago, it is managed by a Scandinavian-born art
historian, Bertil Long. A fine-arts and portrait gallery, with
European connections and an emphasis on quality, it deals in
original oils, pastels, watercolors, and graphics in both traditional
and contemporary styles. The gallery offers a full range of
services, which include acquiring art for corporate and private
collections, executive and family portraiture, appraisals,
restorations, and custom framing.

The works shown are diverse in style and represent a broad
selection of internationally known artists, such as Henry Moore,
Robert Vickrey, exceptional graphic artists Simo Hannula and
Vaino Rouvinen, and the young and nontraditional fresh talents of
Ben Howatt, Kathy Suffel, and Eleanor Irvin.

The gallery includes a special portrait studio where works by
Mary Koski and Kathy Long, who have done commissioned
portraits of dignitaries, royalty, and corporations in the U.S.,
Europe, and Scandinavia can be seen. Along with the portrait
samples, a collection of their oils and pastels are on display.
Traditional pieces, in oil, by English women Carol Roberts and
Berry Fritz are also shown.

There is a wide selection of works on paper. Wyndell Taylor's
sensitive southern landscapes contrast with the dramatic
watercolors by Birgit Sillen of Sweden. There are brilliant colors of
Austrian-born Erika Just, Houstonian Geomonte, Fred Samuelson,
who lives and works in Mexico, and unique etchings by Marci
Harnden and New Yorker Kaarin Holmberg.

Exhibitions are held monthly in one or both of the main
exhibition rooms, with major Christmas and summer showings that
include most of the gallery artists.

Janie C. Lee Gallery   2304 Bissonnet   Houston 77005 (713)
523-7306   Tuesday-Saturday: 10-6

Janie C. Lee

Gallery goers who are well traveled will instantly spot that this
Texas space is not at all what Texas art is about, though it is hardly
a discredit to the excellent art and artists of the gallery. The space
is large, modern, with a high-tech look, and the atmosphere is
about as Texan as Manhattan.

With the exception of Jim Love's sculptures, the gallery almost
never shows works of Texans. In fact, one gets the feeling the
gallery is not at all interested in any art out of New York. They
claim to shown European art as well as American, yet their lists of
artists shows not even one European, unless you would count
pioneer Abstract Expressionists Hans Hofmann or Willem de

Kooning who are shown occasionally. Both are European-born
painters who flowered in New York and influenced, and in fact
founded, the New York school of painting.

Most of the painters work in nonrepresentational veins
excepting Jasper Johns. Quality works of Helen Frankenthaler,
Frank Stella, Robert Motherwell, and Nancy Graves may be
found. Assemblage sculptors Mark di Suvero and David Smith
show their works as well.

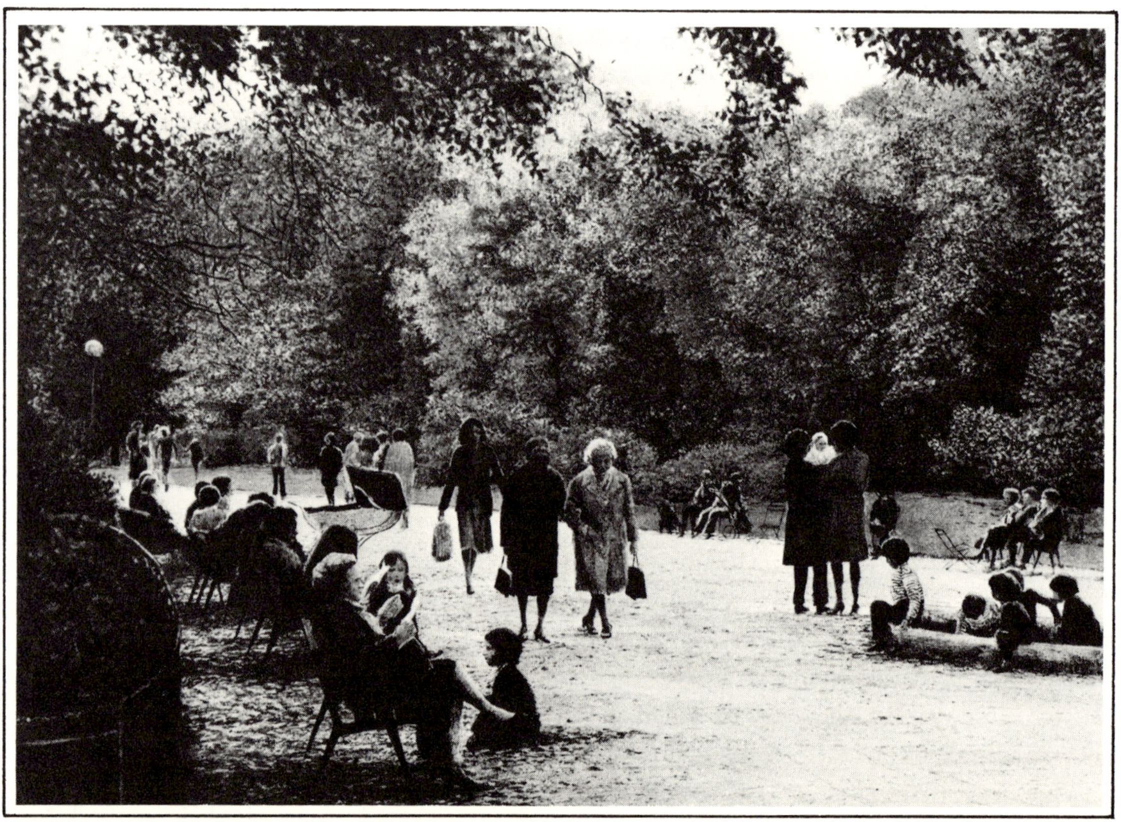

Harold Altman, *Parc Monseau,* 21½" x 30", lithograph. Marjorie Kauffman Galleries.

First-time visitors should be aware that Janie C. Lee operates a
"focused" gallery in that the art shown covers just one narrow, but
splendid area of contemporary art. But this the staff seems to know
quite well and offers painting, prints and drawings of good quality.
As expected, the works of the "super stars" of the art world which
make up the gallery's offering can be purchased or viewed at
many galleries throughout the U.S., but it is Janie C. Lee who
brings their current works to Houston.

Meredith Long & Co.   2323 San Felipe   Houston 77019
(713) 523-6671   Tuesday-Saturday: 10-6

Meredith Long specializes in American nineteenth- and twentieth-century artists, both New York and local. The gallery, which has been in business for 22 years, has an extremely good following.

Although George Inness is of special interest here, the painting turnover is very good, and the stock of American artists is excellent. Winslow Homer, Albert Bierstadt, and Impressionists such as Lilla Cabot Perry, Robert Henri, Maurice Prendergast, and Childe Hassam are well represented.

Contemporary artists fill another gallery. New York-based painters are Dan Christensen, Darryl Hughto, Stanley Boxer, and Wolf Kahn; Boston is represented by Richard Yarde. Texas talent includes realists William Anzalone, Gael Stack, Dorothy Hood, and Richard Stout, and sculptors Masaru Takiguchi, Michael Steiner, Anthony Caro, and Thomas Wolfe. A number of wildlife artists of prominence exhibit at Meredith Long: John P. Cowan, Herb Booth, and Al Barnes. The gallery also handles the estates of Burgoyne Diller and Edmund Greacen.

Although the gallery shows various aspects of its artists' work, including acrylics and watercolors, the inventory continues to change and reflect the art market. There have been several shows with such American artists as A.E. Gallatin, Louis Schanker, George L. K. Morris, Max Weber, and other abstract artists of the twenties, thirties, and forties, who are finally coming into their own as viable forces in the art world.

Exhibitions change at least monthly—sometimes with more frequency—and they are held in one or both of the gallery spaces.

Mancini Gallery   5020 Montrose   Houston 77006   (713) 522-2949   Wednesday-Saturday: 10-5 (Closed in August)

The Mancini Gallery specializes in vintage and contemporary photography from Europe and the United States, and original print portfolios. In addition, the gallery carries a selection of rare and out-of-print photography books.

Selected artists represented are: George Krause, twice recipient of a National Endowment for the Arts grant, and two Guggenheim Fellowships. He was the winner of the Prix de Rome 1980. He photographs a wide variety of subjects, making small, black-and-white toned prints. Peter Brown, who photographs in color and black and white, making studies of the effect light has on the interior of buildings. Joan Myers, who photographs a variety of subjects including figures and landscapes and makes platinum-palladium prints. She also experiments with paper negatives and hand-coloring her images.

Other photographers shown here are: Eugene Atget, Bernice

Abbott, Paul Caponigro, Imogen Cunningham, Louis Davanne,
Robert Doisneau, Frank Eugene, Oliver Gagliani, Andre Kertesz,
Gustave Le Gray, Charles Hugo, Eadward Muybridge, Irving
Penn, C.R. Savage, George Bernard Shaw, Lewis Carroll,
Auguste Sander, Paul Strand, James Vanderzee, Roman Vishniac,
Brett Weston, and Edward Weston.

Prints can also be special-ordered.

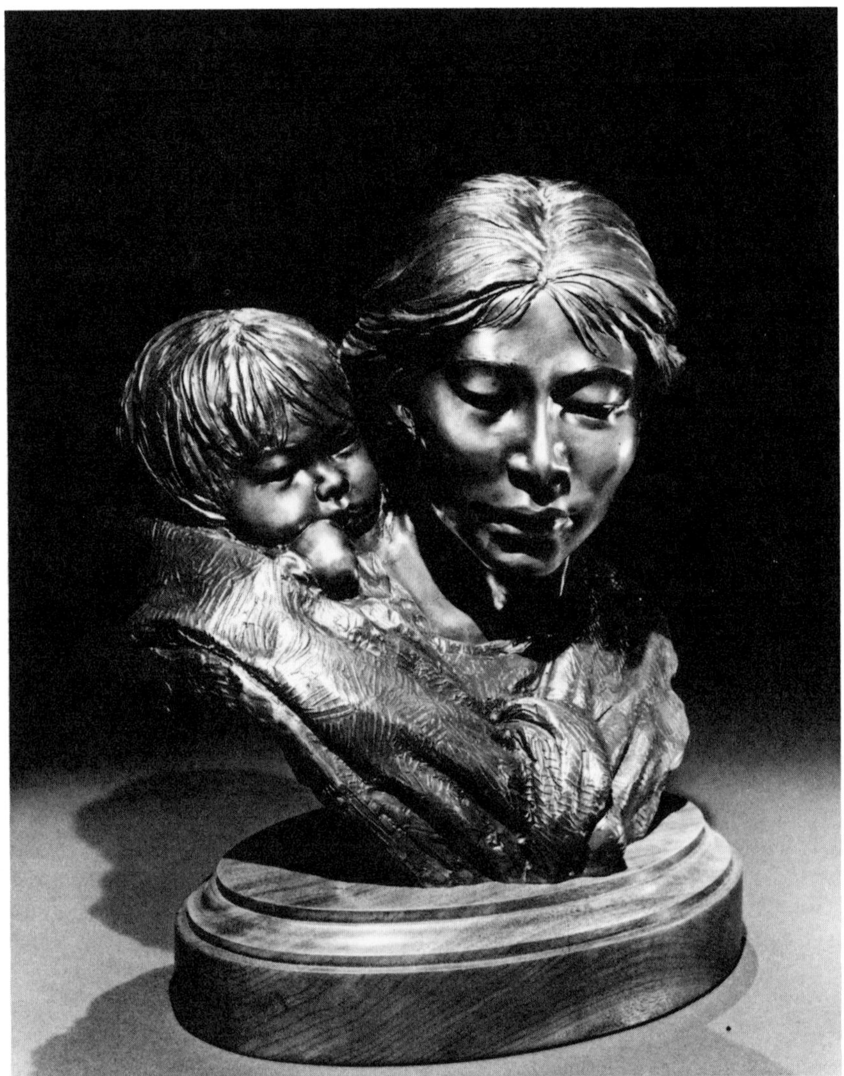

Glenna Goodacre, *Nina,* 15" high, Bronze. Meinhard Galleries.

M.E.'s Gallery   1408 Michigan   Houston 77006   (713) 527-8862   **M.E.'s**
Tuesday-Saturday: 10-4 (Fall and Spring)

M.E.'s Gallery, which opened in March 1976, is owned and
directed by Mary Ellen Whitwork, past president of the Houston
Designer/Craftsmen organization. Located in the heart of the
city's Montrose area, amid cobblestone streets and quaint antique
shops, the gallery specializes in contemporary American crafts.
Single or group exhibitions have included ceramics, jewelry,
leatherworks, hand-blown glass, wearable arts, woodworking,
paper, and soft sculpture. Photography, etchings, drawings, and
watercolors have also graced the gallery's walls on occasion.

The variety of skills and techniques shown have given M.E.'s a
nonstatic, interesting atmosphere. Many native Texans as well as
out-of-state artists have been exhibited. Marilyn Heath, of Clear
Lake City, Texas, executes delicate, nonfunctional porcelain
bowls, each pinched from a single ball of clay, then scraped and
pierced at random. The exceptional translucent quality of the
glaze and its swirling crackle effects produce an airy, motionlike
feeling. Naida Seibel of Fort Collins, Colorado, specializes in
sculpture/weavings. The work features women in clay—
wrapped in earth-toned sisa twines that Seibel dyes herself.
Figures have cast bronze faces. Wrapped bodies are symbolic of
women bound to tradition, an expression of the artist's past. The
combination of metal and fiber provides contrasting textures and
gives a strong visual appeal.

Also included are soft sculptures by Gloria Becker of Michigan,
now a Houston resident. A vivid imagination filled with fantasy and
whimsy is reflected in her dressed animals and mythological
creatures. Creative clay sculptures by Marie Blazek of Bastrop,
Texas, are also seen. In this clay dragon series baby dragons can
be seen hatching out of their eggs.

Paper works by Sue Franklin; watercolors of cats by Laura
Caghan; and drawings and etched prints by Anne Hernandez
round out the inventory.

From time to time the gallery is rented for special group
showings. The Houston Potters Guild, for example, rented the
gallery recently for a one-week juried show.

Jack Meier Gallery   2310 Bissonnet   Houston 77005   **Jack Meier**
(713) 526-2983   Monday-Friday: 10-5:30; Saturday: 10-2   **Gallery**

This contemporary American-oriented gallery, presided over by
Gallery Director Martha Moffitt Meier and her husband Jack, is
located in a small strip-center which also houses the Janie C. Lee
Gallery, a mile west of the two Houston museums and half-dozen
galleries on or near Bissonnet. The group of artists handled by

the gallery, mostly Texans, use oils, watercolors, bronze and stone
to create art that varies from pure abstraction to figurative and
highly representational.

Shirley Romer, a Texan, paints nostalgic Victorian subject
matter in a surrealistic, montage manner. Austin-based Rosemary
Mahoney works mostly in oils, depicting contemporary and
historical people in public and private settings, utilizing a softly
colored, impressionistic style. Virginia Cobb, now a Houstonian,
works exclusively in watercolors, depicting natural forms in a
formal, abstracted manner. Harold Phenix is a watercolorist
specializing in Texas scenes, especially of Houston and the Gulf
Coast "Oil Patch." As one might suspect from the subject matter,
he is a protege of Texas painter Bucky Schiwetz. Ann Hunt is a
Texan specializing in realistic landscapes. Al Brouillette is also
an American Watercolor Society member, painting in that
medium and in acrylics, and rendering interpretive,
impressionistic landscapes and nature studies. William Preston is
a former Maine resident turned Houstonian who paints large oils in
the tradition of Fairfield Porter. H. Y. Peter Shu is a Chinese-
American watercolorist who paints bright landscapes and floral
still lifes in a way that often recalls classic Chinese landscape
painting.

The two more unusual painters in this group are David Grant
Roth, a New Yorker and former TV producer who paints large,
softly colored abstracts in a manner that combines the color sense
of Georgia O'Keeffe with expressionist technique and Jose Perez,
a satirical oil painter.

Sculpture at this gallery is limited to the bronzes of Mikael
Whitley, who uses the ancient material to create her own figurative
allegories and animal studies. Pat Stone, a Santa Fe artist, sculpts
smooth, abstract forms out of, appropriately enough, stones such
as marble, alabaster and onyx.

The Meier Gallery is a member of the Houston Art Dealers
Association and participates in the July "Introductions" show. The
gallery's artists are shown on a rotating basis once every two years
or so, with six to eight shows held in any one year. In all, a large,
airy, comfortable place with a devoted local following of art
buyers.

Meinhard Galleries, Inc.   1614 Post Oak Blvd.   Houston 77056   **Meinhard**
(713) 622-0480   Monday-Friday: 9-5; Saturday: 10-4:30

Meinhard Galleries is one of the oldest galleries in Houston. Since
1940 the galleries have specialized in fine nineteenth- and
twentieth-century traditional and impressionistic art by both
European and American artists—old and contemporary masters,
English portraits and landscapes, the American Western theme in
landscape, figure painting, and bronze sculpture as well as the

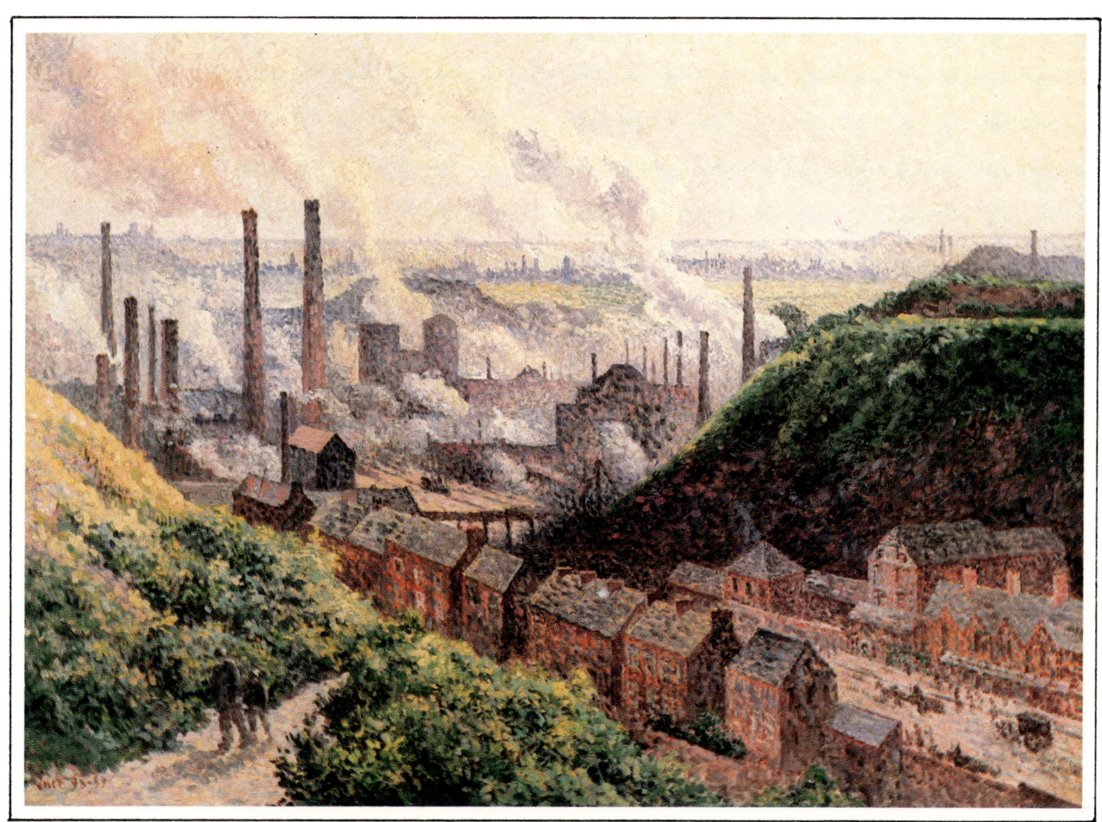

Maximilien Luce, *Factory Chimneys,* Couillet, 1898-1899, 28″ x 40″, oil on canvas.
Robert Rice Gallery.

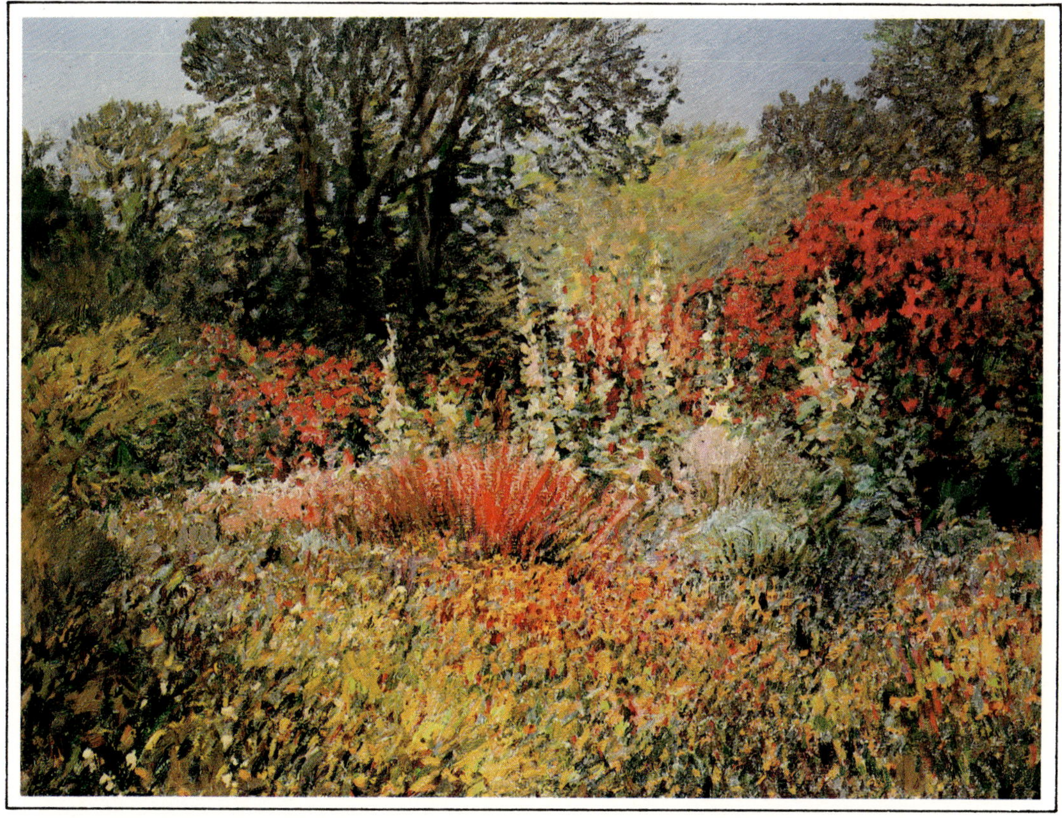

Rod Goebel, *Rainy Day Garden,* 30″ x 40″, oil on canvas. Meinhard Galleries.

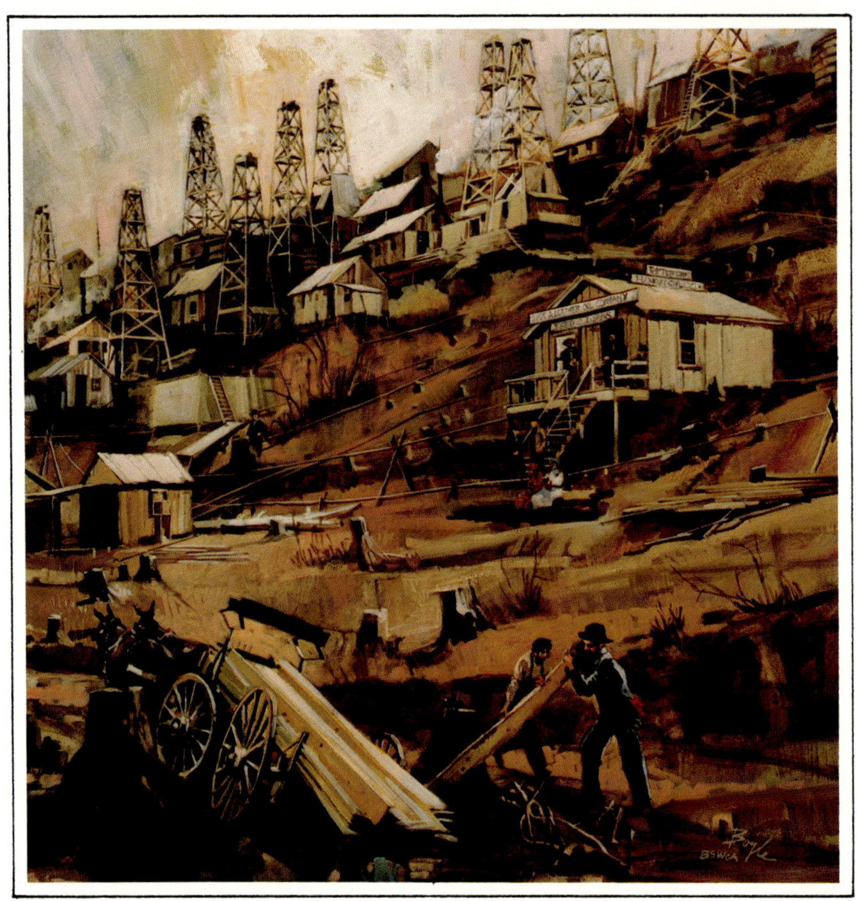

Neil Boyle, *Can't See the Forest,* Lithograph. F.A.M.E. Gallery.

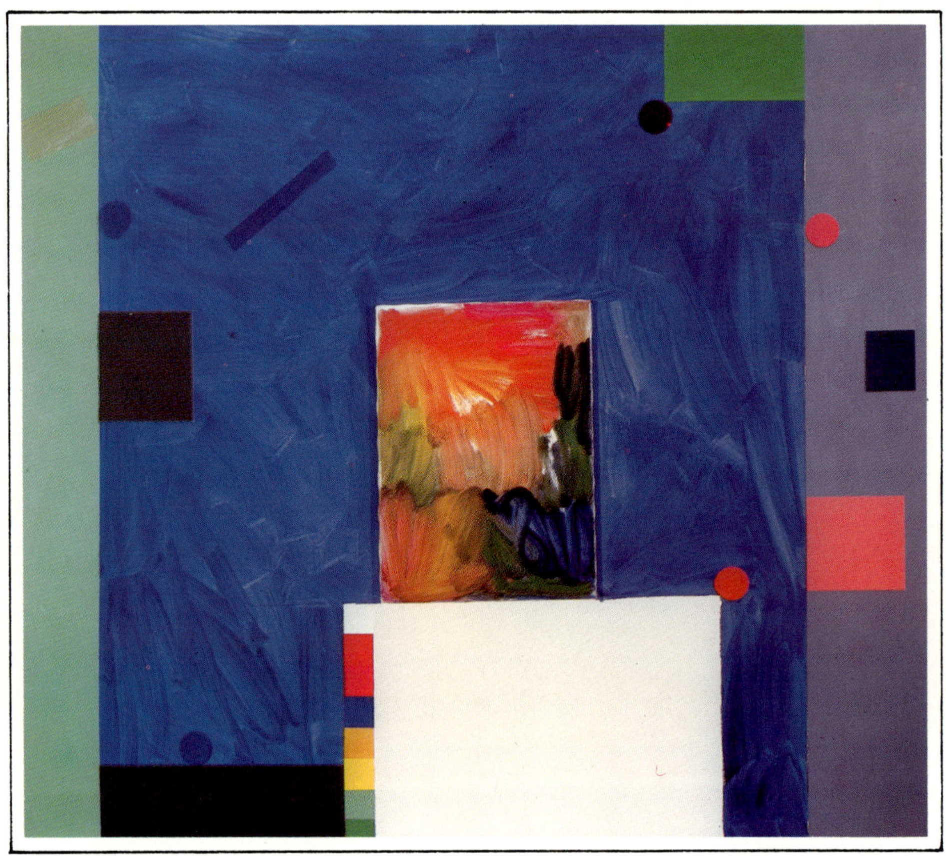

Dick Wray, *Untitled,* 1980, 68″ x 80″, oil on canvas. Moody Gallery.

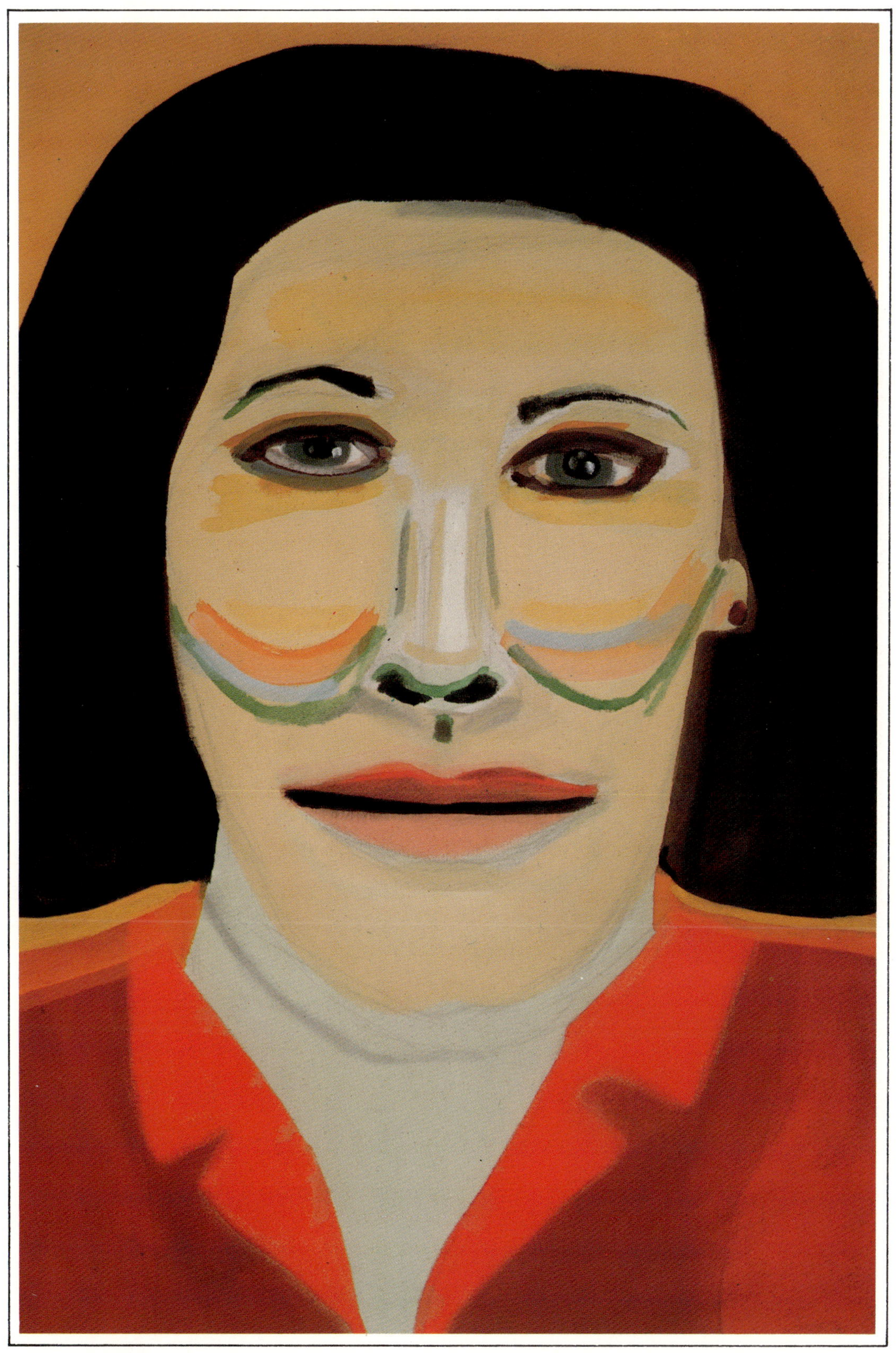

Megan Bowman, *Julie Schuetz,* 36″ x 24″, acrylic on canvas. James-Atkinson, Ltd.

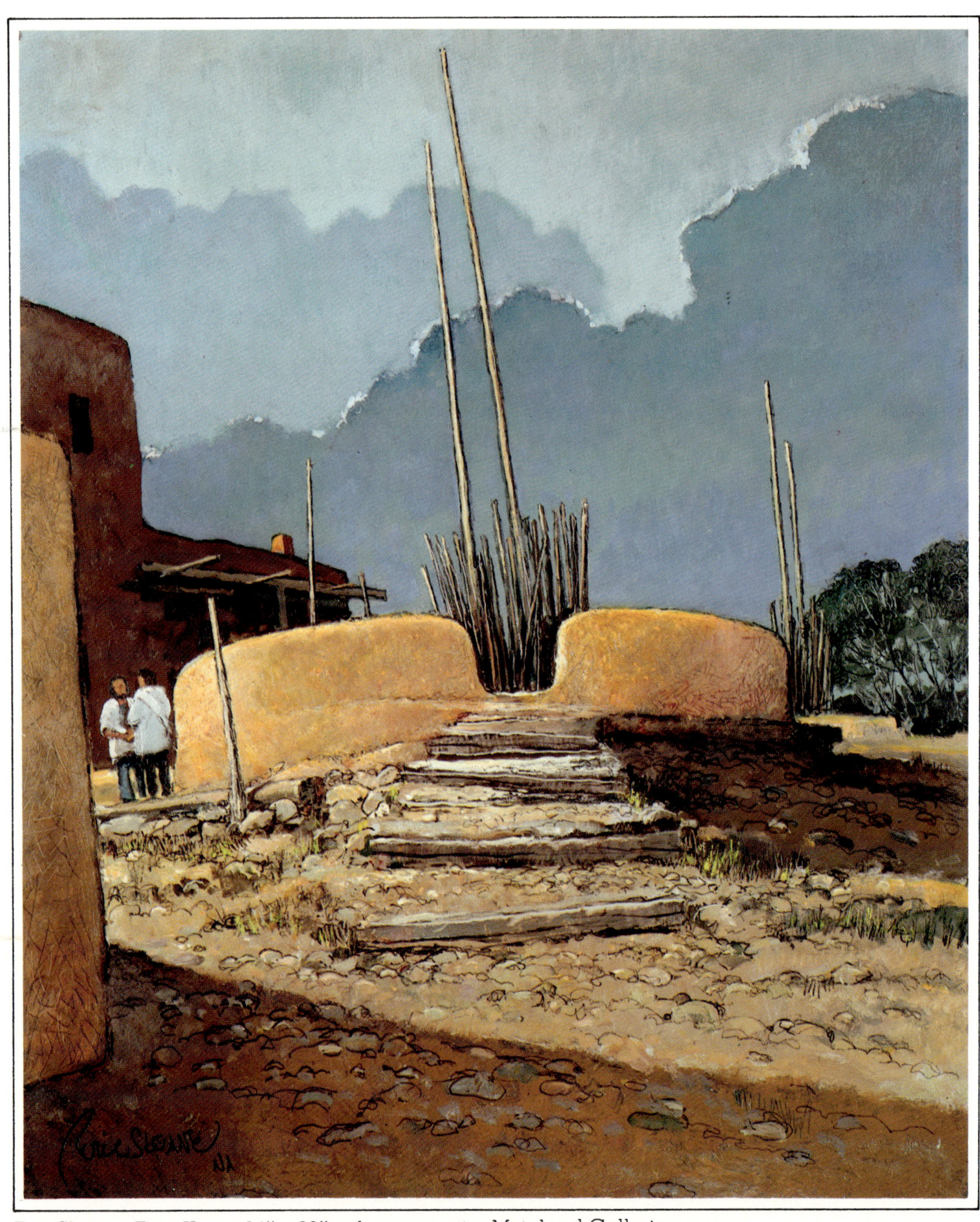

Eric Sloane, *Taos Kivas,* 24″ x 20″, oil on masonite. Meinhard Galleries.

School of Paris and the American Sporting and Wildlife scene are on view to the public. Four to five openings a year are given for gallery artists.

There is strong emphasis on American Impressionist landscapes, particularly in the Western theme. Among those featured are Fremont Ellis, Dane Clark and Rod Goebel. Figure paintings and landscapes by Robert Sarsony are shown as well. Of particular note are oils by contemporary English landscape painter, Ian Houston, and French impressionist Jean Rigaud.

The American Indian of the Old West is represented in the figure landscapes of David Halbach and Shannon Stirnweis. Sensitive portraits in pastel by Ramon Kelley appear along with still lifes, florals and Westerns by watercolorist Bart Lindstrom.

Sculpture ranges from single heads and group figure works by Western sculptress Glenna Goodacre to wildlife bronzes by Clark Bronson and Les Perhacs. Texas landscapes by Bob Wygant as well as sporting and wildlife paintings by Jim Robinson are a special feature.

The gallery also exhibits fine prints, serigraphs and etchings including the sensitive wildlife etchings of Sandy Scott.

Millioud Gallery   4041 Richmond Avenue, Suite 101   Houston   **Millioud**
77027   (713) 621-3330 or 465-4350 (workshop number) Monday-Friday: 10-4; Saturday: 10-5

Director and owner Marguerite Millioud shows a fine collection of original prints of the highest quality. The prints, mostly etchings, lithographs and woodcuts, range over time from the 1500s to the present and represent the artistic output of every country in Europe and North America. The well-established gallery, in existence since 1969 offers a Who's Who in art history selection of Old Masters. Additionally, there are oil paintings, watercolors and occasional sculpture on sale.

The Old Masters include Durer, Rembrandt, Van Dyke, Beham and Goya. The large selection of Impressionist-era artists includes Renoir, Toulouse-Lautrec, Cezanne, Mary Cassatt, Gaugin, Manet, Morisot, Matisse, Pissaro, Bonnard, Villon, Tissot, Robbe, van Dongen and Vuillard. The masters of the early twentieth century include Braque, Picasso, Dali and Roualt.

Contemporary artists include the Danish symbolist Lars Bo, the Austrian figurative artist Brandstaetter, the Israeli geometric abstractionist Yaakov Agam, the Hungarian Vasarely, the Spaniard Clave, a number of French artists such as Lubarow, Dussau, Spitzer, Charnay and Aubry, a Swiss member of the Bauhaus group named Erni, the Italian Baj, the Japanese Hasegawa, and a number of Americans such as Tobey, Friedlander and Downing.

While prints and printmakers are the main body of works offered

by Millioud, Downing employs gouache and watercolor, Charnay
creates drawings and liquid crystal images designed to decorate
entire building facades, and the Houston-based Soviet expatriate
Yakov Vinkovetsky paints in acrylics and oils on canvas, in a
luminous abstract style.

The gallery space itself, located in a commercial office building
near the Greenway Plaza complex, is quite small. Those wishing to
view the works of a specific artist should call Mrs. Millioud ahead
of time and arrange for a special showing as much of the available
stock of prints is not kept at the gallery.

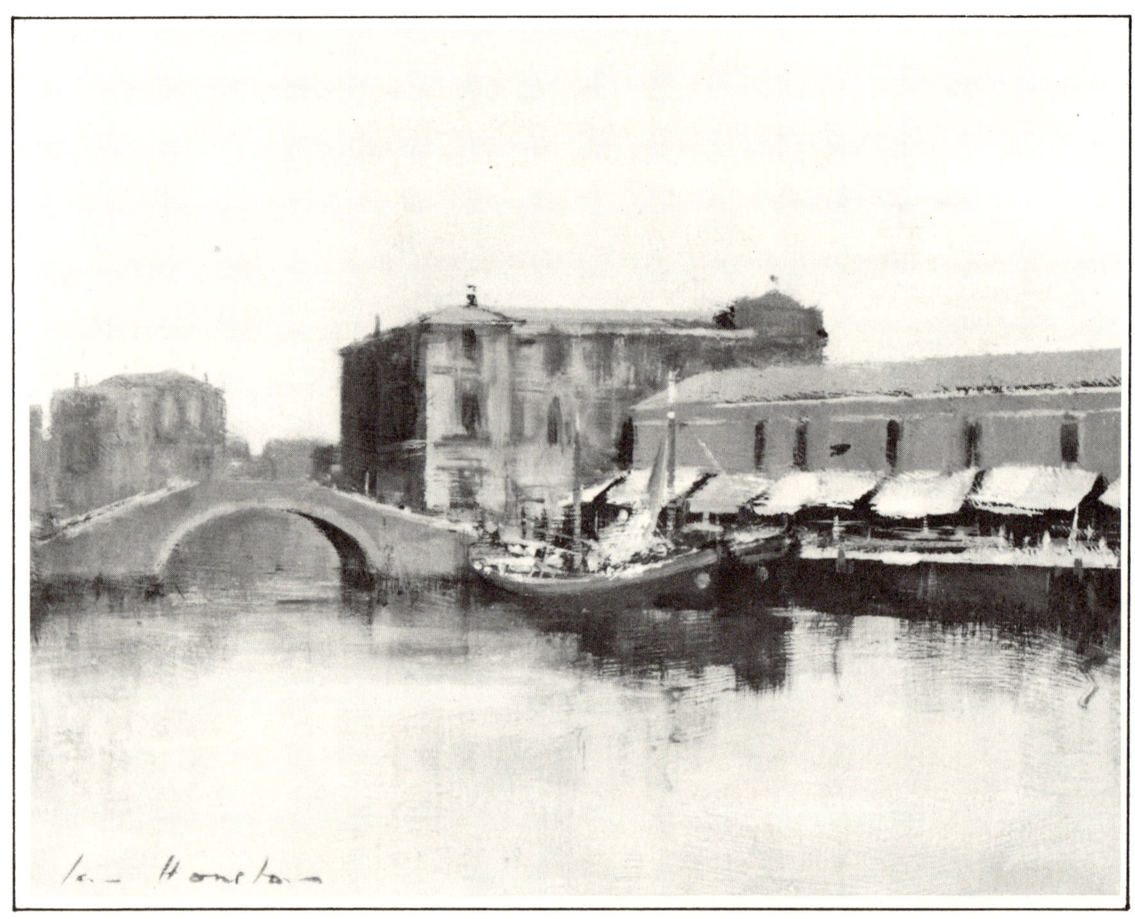

Ian Houston, *The Fishmarket in Chioggia,* 9" x 11" oil. Meinhard Galleries.

Moody Gallery   2105-J West Gray   Houston 77019   (713)
526-9911   Tuesday-Saturday: 10-5:30

**Moody
Gallery**

Moody Gallery, which opened in 1975, represents 12
contemporary artists who do sculpture, painting, and works on
paper.

Dick Wray, for example, does large abstract oil paintings on canvas and colored pencil drawings executed in an all-over-composition style using bright, hot, neon colors. The paintings are based on the juxtaposition of colored planes and quick lines of color—usually straight out of the tube.

Lucas Johnson's paintings, drawings, and monotypes are representational works typically based on a horizon line that delineates the flat foreground and background planes. The figures in the composition relate ambiguously to the space with only very subtle references to dimensionality. The often faceless surreal images emanate from Johnson's involvement with the culture of Mexico, where he lived for a ten-year period.

Donald Roller Wilson paints highly realistic animals, people, and everyday objects arranged in totally whimsical fantasy situations. The characters in his paintings appear in completely unexpected ways—imagine a cat clothed in a dress smoking a cigarette with a dill pickle and match flying overhead!

Bob Cambin usually works in a series related to places he has traveled to (Ireland, for example), and always using a highly personal vocabulary of elements—drawings, watercolors, and oil on canvas paintings.

The other artists represented are: Arthur Turner, abstract drawings and watercolors; Lamar Briggs, large abstract paintings, acrylic on canvas, and monotypes; Don Shaw, steel sculpture and works on paper; Ida Kohlmeyer, large abstract oil paintings on canvas, and silkscreens; Bill Steffy, sculpture and jewelry; Charles Pebworth, sculpture and metal relief; Jack Boynton, works on paper and mixed-media assemblages that often focus on visual puns and wordplay.

The vitality of the artists and the variety of subjects and media make for an intriguing visit.

Off the Wall Graphics

Off the Wall Graphics   7437 Southwest Freeway   Houston 77036   (713) 988-7500   Tuesday-Saturday: 10-5

Off the Wall Graphics opened in December 1978. Graphics—primarily etchings, silkscreens, lithographs, and posters—are the main fare here. Contemporary graphics by international artists such as Alvar, Azoulay, and Charlotte Reine, as well as graphics by many Southwestern regional artists, are the specialty. Ajoulay is a young Moroccan painter from Casablanca who works in Paris now, and does linear studies of horses, nudes, and children. Charlotte Reine is a young Frenchwoman who works in watercolor.

Graphics relating to the oil industry, featuring works by Delmar, Collette, Ewebank, Willis, and Bart Inbes, and posters by Steven Kenny, Charles Bragg, Michael Delacroix, and Boulanger make for a specialized and unusual inventory.

Post Oak Fine Arts   1800 Post Oak Blvd.   Houston 77056
(713) 871-9290   Monday-Saturday: 10-5

Owners Jack and Kathy Reichenthal have been in the present
location for three years. The gallery specializes in contemporary
graphics and paintings executed in many parts of the world.
Director Joan Vaknine is available to work with individuals or
groups in assembling collections.

The late works of Pablo Picasso are featured on a continuing
basis. Many works by Joan Miro are also available, and there is an
excellent selection of works on paper by New York-school artists,
Oldenburg, Stella, Jim Dine, and Larry Rivers. Photographs by
Lucien Clergue are also stocked.

Among the prominent artists represented by the gallery, Lowell
Nesbitt, who works in oil, is one of the most outstanding. Visionary
realist Thomas McKnight also displays spectacular works on
canvas and paper.

Gallery shows feature the work of a different artist each month.

Pritchard Gallery   5015 Westheimer Road, Level 3, The Galleria
Houston 77056   (713) 623-4560   Tuesday, Wednesday, Friday
and Saturday: 10-6; Monday and Thursday: 10-9

The gallery is devoted to realist paintings of the Frederic
Remington and Andrew Wyeth schools. While the gallery is open
the year round, there are only four shows a year held there
devoted to a single painter, with each show lasting two weeks. The
rest of the time a selection of the gallery's artists are shown.
Currently, the gallery represents Roberta Clair, Sherman
Coleman, E.A. Herbes, Helen Hoffman, Geraldine Nunns, Robert
Pierce, William Slaughter, Carl J. Smith, James Verdugo, Jose
Vives-Atsara, Bill Webb and Ronnie Wells. In addition, the works
of deceased Western painters Porfirio Salinas and Robert Wood
are available.

Paintings are almost the exclusive medium shown there, with the
exception of Western bronzes by Dr. Sherman Coleman and
occasional prints produced by the gallery's regular artists.

Random Canyon   855 Frostwood   Houston 77024   (713)
467-3943   Monday, Tuesday, Wednesday, Friday: 10-6;
Thursday: 10-8; Saturday: 10-4:30

Specializing mainly in Southwest and Western art, Random
Canyon offers original graphics by Southwest artists Brent
Thompson, Earl Biss, liese jean scott, Amada Pena, Jr., Ron
Arena, R.C. Gorman, and Norma Andraud; and reproductive
prints by Western artists Robert Summers, Larry Dyke, Ralph
Wall, and Mike Scovel.

A wildlife section features Texas's first duck stamp print.

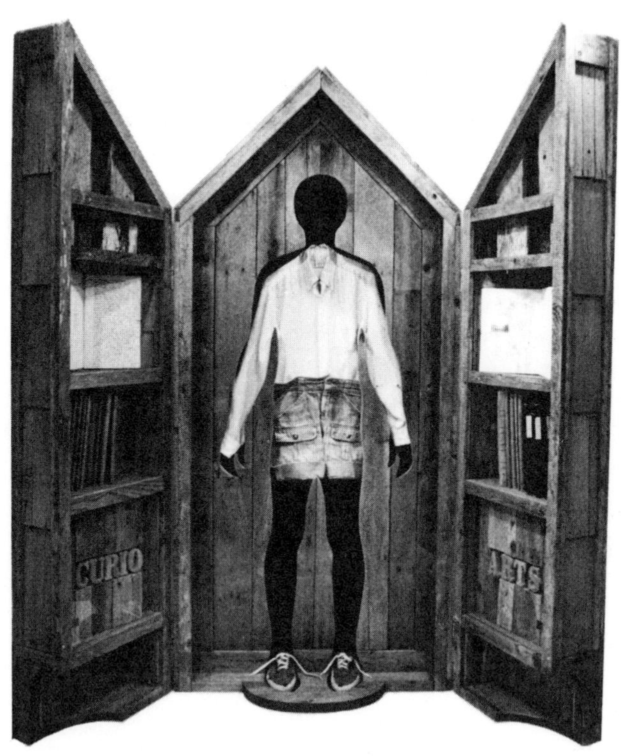

Roy Fridge, *Hermit Shrine,* 8' x 6' x 2', wood and mixed media. Moody Gallery.

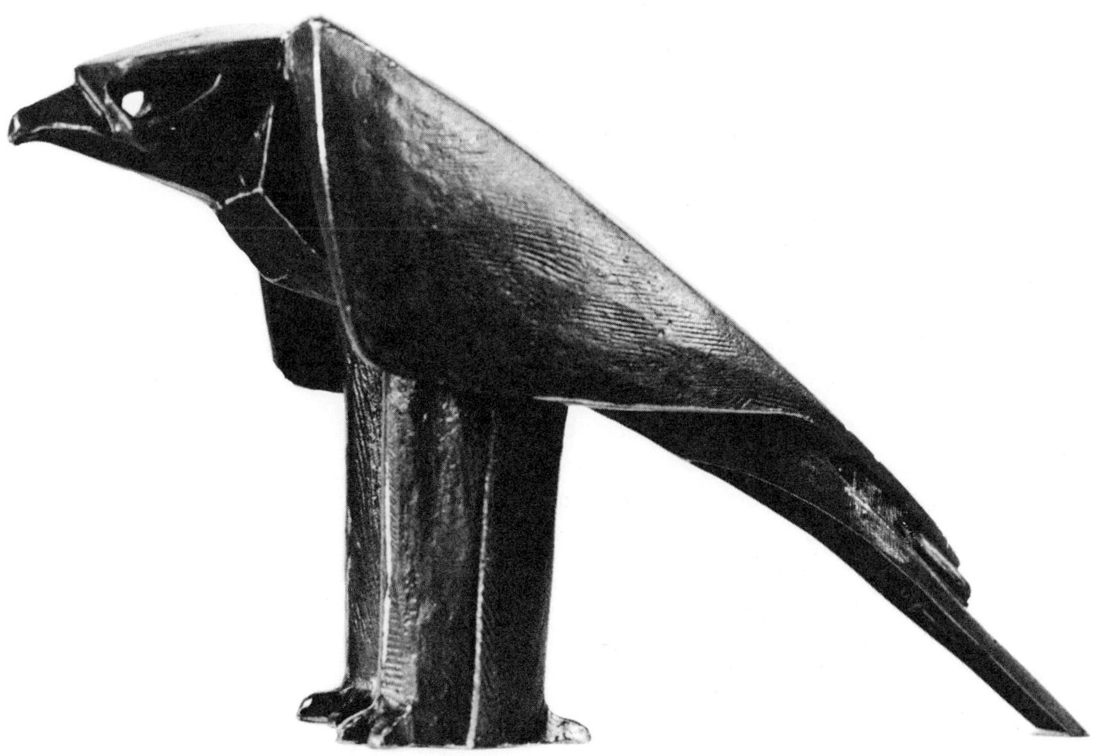

Bill Steffy, *Eagle,* 3½'' x 2'' x 6'' bronze. Moody Gallery.

Bronzes and originals by prominent Western and Southwest
artists are also shown, including Mike Scovel's Mountain Man,
winner of the first-place award in the George Phippen Memorial.
Custom framing is available.

Robert Rice

Robert Rice Gallery   2010 Post Oak Blvd.   Houston 77056
(713) 960-8003   Monday-Saturday: 10-4

Director Robert Rice was, until a few years ago, a New York
collector of nineteenth- and twentieth-century paintings of the
highest quality. Moving to Houston, he and his wife Barbara
Menen opened their gallery and now deal in a highly selective
group of European and American paintngs, all top-quality works,
carefully documented and splendidly displayed. The clientele of
the gallery tends to be serious collectors, dealers and museums.

The works shown span the period of the 1800s to the present,
though most of the works tend to be pre-turn-of-the-century
American. There is also a small, but highly selective
representation of French Impressionists. Occasional contemporary
works show up as well as estates of American and European artists.

Most prominent of the gallery's inventory are works of the
Hudson River School, a group of landscape painters best known
for depicting the wilds of what is now the densely populated state of
New York from "upstate" down to almost the suburban reaches of
the New York City metropolitan area, though one would never
recognize the landscapes today. Their paintings are alive with
light, deep in tone, and rich in content. Important works may be
found of some of the greats of this movement including those
of Albert Bierstadt, Frederic Church and J.F. Cropsey.
Other important painters continually on exhibit or available
for purchase are A.T. Brichter, Edward Shinn, Reginald Marsh,
Edouard Vuillard, L. Valtat, and Robert Vonnoh.

Robinson Galleries

Robinson Galleries   1200 Bissonnet   Houston 77005   (713)
521-9221   Tuesday-Saturday: 10-5:30 (Closed in August)

Established in 1969, Robinson Galleries features the work of
nineteenth- and twentieth-century American artists—painting,
sculpture, drawing, prints, and mixed media with neon. The
Hudson River School, American Impressionists, Ash Can School,
Social Realists, twentieth-century Mexican artists, and regional
contemporary artists are represented here.

Robinson is also the publisher/distributor of original graphics
and multiples and has organized traveling exhibitions both here
and abroad.

The following artists have been featured: Ben Shahn, Rattner,
Baskin, Bellows, Burchfield, and figurative artists Gregory
Palmer, Helen Bickham, and John Dawson.

The gallery also features the work of artists working in
abstraction based on the figure or on nature: Arthur G. Dove, Dan
Foster, Reginald Rowe, and Vera Simons.

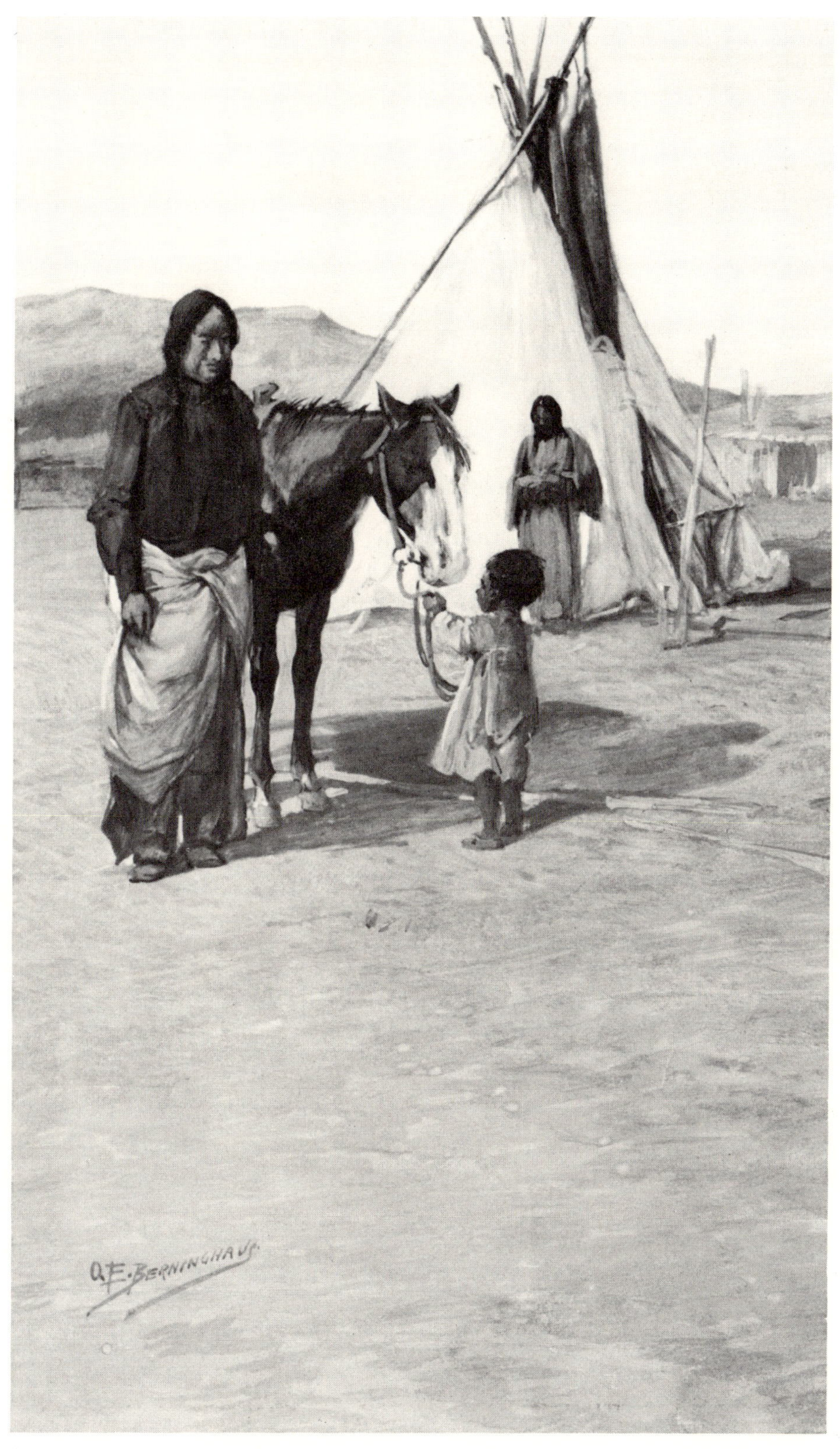

O. E. Berninghaus, *Indian Campsite,* 5½″ x 8¼″ gouache. Robert Rice
Gallery.

Sotheby Parke Bernet   2501 River Oaks Blvd.   Houston 77019
(713) 528-2863   Monday-Friday: 9-5:30

Sotheby's is an auction firm and not a traditional art gallery,
although it transacts millions of dollars worth of art sales a year. It
is the perfect place to buy or sell rare art treasures of distinction
ranging from the most noble of antiquities to Old Master paintings
from royal estates. On a less rarefied level, it is *the place* to
purchase and sell prints, antiques, jewelry, silverware and
collectibles of all sorts.

   The Houston office, located at the foot of the city's most
exclusive residential street, is a large, grey room presided over by
Assistant Vice President Flo Crady. No auctions transpire there. It
is strictly a liaison office, with a selection of catalogs of all
upcoming sales to be held in the firm's auction rooms in Los
Angeles, New York, London, and other cities on the Continent and
South Africa. Those wishing may contact the office to receive a
monthly newsletter on upcoming sales.

   As a liaison office, bids on items coming up for sale around the
world are accepted, and free estimates of the auction value of
property brought into the office will be given. For flat artworks, a
photograph and pertinent information are sufficient for an estimate.
Before you run down with a trunkload of family heirlooms, be
forewarned that Sotheby's only accepts those items for sale which
have "an established position in the marketplace."

Watson/de Nagy & Company   1106 Berthea   Houston 77006
(713) 526-9883   Tuesday-Saturday: 10-6

Watson/deNagy & Company (the second surname is pronounced
"deh-NAZH") has been operating out of a converted and enlarged
home on a quiet side street one block northwest of the
Contemporary Arts Museum since November 1973. Owner Marvin
Watson, Jr. and Director Clint Wilhour are the Houston dealers for
a select group of contemporary North American artists working in
paint, collage and metal sculpture primarily. While the group can
be characterized as falling into the categories of painterly realism,
color-field painting or abstract sculpture, owner Watson defined
the gallery's philosophy as showing "whatever looks interesting to
us." Whatever the formal labels, Watson and Wilhour are
interested in that difficult to define, but unmistakable, look called
"quality." All the art exhibited bespoke the artists' technical skills
and lengthy labors.

   Houston-area artists include Bas Poulos, who divides his time
between painting large, Abstract Expressionist canvases and
acting as the Chairman of Rice University's Art Department; Jane
Allensworth, who produces poured canvases containing up to
thirty layers of paint and possessing a deep, luminous quality;

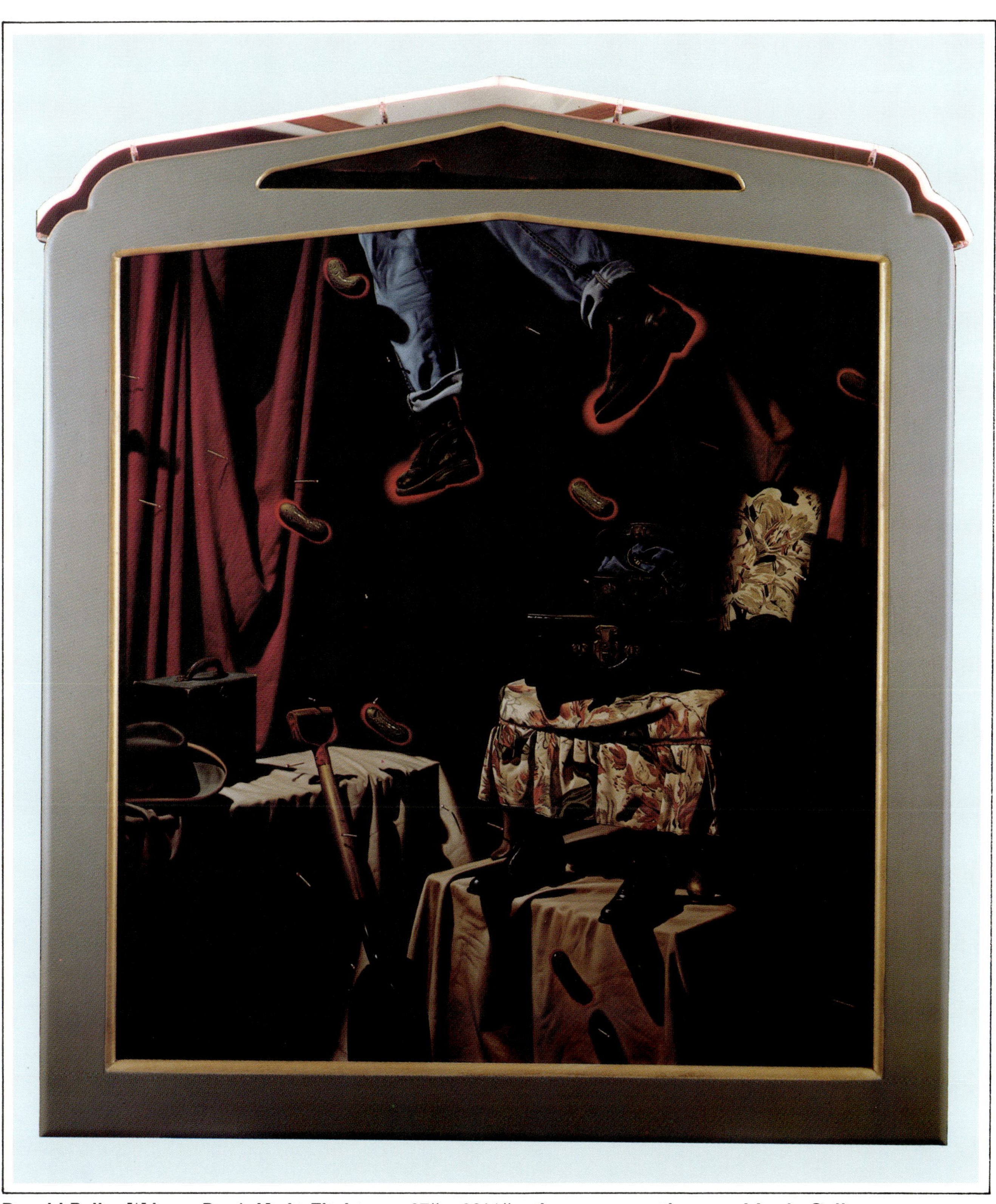

Donald Roller Wilson, *Don's Night Flight . . .,* 67" x 60½", oil on canvas with neon. Moody Gallery.

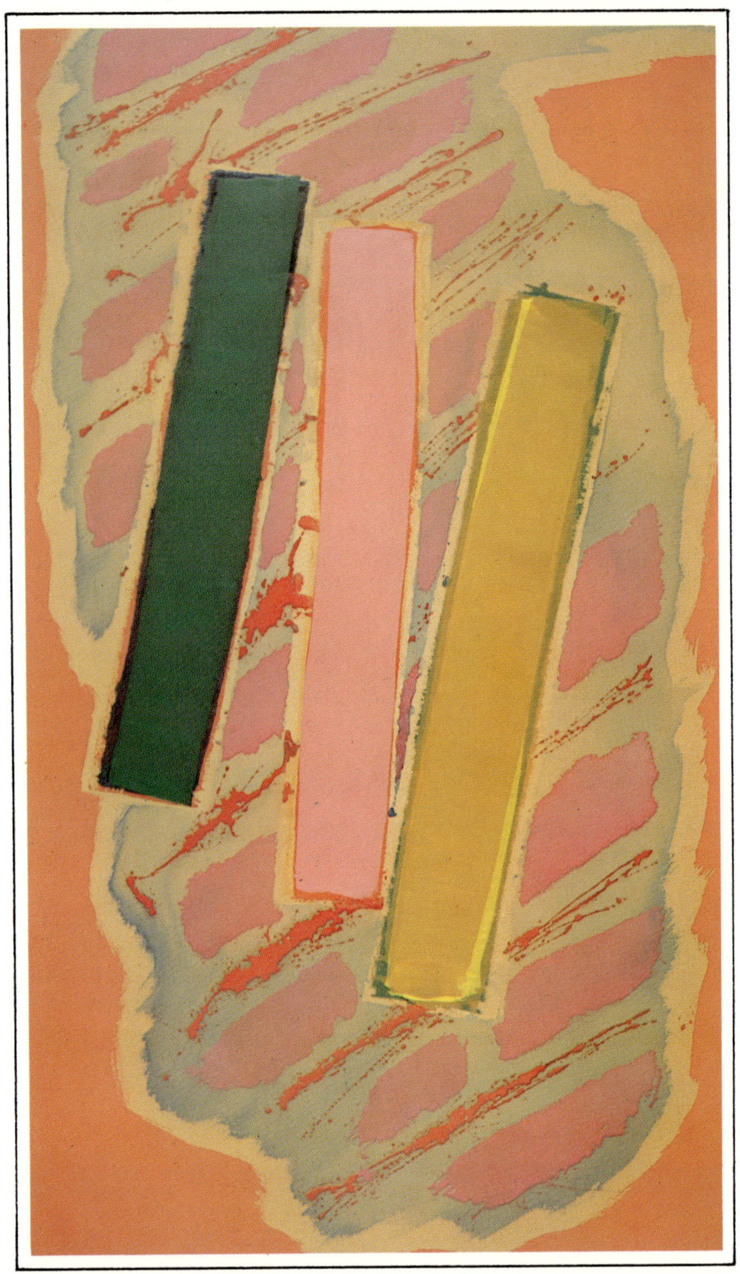

Basilios Poulos, *Satsuma,* 1982, 76″ x 45″, acrylic on canvas.
Watson/de Nagy & Company.

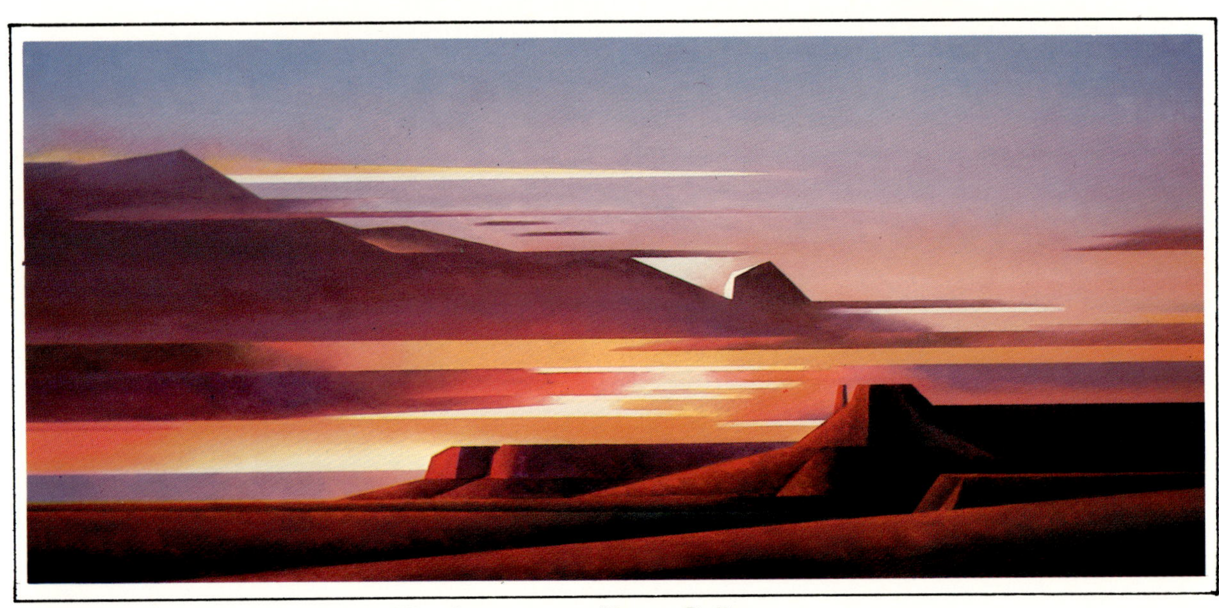

Ed Mell, *Desert Distance,* 24″ x 48″, oil on canvas. Harris Gallery.

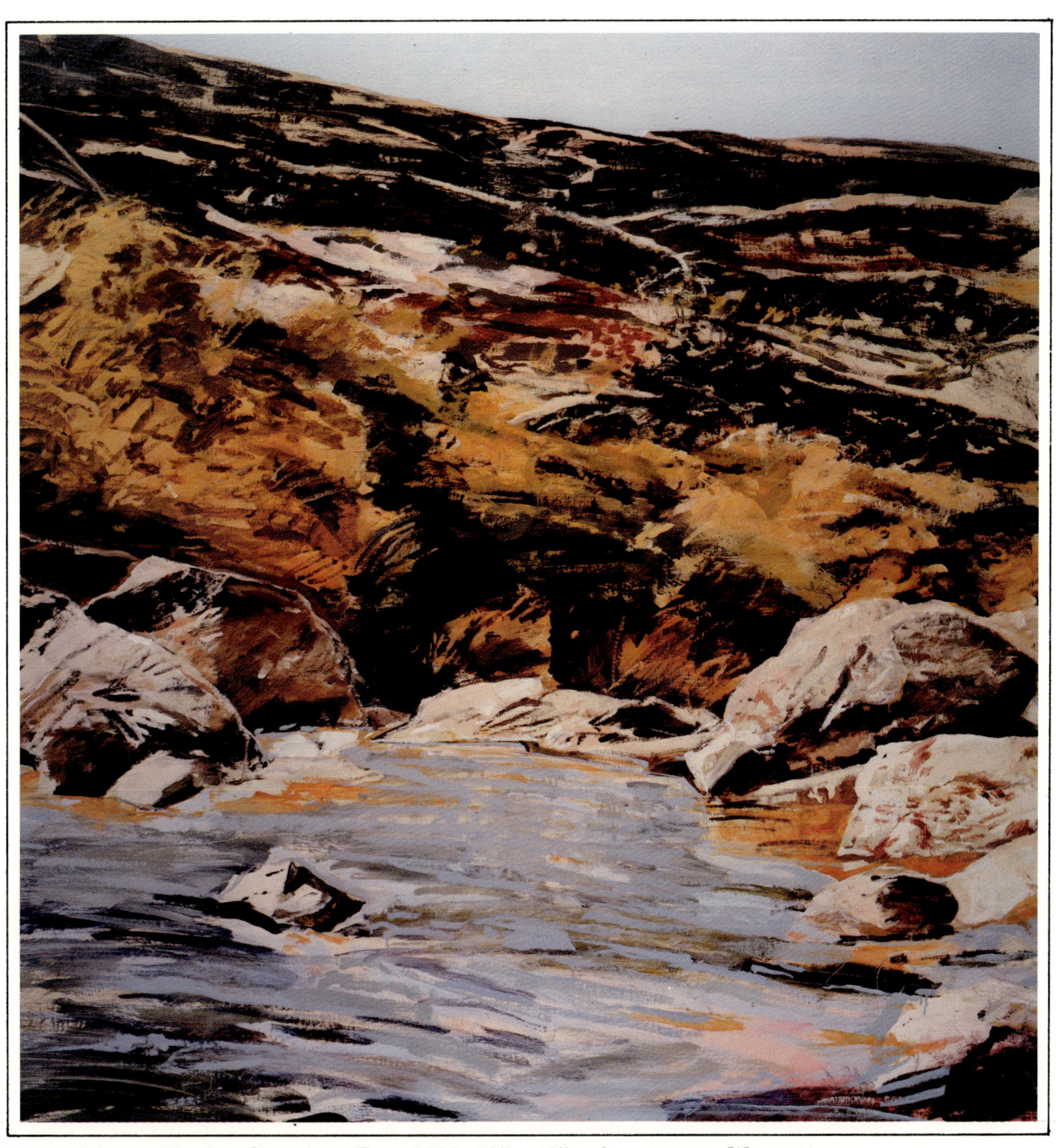

Forrest Moses, *The Rio Grande at Taos,* 1982, 50″ x 48″, oil on canvas. Watson/
de Nagy & Company.

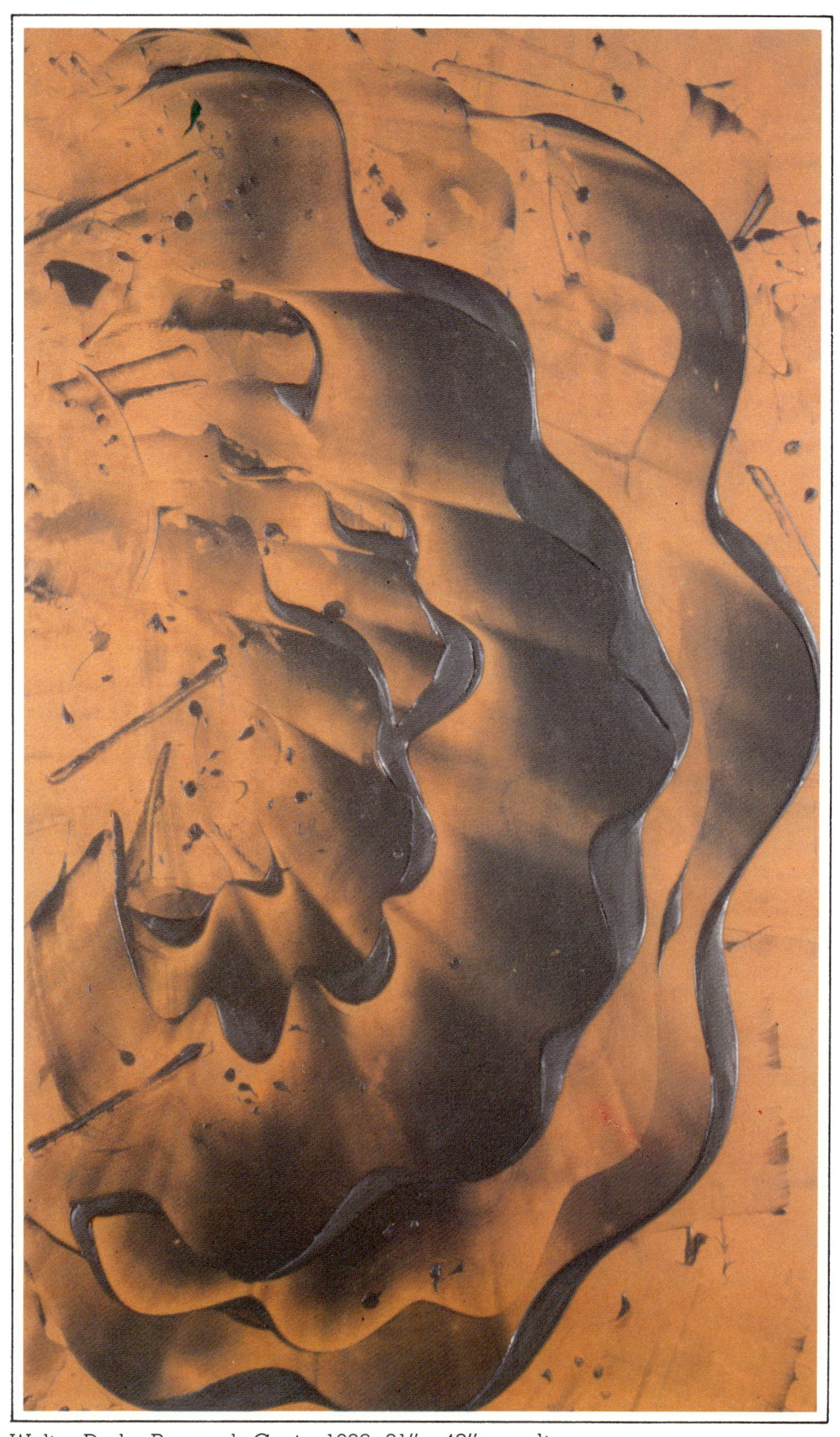

Walter Darby Bannard, *Gusto,* 1982, 81″ x 48″, acrylic on canvas.
Watson/de Nagy & Company.

Robin Utterback, who in his career has gone from Abstract
Expressionist canvases to subtle, lightly impastoed color-field
works; Earl Staley, a figurative painter who uses images
reminiscent of children's art; and Tom Sayre, a sculptor producing
small, precise abstract pieces in metal painted various neutral
shades.

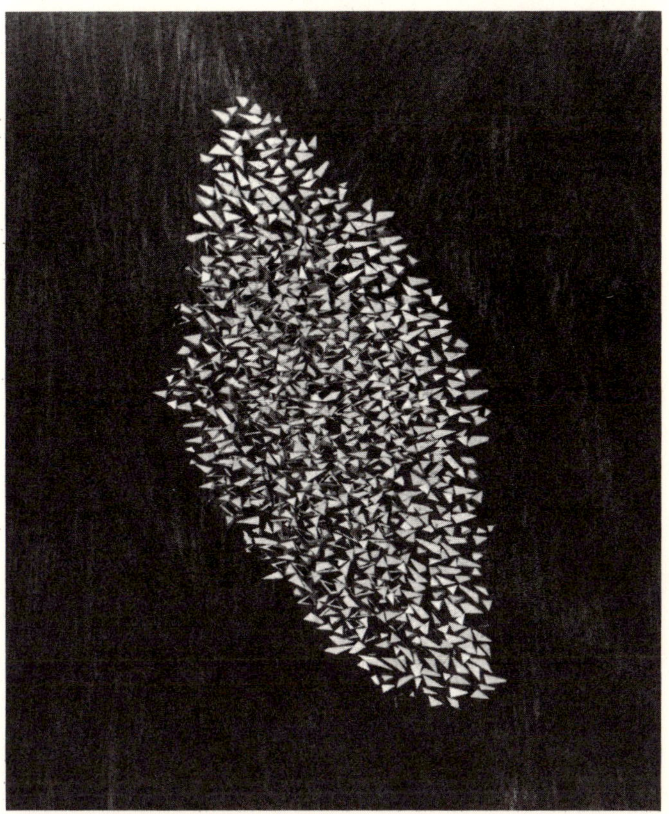

Robert Goodnough, *Gray Blue,* 56" x 66", oil on canvas.
Watson/ de Nagy and Company.

Additional artists include the abstract painters Darby Bannard,
Robert Goodnough, Merrill Wagner, and steel sculptor Peter
Reginato. Representational painters include Jane Frielicher, who
works in the tradition of Fairfield Porter; Santa Fe landscape artist
Forrest Moses; and Hal Reddicliff, a Columbus Ohio artist who
produces precise, painterly still lifes.

A number of collage artists show here as well. Stephanie Cole
works with stamps and cloth. Mary McCleary creates large
collages and constructions of brightly painted geometric forms.
Dallas artist Dan Rizzie's collages are usually small (mostly
6" x 8" or so), bright, geometric works. Dee Wolf, who is shown
exclusively by Watson/deNagy, produces pieces that are between
collage and paintings, consisting of layers of gouache and gold
leaf over a black base and representing a personal sign system.

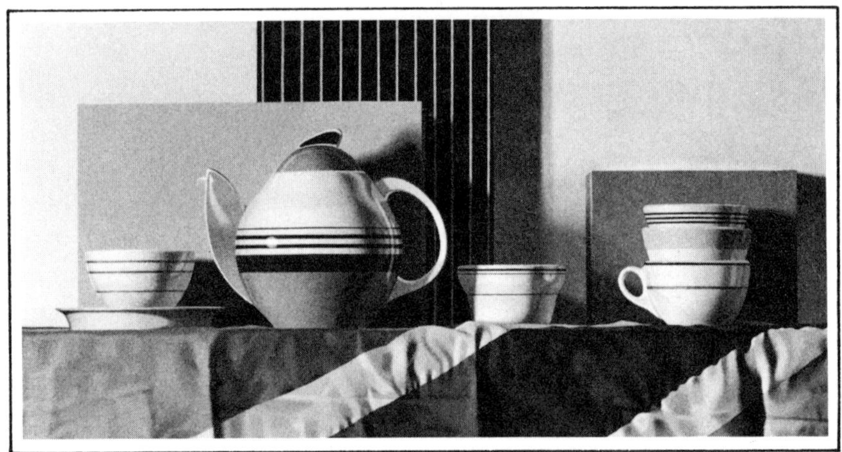

Hal Reddicliffe, *Still Life with Orange Teapot,* 14″ x 28″, oil on canvas.
Watson/de Nagy and Company.

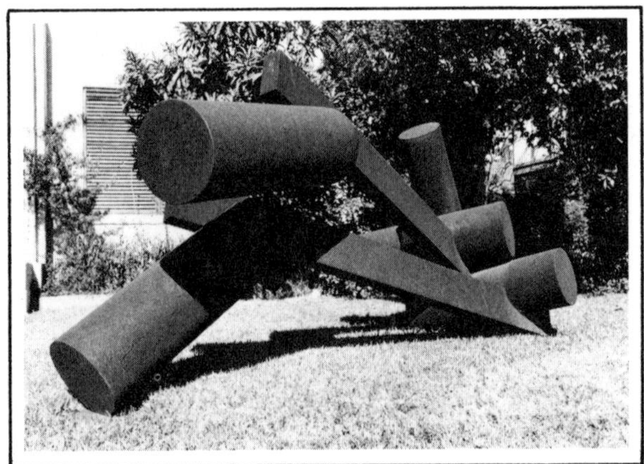

Tom Sayre, *Eclipse,* 6′ 2″ x 17′ x 5′ 5″, Cor-Ten steel.
Watson/ de Nagy and Company.

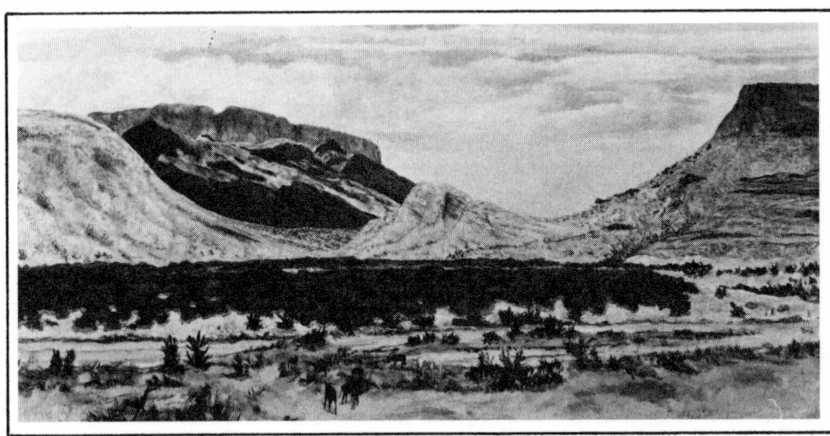

Earl Staley, *The Rio Grande at Lajitas, Texas,* 60″ x 120″, acrylic on canvas.
Watson/de Nagy and Company.

Gerhard Wurzer Gallery   5085 Westheimer Road, Suite 3707,   **Wurzer**
The Galleria   Houston 77056   (713) 961-9888   Monday-Friday:
10-9; Saturday: 10-6

Located on the third level of the Galleria shopping mall, Wurzer
shows a good selection of nineteenth and twentieth century
European master prints by a group of over fifty deceased
printmakers and nine living artists.

The major emphasis is on the master prints of the late nineteenth
century created by French and English artists. Available artists
include such well-known names as Henri de Toulouse-Lautrec,
Pierre Auguste Renoir, James Whistler, Alphonse Mucha, John
Martin, Pierre Bonnard and Camille Pissarro. The twentieth
century is represented by such giants as Pablo Picasso, Joan Miro
and Marc Chagall. The gallery is also strong in the works of artists
such as Buhot, Chahine and Cheret, with examples of printmaking
by artists ranging from Albers to Zorn.

The nine living artists, all of whom are shown in Houston
exclusively by Wurzer, include two photographers, two Mexican
artists and five Americans. Michael Rubin and Ronald Wohlauer
are the photographers. Wohlauer, especially, works in the
tradition of California's "f-64 group." The Mexican artists are
Gustavo and Arias- Muruetta. Of the American printmakers,
Robert Kipniss and Thom Kapheim are especially well
represented. Kapheim is known for his large, colorful, playfully
erotic lithographs reminiscent of Chagall's use of line and color.

The gallery mounts one major exhibition a year of nineteenth
century master prints and six other shows a year featuring the
works of a particular group of either master or contemporary
printmakers.

Index

190